'Rolf Dobelli has a gift for identifying the best ideas in the world and then putting them together in ways that make the whole even more valuable than the sum of the parts. He's done it for the art of thinking. Now he does it for the art of living.'

Jonathan Haidt, author of *The Righteous Mind*

'Gives us as valuable advice about how to live as he did about how to think'   James R. Flynn, Professor Emeritus,
University of Otago, and discoverer of the Flynn Effect

'Rolf Dobelli is brilliant at converting evidence from scientific research into practical steps that improve personal outcomes.'
Robert Cialdini, author of the international bestseller, *Influence*

'Dobelli writes clearly, intelligently and convincingly'
Gerhard Schroder, former Chancellor of Germany

'Rolf Dobelli has done it again! Not only does he open our eyes, now he wakes us up. Because of his rigorous scientific analysis combined with his shattering philosophical approach he is never satisfied with the superficial. So, grab Rolf's book and don't let it go!'   Tenley E. Albright,
Professor Emeritus, Harvard Medical School

'Rolf Dobelli is a virtuosic synthesizer of ideas. With wit, grace, and precision he melds science and art in his joyful pursuit of wisdom.'
Joshua Greene, Professor of Psychology,
Harvard University, and author of *Moral Tribes*

'Rolf Dobelli's works are informative, insightful, and accessible. In an age of celebrity ignoramuses, he is a true public intellectual.'
Lou Marinoff, Professor of Philosophy
at the City College of New York

'Dobelli possesses one of Europe's finest minds'
Matt Ridley, author of *The Evolution of Everything*

Also by Rolf Dobelli

The Art of Thinking Clearly

The Art of the Good Life

Clear Thinking for Business and a Better Life

ROLF DOBELLI

TRANSLATED FROM THE GERMAN
BY CAROLINE WAIGHT

SCEPTRE

Originally published in Germany in 2017
by Piper Verlag GmbH, München / Berlin

First published in Great Britain in 2017 by Sceptre
An Imprint of Hodder & Stoughton
An Hachette UK company

1

A CIP catalogue record for this title
is available from the British Library

Hardback ISBN 978 1 473 66748 8
eBook ISBN 978 1 473 66749 5

Printed and bound in Great Britain by Clays Ltd, St Ives plc

Hodder & Stoughton policy is to use papers that are natural, renewable and
recyclable products and made from wood grown in sustainable forests. The
logging and manufacturing processes are expected to conform to the environmental regulations of the country of origin.

Hodder & Stoughton Ltd
Carmelite House
50 Victoria Embankment
London EC4Y 0DZ

www.sceptrebooks.co.uk

CONTENTS

CONTENTS

For my wife, Sabine, and our twins, Numa and Avi

FOREWORD

Since antiquity—in other words, for at least 2,500 years, but probably much longer—people have been asking themselves what it means to live a *good life*. How should I live? What constitutes a *good life*? What's the role of fate? What's the role of money? Is leading a *good life* a question of mindset, of adopting a particular attitude, or is it more about reaching concrete life goals? Is it better to actively seek happiness or to avoid unhappiness?

Each generation poses these questions anew, and somehow the answers are always fundamentally disappointing. Why? Because we're constantly searching for a *single* principle, a *single* tenet, a *single* rule. Yet this holy grail of the *good life* doesn't exist.

Over the past few decades, a silent revolution has taken place within various fields of thought. In science, politics, economics, medicine and many other areas, scholars have come to realize that the world is far too complicated to summarize in one big idea or handful of principles. We need a mental toolkit with a range of tools in order to understand the world, but we also need one for practical living.

Over the past two hundred years, we have created a world we no longer understand intuitively. This means that entrepreneurs, investors, managers, doctors, journalists, artists, scientists, politicians and people like you and I will inevitably stumble our way through life unless we have a sound box of mental tools and models to fall back on.

You might also call this collection of methods and attitudes an "operating system for life," but I prefer the old-fashioned toolkit metaphor. Either way, the point is that these tools are more important than factual knowledge. They are more important than money, more important than relationships and more important than intelligence.

A few years ago I began assembling my own collection of mental tools designed to build a *good life*. In doing so I drew on a wealth of half-forgotten tools from classical antiquity, as well as on cutting-edge psychological research. You could even describe this book as classical life philosophy for the twenty-first century.

I've been using these tools in my daily life for years, and they've helped me cope with many challenges, great and small. Because my life has improved in almost every respect (my thinning hair and laughter lines have made me no less happy), I can recommend them to you with a clear conscience: these fifty-two intellectual tools may not guarantee you a *good life*, but they'll give you a fighting chance.

1

MENTAL ACCOUNTING

How to Turn a Loss into a Win

I should have known. Shortly before the motorway exit in Bern, there's a gray speed camera that lies in wait for unwary drivers. It's been there for years. No idea what I was thinking. The flash jolted me out of my reverie, and a quick glance at the speedometer confirmed my fears: I was going at least 10 mph too fast, and there was no other car for far and wide, nobody else I could pin the flash on.

The next day in Zurich, I watched from a distance as a police officer tucked a ticket underneath the windscreen wiper of my car. Yes, I was parked illegally. The car park was full, I was in a rush, and finding a legal parking space in central Zurich is like finding a deckchair in the Antarctic. For a moment I considered running over. I pictured myself standing in front of the officer, gasping for breath, hair disheveled, trying to make him understand my dilemma. But I let it go: years of experience have taught me that such things only make you feel silly. You look small, and you end up losing sleep.

Parking tickets used to infuriate me. These days I pay them with a smile. I just debit the sum from the account I've earmarked for donations. Each year I set aside 10,000 francs for good causes, and I pay all my fines out of that. In the world of psychology, this simple trick is known as mental accounting. I borrowed it from Richard Thaler, one of the founding fathers of behavioral economics. Mental accounting is considered a classic logical fallacy. People treat money differently depending on where it's coming from, so if you find money on the street, you treat it more casually and spend it more quickly and more frivolously than money you've actually earned. The parking-ticket example illustrates how you can turn this logical fallacy to your advantage. You're deliberately tricking yourself—for the sake of your own peace of mind.

Say you're traveling in an impoverished country, and your wallet disappears. Minutes later you find it again, and all that's missing is the cash. Do you see this as theft, or as a donation to somebody who's probably far worse off than you are? No amount of mental gymnastics will alter the fact that your money was stolen, but the significance of what happened, the interpretation of the event—*that* you can influence.

Living a *good life* has a lot to do with interpreting facts in a constructive way. I always mentally add 50 percent to prices in shops and restaurants. That's the amount this pair of shoes or sole *à la meunière* will actually cost me—taking income tax into account. If a glass of wine costs 10 dollars, I'll have to earn 15 in order to afford it. For me, that's good *mental accounting*, because it helps me keep my expenditure in check.

I prefer to pay for hotels in advance. That way I won't spoil a romantic weekend in Paris by being confronted with the bill at the end. The Nobel Laureate Daniel Kahneman calls this the peak–end rule: you remember the high point and the end point of your holiday, but the rest is forgotten. We'll take a closer look at this effect in Chapter 20. If the end of the trip is a big fat bill, presented to you like marching orders by a snooty French receptionist and complete with mysterious extras he has probably added on purpose (to punish you for not speaking accent-less French), your memory of the romantic getaway will be forever tarnished. Precommitment, they call it in psychology: pay first, consume later. It's a form of *mental accounting* that takes the sting out of payment.

I pay taxes with equal nonchalance. After all, I can't upturn the taxation system single-handed. So I compare what I get in return for my money in the lovely city of Bern with cities like Kuwait, Riyadh, the jam-packed concrete wasteland of Monaco or the surface of the moon—all places without income tax. Conclusion? I'd rather stay in Bern. People who move to ugly cities for tax reasons make themselves seem petty and stubborn—not exactly solid bedrock for a *good life*. Interestingly, my transactions with such individuals have thus far all been bad.

That money can't buy happiness is a truism, and I'd certainly advise you not to get worked into a lather over incremental differences in price. If a beer's two dollars more expensive than usual or two dollars cheaper, it elicits no emotional response in me whatsoever. I save my energy rather than my money. After all, the value of my stock portfolio fluctuates every minute by significantly more than two dollars, and if the Dow Jones falls by a thousandth of a percent, that doesn't faze me either. Try it for yourself. Come up with a similar number, a modest sum to which you're completely indifferent—money you consider not so much money as white noise. You don't lose anything by adopting that attitude, and certainly not your inner poise.

There was a period around the time I turned forty, after a long spell as an atheist, when I started doggedly trying to find God again. For several weeks the obliging Benedictine monks at Einsiedeln put me up as their guest. I have fond memories of this time, remote from worldly hustle and bustle—no TV, no internet and barely any phone signal, thanks to the thick medieval walls. Most of all I enjoyed the silence during meals—the monks were forbidden from speaking. I may not have found

God, but I did learn another *mental accounting* trick, this time temporal rather than monetary. In the refectory, as they called the dining hall, the cutlery is placed in a small black casket about eight inches long. At the beginning of the meal, you open the lid and extract the neatly bundled fork, spoon and knife. The message? You're basically already dead, and everything that follows is a gift. *Mental accounting* at its best. It taught me to value my time—and not to waste it getting into a tizzy.

Do you hate queuing at the supermarket till, waiting at the dentist's, and sitting in traffic jams on the motorway? Your blood pressure reaches 150 in seconds, and you start frantically releasing stress hormones. But instead of getting upset, consider the following: without this unnecessary agitation eating away at your body and soul, you'd live a whole year longer. That extra year would more than make up for all the time you spent in queues. The upshot? You can't nullify the loss of time and money, but you can reinterpret it. Open your box of *mental accounting* tricks and see for yourself: the more practiced you are at dodging fallacies, the more fun it is to occasionally commit one on purpose. Remember, it's for your own good.

2

THE FINE ART OF CORRECTION

Why We Overestimate Set-Up

You're sitting on a plane from London to New York. How much of the time is it sticking to the flight path, do you think? 90 percent of the time? 80 percent of the time? 70 percent of the time? The correct answer is never. Sitting beside the window, gazing out at the edge of the wing, you can watch the jumpy little ailerons—they're there to make constant adjustments to the flight path. Thousands of times per second, the autopilot recalculates the gap between where the plane *is* and where it *should* be and issues corrective instructions.

I've often had the pleasure of flying small planes without autopilot, when it's my job to carry out these minuscule adjustments. If I release the joystick even for a second, I drift off course. You'll recognize the feeling from driving a car: even on a dead-straight motorway, you can't take your hands off the wheel without veering out of your lane and risking an accident.

Our lives work like a plane or a car. We'd rather they didn't—that they ran according to plan, foreseeable and undisturbed. Then we'd only have to focus on the set-up, the optimal starting point. We'd arrange things perfectly at the beginning—education, career, love life, family—and reach our goals as planned. Of course, as I'm sure you know, it doesn't work like that. Our lives are exposed to constant turbulence, and we spend much of our time battling crosswinds and the unforeseen caprices of the weather. Yet we still behave like naïve fair-weather pilots: we overestimate the role of the set-up and systematically underestimate the role of correction.

As an amateur pilot I've learned that it's not so much the beginning that matters but the art of correction following take-off. After billions of years, nature knows it too. As cells divide, copying errors are perpetually being made in the genetic material, so in every cell there are molecules retroactively correcting these errors. Without this process of DNA repair, as it's known, we'd die of cancer hours after conception. Our immune system follows the same principle. There's no master plan, because threats are impossible to predict. Hostile viruses and bacteria are constantly mutating, and our defenses can only function through perpetual correction.

So next time you hear that an apparently perfect marriage between two perfectly well-matched partners is on the rocks, don't be too surprised. It's a clear case of set-up overestimation. Frankly, anyone who's spent more than five minutes in a relationship should already know that without ongoing fine-tuning and repairs, it doesn't work. All partnerships have to be consistently nurtured. The most common misunderstanding I encounter is that the *good life* is a stable state or condition. Wrong. The *good life* is only achieved through constant readjustment.

Then why are we so reluctant to correct and revise? Because we interpret every little piece of repair work as a flaw in the plan. Obviously, we say to ourselves, our plan isn't working out. We're embarrassed. We feel like failures. The truth is that plans almost never work out down to the last detail, and if one does occasionally come off without a hitch, it's purely accidental. As the American general—and later president—Dwight Eisenhower said, "Plans are nothing. Planning is everything."

It's not about having a fixed plan, it's about repeated re-planning—an ongoing process. The moment your troops meet your opponents', Eisenhower realized, any plan is going to be obsolete.

Political constitutions lay out the fundamental laws on which all other legislation rests, and in theory should be time-less. Yet not even constitutions go unrevised. The constitution of the United States—originally signed in 1787—has been amended twenty-seven times so far. The Federal Constitution of the Swiss Confederation has undergone two thorough-going revisions since 1848 and dozens of partial ones. The German constitution of 1949 has been altered sixty times. This isn't an embarrassment; it's eminently sensible. A capacity for correc-tion is the foundation of any functional democracy. It's not about electing the right man or the right woman (i.e., the "right set-up"); it's about replacing the wrong man or the wrong woman without bloodshed. Democracy has a built-in correc-tion mechanism—and it's the only form of government that does.

In other areas, unfortunately, we're even less willing to cor-rect ourselves. Our school system is largely geared toward the set-up: the emphasis on factual knowledge and certifications makes it seem like life is primarily about getting the best possi-ble grades and giving our careers the best possible jump-start. Yet the connection between degrees and workplace success is growing ever more tenuous, while the ability to self-correct is growing ever more important—even though it's hardly taught at school.

The same phenomenon is apparent in the development of our characters. I'm sure you know at least one person you'd consider a wise and mature individual. What do you think: was it the set-up—the perfect genes, an ideal upbringing, a first-class education—that made this person so wise? Or was it acts of correction, of constant work on their own issues and shortcomings, a gradual elimination of these inadequacies from their lives?

The upshot? We've got to get rid of the stigma attached to correction. People who self-correct early on have an advantage over those who spend ages fiddling with the perfect set-up and crossing their fingers that their plans will work out. There's no such thing as the ideal training. There's more than one life goal. There's no perfect business strategy, no optimal stock portfolio, no one right job. They're all myths. The truth is that you begin with one set-up and then constantly adjust it. The more complicated the world becomes, the less important your starting point is. So don't invest all your resources into the perfect set-up—at work or in your personal life. Instead, practice the art of correction by revising the things that aren't quite working—swiftly and without feeling guilty. It's no accident that I'm typing these lines in Word 14.7.1. Version 1.0 hasn't been on the market for years.

3

THE PLEDGE

Inflexibility as a Stratagem

In 1519 the Spanish conqueror Hernán Cortés reached the coast of Mexico from Cuba. He summarily declared Mexico a Spanish colony, and himself the governor. He then destroyed his ship, eliminating any chance of return for himself and his men.

From an economic perspective, Cortés's decision makes no sense. Why exclude the possibility of returning right from square one? Why exclude alternatives? One of the most important principles of economics, after all, is that the more options you have, the better. So why did Cortés abandon his freedom of choice?

Two or three times a year, I meet the CEO of a major international corporation at various obligatory dinners to which we've both been invited. For years I've found it striking that he always turns down dessert. Until recently, I considered his behavior illogical and ascetic. Why exclude the sweet option on principle? Why not decide on a case-by-case basis? Why not make his decision dependent on how much he weighs, how filling the main course was, or how tempting the dessert looks? A blanket refusal of pudding may be a less dramatic decision than barring your return home, but at first glance they both seem unnecessary.

One of the world's most important experts on management is Clayton Christensen, the Harvard professor known for his international bestseller *The Innovator's Dilemma*. A committed Mormon, Christensen leads his life according to *pledges*—an old term for a promise one cannot break. If *pledge* sounds too fusty, call it "absolute commitment." I'm a fan of the older term, because these days "commitment" is subject to inflation and often used insincerely (e.g., "we are committed to improving the state of the world"). Only an individual, not an organization, can make such a *pledge*.

In his younger years, Christensen saw many managers sacrifice the first stage of their lives to their careers so that they could dedicate the second half—by now financially independent—to their families, only to discover that their families had either fallen apart or long since flown the coop. So Christensen made a *pledge*, promising God not to work at the weekends and to eat dinner at home with his family on weeknights. Sometimes, this meant he'd get to work at three in the morning.

When I first heard this, I found Christensen's behavior irrational, obstinate and uneconomical. Why be so inflexible? Why not decide on a case-by-case basis? Sometimes you simply *have* to work on the weekend, and then you can make up for it by working a bit less on Monday and Tuesday. Flexibility is an asset, surely, especially at a time when everything is in flux.

Today I have a different perspective. When it comes to important issues, flexibility isn't an advantage—it's a trap. Cortés, the dessert-averse CEO and Clayton Christensen: what all three of them have in common is that they use radical inflexibility to reach long-term goals that would be unrealizable if their behavior were more flexible. How so? Two reasons. First: constantly having to make new decisions situation by situation saps your willpower. *Decision fatigue* is the technical term for this. A brain exhausted by decision-making will plump for the most convenient option, which more often than not is also the worst one. This is why *pledges* make so much sense. Once you've *pledged* something, you don't then have to weigh up the pros and cons each and every time you're faced with a decision. It's already been made for you, saving you mental energy.

The second reason inflexibility is so valuable has to do with reputation. By being consistent on certain topics, you signal where you stand and establish the areas where there's no room for negotiation. You communicate self-mastery, making yourself less vulnerable to attack. Mutual deterrents during the Cold War were based largely on this effect. The USA and the USSR both knew that a nuclear strike would mean instant retaliation. No deliberation, no situational weighing up of pros and cons. The decision for or against the red button had already been taken. Pressing it first simply wasn't an option.

What applies to nations applies equally to you. If you lead a life consistent with your *pledges*—whatever those look like— people will gradually start to leave you in peace. Legendary investor Warren Buffett, for instance, refuses on principle to negotiate. If you want to sell him your company, you've got exactly one shot. You can make precisely *one* offer. Buffett will either buy the company at the price you suggest, or he won't buy it at all. If it's too high, there's no point lowering it. A no is a no, and everybody realizes that. Buffett has acquired such a reputation for inflexibility that he's now guaranteed to be offered the best deal right from the word go, without wasting any time on haggling.

Commitments, *pledges*, unconditional principles—it sounds simple, but it's not. Say you're driving a truck full of dynamite down a ramrod-straight, single-lane road. Another truck is coming toward you, also loaded with dynamite. Who swerves first? If you can convince the other driver that you've made the stronger commitment, you'll win. In other words, the other driver will swerve first (assuming he's acting rationally). If, for example, you can convince the other driver that your steering wheel is locked and you've thrown the key out of the window, you're signaling an extremely strong commitment. That's how strong, believable and radical your pledges have to be in order for your signals to be effective.

So say good-bye to the cult of flexibility. Flexibility makes you unhappy and tired, and it distracts you from your goals. Chain yourself to your *pledges*. Uncompromisingly. It's easier to stick to your *pledges* 100 percent of the time rather than 99 percent.

4

BLACK BOX THINKING

Reality Doesn't Care About Your Feelings; or, Why Every False Step Improves Your Life

The British de Havilland Comet 1 was the world's first commercially produced jetliner. In 1953 and 1954, it was involved in a number of mysterious accidents in which the machines broke up in midair. One plane crashed shortly after take-off from Calcutta airport; another split apart as it flew over the Italian island of Elba. A few weeks later, a Comet 1 plummeted into the sea outside Naples. In all three cases, there were no survivors. The fleet was grounded, but investigators couldn't determine what caused the crashes, so flights were resumed. Just two weeks later, another plane tumbled from the sky just outside Naples (again)—the final nail in the Comet 1's coffin.

Eventually the flaw was identified: hairline cracks had formed at the corners of the plane's square windows, spreading across the fuselage and eventually causing the whole machine to come apart. The Comet 1 is the reason why passengers these days only ever peer through oval windows. But there was another, more significant consequence: after the disaster, accident investigator David Warren suggested that a near-indestructible flight data recorder (later dubbed a black box) be installed in each and every jetliner—an idea that was later implemented. A black box records thousands of pieces of data per second, including the pilots' conversations in the cockpit, making it easier to determine the exact cause of a crash.

No industry takes mistakes more seriously than airlines. After his spectacular emergency landing in the Hudson River, Captain Sullenberger wrote: "Everything we know in aviation, every rule in the rule book, every procedure we have, we know because someone somewhere died." With each crash, future flights become safer. This principle—let's call it *black box thinking*—is an exquisite mental tool that can be applied to any other area of life. The term *black box thinking* was coined by Matthew Syed, who dedicated a whole book to it.

Human beings are the exact opposite of the aviation industry. Say, for instance, you bought shares several years ago for 100 dollars each. Now they're valued at a measly 10 dollars. What's going through your head? You're hoping—probably praying—that the stock price rebounds as soon as possible. Or you're cursing the company management. Or you're reaching for the bottle to take the edge off your frustration. Very few people simply accept reality and analyze their own flight recorders. This requires precisely two things: a) *radical acceptance* and b) *black box thinking*. First one, then the other.

Overdraft at the bank? It's staying put, I'm afraid, regardless of your feelings. Angry e-mail to the boss? There's no getting it back, no matter how many glasses of wine you drink trying to justify your tantrum. Nor does the cancer growing inside you care if you think about it or ignore it.

Psychologist Paul Dolan at the London School of Economics

has observed how people who are gaining weight will gradually shift their focus to areas of their lives where the number on the scale is less relevant—to their jobs, for instance. Why? Because it's easier to redirect your focus than to lose weight. Yet the fat couldn't care less about your focus, your interests or your motivation. The world isn't remotely interested in what you think of it or how you feel. Banish all such obscurantist tactics from your brain.

"Nothing is more fatiguing nor, in the long run, more exasperating than the daily effort to believe things which daily become more incredible. To be done with this effort is an indispensable condition of sure and lasting happiness," wrote mathematician and Nobel Prize winner Bertrand Russell. This is an exaggeration, of course, because sure and lasting happiness does not exist. Yet Russell is correct in his observation that self-deception is incompatible with the *good life*. Accepting reality is easy when you like what you see, but you've got to accept it even when you don't—*especially* when you don't. Russell follows up with an example: "The playwright whose plays never succeed should consider calmly the hypothesis that they are bad plays." You may not write plays, but I'm sure you can come up with examples from your own life. Perhaps you have no talent for foreign languages? Not a natural manager or athlete? You should take these truths into account—and consider the consequences.

Radical acceptance of defeats, deficiencies, flops—how does that work? If we're left to our own devices, it's a bit of a chore. Often we see other people far more clearly than we see ourselves (which is why we're so frequently disappointed by others but rarely by ourselves), so your best shot is to find a friend or a partner you can rely on to give you the warts-and-all truth. Even then, your brain will do its best to soft-pedal the facts it doesn't like. With time, however, you'll learn to take seriously the judgments of others.

Alongside radical acceptance, you'll need a black box. Build your own. Whenever you make a big decision, write down what's going through your mind—assumptions, trains of thought, conclusions. If the decision turns out to be a dud, take a look at your flight data recorder (no need to make it crash-proof; a notebook will do just fine) and analyze precisely what it was that led to your mistake. It's that simple. With each explicable fuck-up, your life will get better. If you can't identify your mistake, you either don't understand the world or you don't understand yourself. To put it another way, if you can't spot where you put a foot wrong, you're going to fall flat on your face again. Persistence in your analysis will pay off.

Side note: *black box thinking* works not only on a personal level but also in the business world. It ought to be standard practice for every corporation.

By themselves, *radical acceptance* and *black box thinking* are not enough. You've got to rectify your mistakes. Get future-proofing. As Warren Buffett's business partner Charlie Munger has observed, "If you won't attack a problem while it's solvable and wait until it's unfixable, you can argue that you're so damn foolish that you deserve the problem." Don't wait for the consequences to unfold. "If you don't deal with reality, then reality will deal with you," warns author Alex Haley.

So accept reality—accept it radically. Especially the bits you don't like. It might be painful in the moment, but it's got to be done. It'll be worth it later on. Life isn't easy. Even living a *good life*, you'll have to deal with your fair share of failure, and it's okay to put a foot wrong every now and then. The key is to discover why it happened and tackle the issue at its root. Because problems aren't like great Bordeaux wines—they don't improve with age.

5

COUNTERPRODUCTIVITY

Why Timesavers Are Often Timewasters

The automobile. There's no question that, compared to walking or the horse-drawn carriage, it was a quantum leap in terms of efficiency. Instead of sauntering around at 4 mph or rattling over hill and down dale at 10 mph, today you can reach an easy 100 mph on the (German) motorway without any effort at all. Even given the occasional red light, what would you say is the overall average speed of your car? Write down your estimate in the margin of this page before you read on.

How did you make that calculation? Presumably you divided the total number of miles driven per year by the approximate number of hours spent on the road per year. That's a figure, incidentally, that your car's on-board computer can provide. My Rover Discovery calculates it at about 30 mph. Yet this calculation is incorrect. There are other factors to take into account: a) the number of hours you had to work in order to buy the car; b) the number of hours you have to work in order to pay for the insurance, maintenance, petrol and parking tickets; and c) the time you spend traveling to work for a) and b), including sitting in traffic jams. The Catholic priest Ivan Illich totted up all this for cars in the USA. The result? An American car has an average speed of exactly 3.7 mph—walking pace, in other words. And this was in the seventies, when the USA had 40 percent fewer inhabitants but just as many motorways. Today the average speed is almost certainly below 3.7 mph.

Illich called this effect *counterproductivity*. The term refers to the fact that while many technologies seem at first glance to be saving us time and money, this saving vanishes into thin air as soon as you do a full cost analysis. No matter how you prefer to travel, *counterproductivity* is a decision-making trap, and you're better off giving it a wide berth.

Take e-mail, for example. Viewed in isolation, it's brilliant. You can type and send it off within seconds—and for free, at that! But appearances can be deceptive. Every e-mail address attracts spam that has to be filtered out. Worse yet, most of the messages landing in your inbox are irrelevant, but you still have to read them in order to decide whether they require action on your part. It's hugely time-consuming. Strictly speaking, you should factor in a slice of the cost of your computer and smartphone, plus the time it takes to update your software. A rough estimate puts the cost at one dollar per relevant e-mail—i.e., just as much as an old-fashioned letter.

Let's take presentations as an example. A talk—given to management or customers—used to consist of a series of coherent arguments. Handwritten notes sufficed, enlivened, perhaps, with a few lines on an overhead projector. In 1990, PowerPoint launched onto the market. All at once, millions of managers and/or their assistants starting sinking millions of hours into their presentations, adding garish colors, bizarre fonts and oh-so-hilarious animation effects. Net gain: nil. Suddenly, everybody was using PowerPoint, so it soon lost its impact—a classic *arms-race effect* (see Chapter 46). The hidden costs of *counterproductivity* come into play, in the form of millions of hours squandered on learning the software, installing endless upgrades and, finally, designing and prettifying the slides. PowerPoint is generally considered "productivity" software. Properly, however, it should be called "counterproductivity" software.

The negative effect of *counterproductivity* may often catch us unawares—but it comes as no surprise to biologists. The effects have been apparent in nature for millions of years. The male peacock—furnished, in a kind of esthetic arms race with the competition, with increasingly long and beautiful plumage—is faced with the impact of *counterproductivity* as soon as he runs into a fox. The longer and more magnificent his feathers, the better his chances with the ladies—and the easier he becomes for predators to spot. Over millions of years, a balance has developed between sexual attractiveness and inconspicuousness, which ensures survival. Every extra centimeter of plumage has a *counterproductive* effect. The same is true, incidentally, of a stag's antlers or the vocal skills of songbirds.

So be on your guard against *counterproductivity*. It's apparent only at a second glance. I've got used to only using *one* laptop (there's no network at my house), keeping the number of apps on my smartphone to an absolute minimum and only rarely replacing still-functional older gadgets. I avoid all other technology. No TV, no radio, no gaming consoles, no smart watch, no Alexa. From where I sit, smart homes are a horror-movie scenario. I'd rather switch my lights on and off manually than use an app I have to install, connect to the internet and continually update. Plus, my old-fashioned light switches can't be hacked—another *counterproductive* factor that can be eliminated.

Do you remember when digital cameras came on the market? Liberation! At least, that's how it felt at the time. No more expensive film, no more waiting for it to be developed, no more unflattering photographs—you can easily take a dozen more. It looked like a huge simplification, but in hindsight it's a clear case of *counterproductivity*. Today we're sitting on a mountain of photos and videos, 99 percent of which are superfluous, without the time to sort through them, yet compelled to schlep them all over the place in local back-up drives and in the cloud, visible and exploitable by large internet corporations. On top of that is the time you now have to spend working on the images, the complex software that periodically demands updates, and the labor-intensive transfers required when you buy a new computer.

The upshot? Technology—usually heralded as full of promise—often has a *counterproductive* effect on our quality of life. A basic rule of the *good life* is as follows: if it doesn't genuinely contribute something, you can do without it. And that is doubly true for technology. Next time, try switching on your brain instead of reaching for the nearest gadget.

6

THE NEGATIVE ART OF THE GOOD LIFE

Do Nothing Wrong and the Right Thing Will Happen

"There are old pilots and there are bold pilots, but there are no bold old pilots." As an amateur pilot myself, I'm often put in mind of this saying. I quite like the idea of being an old pilot someday. It's certainly better than the alternative.

When I clamber into the cockpit of my old single-engine plane (a 1975 vintage), I'm not aiming for anything spectacular. I'm just trying not to crash. The potential causes of a crash are well established: flying in bad weather, flying without a checklist, flying when you're too tired, flying without proper fuel reserves.

Investing in the stock market might not put your survival at risk, but there's plenty of money at stake. Investors often talk about "upside" and "downside." By "upside," they mean the total conceivable positive results of an investment (such as an above-average yield), while "downside" encompasses all possible negative results (such as bankruptcy). These terms can also be applied to flying. Before and during a flight, I focus almost exclusively on the potential downside and how to avoid it. The upside, on the other hand, gets very little of my attention. The majesty of the snowy Alps, the gorgeous cloud formations, the way my sandwich tastes at this dizzying height—all that will come. As long as I keep the downside at bay, the upside will take care of itself.

Investor Charles Ellis recommends the same approach for amateur tennis players. Unlike pros, who can place virtually every shot wherever they choose, amateurs make endless mistakes. They smash the ball into the net. They aim too long, too high, at the wrong area of the court. Professional tennis is an entirely different game from the amateur variety: pros *win* points; amateurs *lose* points. This means that if you're playing against an amateur, your best option is to focus on not making any mistakes. Play conservatively, and keep the ball in play as long as possible. Unless your opponent is deliberately playing equally conservatively, he or she will make more mistakes than you do. In amateur tennis, matches aren't *won*—they're *lost*.

Concentrating on the downside instead of the upside is a valuable intellectual tool. Greek, Roman and medieval thinkers even had a name for this approach: negative theology—the negative path, the way of renunciation, of omission, of reduction. The basic idea is that you can't say what God is, you can only say what God isn't. Or, in our terms, you can't say what a *good life* guarantees; you can only say what a *good life* prevents—but you can say that for sure.

For 2,500 years, philosophers, theologians, doctors, sociologists, economists, psychologists, brain researchers and advertising executives have been trying to figure out what makes people happy, yet the body of knowledge they've produced is still somewhat puny. Social contacts are important, they tell us. It helps to have a sense of purpose. Sex is probably a good idea, as is moral behavior. Well, great. I think we could probably have worked that out for ourselves. Their results could hardly be less precise. In terms of concrete contributing factors to happiness—the happiness upside—we're still fumbling around in the dark.

But when we ask what factors have a significant *negative*

impact on the *good life*—which factors *jeopardize* it—we can pinpoint them exactly: alcoholism, drug addiction, chronic stress, noise, a lengthy commute, a job you despise, unemployment, a dysfunctional marriage, stupidly high expectations, poverty, debt and financial dependence, loneliness, spending too much time with moaning Minnies, overreliance on external validation, constant self-comparisons with others, thinking like a victim, self-loathing, chronic sleep deprivation, depression, anxiety, rage and envy. You don't need science to tell you that. You can see it for yourself—in your own mind, in friends, in your community. The downside is always more concrete than the upside. The downside is like granite—hard, tangible, solid. Whereas the upside is like air.

So do your best to systematically eliminate the downside in your life—then you'll have a real chance of achieving a *good life*. Of course, fate may intervene at any time: a meteorite destroys your house, a war breaks out, your child drowns, your company goes bust. But fate, by definition, is immune to influence. So don't dwell on it.

You're probably thinking I left out a thing or two from the list above: disease, disabilities, divorce. However, countless studies have shown that the impact of these factors dissipates more quickly than we imagine. In the initial months after an injury, paraplegics focus almost exclusively on their disability—understandably so—and they feel correspondingly miserable. Yet after just a few months, their mood normalizes. Ordinary, everyday issues return to the forefront of their minds, while their physical injuries fade into the background. The same is true of divorce. After a year or two's travail, you reach the other side of the valley of tears. But alcoholism, drug addiction, chronic stress, noise, lengthy commutes—indeed, any of the factors on the first list: those aren't things people learn to live with. Those cannot simply be normalized. They're always present, and they make a *good life* impossible.

Investors who have been successful in the long term, such as Warren Buffett and Charlie Munger, work with mental tricks, tools and attitudes that are eminently applicable to everyday life. Step one: avoid the downside. In their investments, Buffett and Munger are careful first and foremost about what to avoid—i.e., what *not* to do—before they even think about the upside. Buffett observes: "Charlie and I have *not* learned how to solve difficult business problems. What we have learned is to avoid them." You don't have to be a genius to do that. Charlie Munger has commented, "It is remarkable how much long-term advantage people like us have gotten by trying to be consistently not stupid, instead of trying to be very intelligent."

So what should we take away from all this? That a big part of the *good life* is about steering clear of stupidity, foolishness and trends instead of striving for ultimate bliss. It's not what you add that enriches your life—it's what you omit. Or as Munger once quipped (revealing that he's not lacking intelligence in the humor department, either): "All I want to know is where I'm going to die, so I'll never go there."

7

THE OVARIAN LOTTERY

Why You Didn't Earn Your Successes

Happiness is something you have, but success you've got to earn—or so we think. Take stock and ask yourself: how successful has my life been so far? Use a scale from +10 (superstar) to -10 (total loser). Jot down your answer in the margin. Then ask yourself a follow-up question: how much of this success can be attributed to your own actions—to your effort, your work, your input? In other words, how much of your success is truly your own? And how much is down to chance, to factors beyond your control? Note down these two as percentages. I'd guess you attributed something like 60 percent to your own achievement and 40 percent to factors beyond your control. At least, that's the answer I get from most people.

Now I want you to run a little thought experiment I got from Warren Buffett: "Imagine there are two identical twins in the womb, both equally bright and energetic. And the genie says to them, 'One of you is going to be born in the United States, and one of you is going to be born in Bangladesh. And if you wind up in Bangladesh, you will pay no taxes. What percentage of your income would you bid to be the one that is born in the United States?'" Buffett is speaking here about the *ovarian lottery*. You could substitute Great Britain, Germany or any other developed nation for the USA, of course. How would you reply?

Most people I ask put the figure at 80 percent. I'd say the same. In other words, we're prepared to sacrifice an extremely high proportion of our income to grow up in our preferred country. The fact that our place of birth is worth that much money to us makes it clear how greatly it influences our success.

The *ovarian lottery* doesn't end with your country of origin. You weren't just born in a particular nation, but in an area with a particular postcode and into a particular family. None of that is within your control. You have been given values, behaviors and principles that help or hinder you in everyday life, and again these are beyond your control. You were slotted into an educational system with teachers you didn't choose. You got sick, suffered fortune's slings and arrows (or were spared them), and were responsible for absolutely none of it. You slipped into a series of roles and you made decisions—based on what? Perhaps you read a book that changed your life—but how did you come to hear about it? Say you met somebody who opened doors for you, without which you wouldn't have got where you are today. Who do you have to thank for this acquaintance?

Even if you've had your fair share of tussles with fate, you've got to admit that you're enormously lucky. Six percent of all the people who have ever lived on Earth are alive at this moment. To put it another way, six percent of all the people who have been born over the last 300,000 years—since Homo sapiens populated the world—are alive in the present day. They could just as easily have been born into another era; indeed, the probability of that is 94 percent. Imagine yourself as a slave in the Roman Empire, a geisha during the Ming Dynasty, a water-carrier in ancient Egypt. How many of your inborn talents would have been worth much in those environments?

My wife and I have twins, the non-identical kind. The one

who's forty seconds older has blonde hair and blue eyes, while the second has black hair and dark eyes. Although we made every effort to bring up both boys in the same way, their personalities are fundamentally different. One is always in a good mood; he's warm and open with other people. The second finds it difficult to socialize, but he's extremely skillful at anything that involves using his small hands. He has been since birth. The haphazard mixing of my wife's genes and mine produced two new human beings. Similarly, your genes are a coincidental blend of your parents', which in turn are a coincidental blend of your grandparents' genes, and so on and so forth. During the reign of Louis XIV, the Sun King, there were approximately four thousand people alive who contributed genetic material to your contemporary mixture. You are their descendant. Did you recruit any of these four thousand people? No. Think about that next time you visit Versailles.

What you are, you owe to your genes—and the environment in which your genetic blueprint was realized. Even your level of intelligence is largely determined by your genes. So is whether you're introverted or extroverted, open-minded or anxious, reliable or sloppy. If you believe your success is based on relentlessly hard work, on driving tenacity and far too many night shifts, you're not necessarily wrong. It's just that you owe the willpower you're so proud of to the interplay between your genes and environment.

So, given all that: what proportion of your success would you ascribe to your own achievement? Correct. The logical answer is zero percent. Your successes are fundamentally based on things over which you have no control whatsoever. You haven't really "earned" your achievements.

Two consequences. First: stay humble—especially if you're successful. The greater your success, the less you should toot your own horn. Modesty has fallen out of fashion these days, and there's nothing we like better than showing off on social media. Restrain yourself. I'm not talking about false modesty here, but the genuine article. The thing is, you see, that people who pat themselves on the back—even if they do so quietly—have been taken in by an illusion. Pride is not only pointless; it's also factually misplaced. Getting rid of it is a fundamental cornerstone of the *good life* (more on that in Chapter 51). Remind yourself daily that everything you are, everything you have and can do, is the result of blind chance. For those of us blessed with good luck—i.e., for you and me—gratitude is the only appropriate response. One nice side effect is that grateful people are demonstrably happier people.

Second: willingly and ungrudgingly surrender part of your (unearned) success to people who were born with the wrong genes into the wrong families, in the areas with the wrong postcodes. It's not just noble; it's commonsensical. Donations and taxes aren't financial matters. First and foremost, they're issues of morality.

8

THE INTROSPECTION ILLUSION

Take Feelings Seriously—Just Not Your Own

What can you see right now? What objects are in front of you? Try to describe them as precisely as possible. Take a minute before you read on.

Another question: how do you feel right now? What emotions can you identify? Try to describe them as precisely as possible. Take a minute before you read on.

In the first case, I'm sure your answers were very precise. You see the page of a book, black letters on a white background. Perhaps you looked up and let your gaze sweep around the room: furniture, potted plants, pictures on the wall. No matter what you saw, it was easy to describe.

Now look at your answers to the follow-up question about your emotions. They're probably somewhat nebulous. Maybe you're in a bad mood right now, but what precisely do you feel? Are you angry, disappointed, sulky, peevish, bitter? And if so, then why? If you're in a good mood, where exactly has it come from? Perhaps you sensed no current emotions in particular, or they only surfaced once I asked about them.

Don't be frustrated if you had a hard time describing your feelings. It's not that you're inarticulate. English has more than three hundred adjectives to identify different emotions. We have more words for emotions than for colors—yet we cannot express them clearly. "The introspection of current conscious experience, far from being secure, nearly infallible, is faulty, untrustworthy, and misleading—not just *possibly* mistaken, but massively and pervasively. I don't *think* it's just me in the dark here, but most of us," Stanford professor Eric Schwitzgebel has observed of this inability.

It would be easy enough to live with if the whole world wasn't endlessly badgering us to follow our hearts. Trust your emotions! Listen to your inner voice! My advice? Don't bother. Don't make your emotions your compass. Your inner voice—if we continue with the compass metaphor—consists of a dozen magnetic needles, all pointing in different directions and swiveling incessantly around and around. Would you set sail across an ocean with a compass like that? Exactly. So don't use it to navigate your life.

You won't find the *good life* through introspection. Psychologists call it the *introspection illusion*—the mistaken belief that we can learn what we truly desire through sheer intellectual contemplation. That we can discover the purpose, the meaning of our lives, dig down to some golden, blissful core. The fact is that chasing your heart deep into the forest—to use a common poetic description of our inner landscape—is guaranteed to get you hopelessly lost. You'll end up bogged down in moods, fragments of thought and fits of emotion.

If you've ever given a job interview, you'll be familiar with the problem. You chat to the candidate for half an hour, then you're expected to pronounce judgment on this basis. Research has shown that such interviews are useless, and you're better off analyzing the candidate's track record. Makes sense. After all, what's more meaningful: thirty brief minutes of conversation or thirty years' overall accomplishment? Introspection is nothing but a job interview with yourself—highly unreliable. What you *should* be exploring is your past. What are the recurring themes in your life? Examine the evidence, not your subsequent interpretation of it.

But why, then, is introspection so unreliable? Two reasons. First, listening to your inner voice ever more deeply and often isn't going to help you replicate your genes in the next generation. From an evolutionary perspective, it's far more crucial that you be able to read the emotions of *others*. Which is reassuring, because we're demonstrably more skillful at that. In practical terms, this means your best bet is to ask a friend or a partner what's going on inside your head. He or she will be a more objective judge.

The second reason why introspection is so unreliable? It's that people love nothing better than being the sole authority in the room. Whatever we decide we feel deep down, there's nobody around to contradict us. That might feel pleasant, but it's not very helpful, because there's no mechanism for correction.

Because our emotions are so unreliable, a good rule of thumb is to take them less seriously—especially the negative ones. The Greek philosophers called this ability to block things out *ataraxia*, a term meaning serenity, peace of mind, equanimity, composure or imperturbability. A master of *ataraxia* will maintain his or her poise despite the buffets of fate. One level higher is *apatheia*, the total eradication of feeling (also attempted by the ancient Greeks). Both—*ataraxia* and *apatheia*—are ideals virtually impossible to attain, but don't worry: I'm not asking you to try. I do, however, believe we need to cultivate a new relationship with our inner voices, one distanced, skeptical and playful.

I, for example, treat my feelings as though they don't belong to me. They arrive from somewhere else, pay me a visit, then retreat. If you'd like it in metaphorical terms, I see myself as a huge and airy covered market, in which birds of all varieties flit from spot to spot. Sometimes they simply flutter through the marketplace, sometimes they dawdle a little longer, and sometimes they even let something fall. But, sooner or later, they all move on. Some I like more, some I like less, but since I sketched out this image in my head I've no longer been "owned" by emotions. I don't even feel like I own them. Some of these visitors aren't exactly welcome, but they don't perturb me overmuch—like the birds in the covered market. I ignore them, or watch them from a distance. And the bird metaphor can be taken further still: if you assign species of birds to your emotions, you can treat them even more playfully. Jealousy, in my imagination, is a small green chirruping sparrow. Anxiety a flapping thrush. And so it goes on—you get the picture.

You probably recognize this from your own experience: if you try to repress negative emotions with sheer force of will, you only make them stronger. Yet if you can figure out a relaxed, unserious way of dealing with them, you might not achieve total equanimity (nobody does) but you will find a certain sense of composure. If the bird metaphor doesn't appeal to you, then picture your feelings as toddlers. Pressure won't get you very far with them, but a playful approach works wonders.

Admittedly, some emotions—especially self-pity, worry and jealousy—are so toxic that a playful approach by itself won't do the trick. They require additional cognitive strategies, which we'll go into in Chapters 24, 29 and 32. Fundamentally, however, the message holds true: don't trust your emotions. You can be much more specific about what's in a Big Mac than about how you feel while you're eating it. So take other people's feelings very seriously, but not your own. Let them flit through you—they'll come and go anyway, just as they please.

9

THE AUTHENTICITY TRAP

Why You Need a Secretary of State

Do you like authentic people? Of course you do. With authentic people you always know where you stand. You know what they think and feel, what they're doing and what they've got in mind. Such guileless individuals make no secret of what's below the surface, which is why personal interaction with them is so intimate, so pleasant and efficient. No wonder authenticity is in vogue. These days you can barely squeak through a training seminar without a unit on it. No leadership book is complete without a chapter on "authentic leadership," no secrets-of-success-type blog without tips about how to be as "raw" and authentic as possible. Just as it's unwise to invest in a forged Picasso, it's unwise to invest in people who aren't "genuine"—neither time nor money.

But how authentic are we talking? Let's run a thought experiment. Say you're meeting your über-authentic friend Lisa for lunch. She turns up twenty minutes late, hair looking like a cat's been scrabbling around in it. She mutters an apology then announces loudly enough for the whole restaurant to hear that she's "not really in the mood" for lunch today, and "definitely not in some restaurant that used to be cool." The diners at the next table lower their forks. After a moment of silence, Lisa starts complimenting your outfit, although she points out that your watch "doesn't really go with it," at least not the way you've put everything together. She leans across the table mid-flow, grabs the glass of wine you've just ordered, and downs it in a single gulp: "Sorry, I was soooo thirsty!" Having finished her starter, she then plonks her head down onto the table and goes to sleep—leaving you caught in the crossfire of strangers' glances. Five minutes later, when the spaghetti is served, she wakes up and stretches with an animal yawn, laughing: "I'm just not myself without my power nap, you know?" Picking up one strand of spaghetti after the next, she dunks them into the sauce with her fingers then lets them fall into her mouth, declaring that it's "so much more fun that way." Then, because she's "simply got to get it off her chest," she tells you everything she dreamt last night, all of which is total nonsense—but you've already asked for the bill. And that, dearest reader, is a rough distillation of authenticity in its purest form.

In his book *Mirror, Mirror*, the British philosopher Simon Blackburn recounts the story of Charles Darwin's burial in Westminster Abbey. William, the great biologist's eldest son (and most important mourner), was sitting in the first row of the cathedral when he felt a sudden draught across his bald head, so he took off his black gloves and draped them over his bare scalp—where they remained for all to see throughout the whole service.

William Darwin may not have been as bad as our fictional lunch date Lisa, but it's safe to say you can have too much authenticity. We expect a certain degree of propriety, of manners, of self-control—of civilized misrepresentation. Face-to-face, at least. Online we've long ago devolved to Lisa's level. If you're not sharing your innermost feelings in an online video before you go to bed, you're considered stuffy and insincere. Yet fundamentally even the most authentic of these displays on social media remains artificial, stage-managed. And the users know it.

My recommendation? Don't buy into the authenticity hype. For several reasons. One: there's the simple fact that we don't really know who we are. As we saw in the previous chapter, our inner voice is anything but a reliable compass. It's more like a hodgepodge of conflicting impulses. We don't understand ourselves, so what exactly is "authentic" behavior supposed to be revealing? Authenticity has a role to play in a romantic relationship or a very close friendship, but it's out of place in a casual acquaintanceship, and certainly in public.

Two: you're making yourself look ridiculous. Name one famous figure you truly respect—a statesman, a general, a philosopher, a captain of industry, a scientist—who regularly blurts out their innermost feelings. You won't find one. People are respected because they deliver on their promises, not because they let us eavesdrop on their inner monologs.

Three: cells are the building blocks of life. Every cell is enclosed by a membrane, the purpose of which is to repel hostile intruders and precisely regulate which molecules are allowed to pass through. We see the same dynamic play out with the organism as a whole—and for the same reasons. Animals have skin, trees bark. An organism with no outer layer would die immediately. On a psychological level, authenticity just means you've given up on this barrier. You're practically inviting people to exploit you. You're making yourself not just silly but vulnerable.

General Eisenhower deliberately crafted a persona for the outside world. *New York Times* columnist David Brooks talks about Eisenhower adopting a "second self," which is at odds with the common contemporary belief that there is only a single, "true" self. This second persona isn't a contrived pose; rather, it's a professional, consistent, and reliable outward-facing stance that leaves no room for doubts, frustrations or disappointments—those are for your diary, your partner or your pillow. I recommend you take a cue from Eisenhower and adopt a second self of your own. Restrict authenticity to keeping your promises and acting according to your principles. The rest is nobody else's business.

If the mental model of a second persona doesn't suit you, try putting it this way: think of yourself as a nation, with a State Department and a secretary of state. Write down the basic precepts of your foreign policy. You'll have to play the role yourself—like a sort of personal union. You don't want a secretary of state who broadcasts every thought in his head, who shows weakness or dissolves into self-doubt. You want a secretary of state who keeps promises, acts according to agreements, behaves professionally, avoids gossip, limits whining and stays polite. Check in from time to time on how well you're doing your job as secretary of state. Ask whether you'd reelect yourself.

Whether you call it a "second persona" or a "secretary of state," you'll soon realize that this barrier, this skin, this bark, not only shields you from toxic influences but also stabilizes what's inside it. Like all boundaries, this external structure establishes a degree of internal clarity. So even if other people—your employees or alleged friends—occasionally demand you show "more authenticity," don't fall into the trap. A dog is authentic. You're a human being.

10

THE FIVE-SECOND NO

Small Favors, Big Pitfalls

Someone's asked you for a small favor. How often do you say yes without thinking twice? How often do you refuse? How often have you kicked yourself later on for agreeing? And how often have you regretted saying no?

When I totted up my own statistics a few years ago in response to these questions, I realized I was agreeing to do favors for people far too often—little things like giving a lecture, providing an article, or doing a short interview. I frequently invested more time than I'd first imagined to produce results significantly less useful than I'd hoped for all concerned. I set out wanting to do the other person a favor, but ended up doing myself none.

Where does this "disease to please" come from? In the 1950s, biologists attempted to find out why animals that weren't blood-related still cooperated with each other. Why, for instance, did chimpanzees share meat with other chimpanzees? Why would a baboon make the effort to groom another baboon's fur? When you're talking about blood-related animals, the answer is obvious: they share a high proportion of the same genes. Cooperation helps sustain this common gene pool, even if it means particular individuals lose out—even if it means they die. But why would animals that aren't blood-related accept this risk? To ask the question another way:

why do non-related animals sometimes behave altruistically? Why doesn't the chimp just eat the meat itself, instead of sharing it with a friend? Why doesn't the baboon just take it easy, instead of expending valuable calories and countless hours picking insects out of a non-relative's coat? These are not trivial questions.

The answer lies in mathematics, and more specifically in game theory. The American political scientist Robert Axelrod once held tournaments in which different computer programs competed against each other. Each program followed a specific strategy when interacting with its opponent—cooperating with it, betraying it, behaving egotistically, always giving way and so on. In the long term, one strategy emerged as the most successful, one Axelrod called *tit for tat*. A simple strategy, it consists of the following instructions: first be cooperative, then imitate the behavior of your opponent throughout the rest of the game. So if—after my first move—my opponent cooperates, then I cooperate too. If my opponent doesn't cooperate, however, if he or she exploits me, then I stop cooperating. If my opponent starts cooperating further down the line, then I adapt my behavior to be cooperative once more.

This is precisely the behavior we see in the animal kingdom. It's called *reciprocal altruism* or *reciprocity*. The chimpanzee shares its meal with another member of the group because it assumes that, next time its friend has food to share, it will return the favor. If the first chimpanzee returns empty-handed from the next hunt, it can still expect to eat.

Reciprocity only works among animals with long memories. A chimpanzee can only pursue this strategy successfully if it remembers whether another member of the group has previously shared food with it. Only a few highly developed species have the necessary capacity for recall—primarily apes.

Of course, chimps aren't conscious of "thinking" strategically; rather, evolution has made this behavior innate. Groups of apes that didn't pursue the *tit-for-tat strategy* have vanished from the gene pool. Since we human beings are merely a highly developed species of animal, this impulse toward *reciprocity* is present in us too.

The *tit-for-tat strategy* is what keeps the global economy going. We cooperate every day with dozens of people to whom we are not related, many of them on the other side of the world, and have profited remarkably from doing so.

But be careful. Reciprocity has its lurking dangers. If somebody does something nice for you, you feel duty bound to pay them back—by doing them a favor, for example. You allow yourself to become manipulable. Moreover, there is a second, far greater danger: every *tit-for-tat strategy* begins with an opening move, a leap of faith, a first, spontaneous yes; and often this is precisely what we come to regret. Once the spontaneous yes has slipped out, we tend to rationalize it. We think about the solid arguments for it, and not about the time it will take to fulfill it. We value arguments above time—an error in reasoning, because there is an infinite number of arguments and a decidedly finite amount of time.

Ever since I realized that spontaneously agreeing to things is a deep-seated biological reflex, I've been using Charlie Munger's *five-second no* as a counter-tactic: "If you say 'No' ninety percent of the time, you're not missing much in the world." If I'm asked for a favor, I mull it over for exactly five seconds before making up my mind—and the answer is mostly no. I'd prefer to systematically turn down most requests and risk unpopularity than the other way around. Why not give it a try? It's rare to find yourself immediately dismissed as a scumbag. In fact, most people will secretly admire your consistency.

Two thousand years ago, the Roman philosopher Seneca wrote: "All those who summon you to themselves, turn you away from your own self." So give the *five-second no* a trial run. It's one of the best rules of thumb for a *good life*.

11

THE FOCUSING ILLUSION

Why You Wouldn't Be Happier
in the Caribbean

Let's say you're living in New York, and it's winter. The streets are carpeted in dirty snow. You're busy scraping the windscreen of your car. The wind keeps blowing runaway shavings of ice into your face, and your shoes are filling with slush. Your fingertips feel as though they're full of needles. With a jerk, you manage to open the frozen door of your car. You sit down on the leather seat, cold as a block of ice, and rest your hands on the chilly steering wheel. Your breath forms white clouds as it leaves your mouth. Question: how much happier would you be if you lived in Miami Beach, where it's a balmy twenty-six degrees with a gentle sea breeze? Put it on a scale from 0 (not even a little bit happier) to 10 (infinitely more happy).

Most people I ask give an answer between 4 and 6.

Having driven out of your parking spot, you set off for work. Moments later you're in a traffic jam on the motorway. You reach the office thirty minutes late, where you're greeted by a flood of e-mail and the usual headache with your boss. After work you do your weekly shopping. Back home you cook your favorite meal (it tastes delicious), settle down on the sofa, watch a good film and go to bed.

Ditto in Florida. Set off, get stuck in a jam, deal with the e-mails and the annoying boss, do the weekly shop, eat tasty food, watch a good film. I'll ask you again: how much happier would you be if you lived in Miami Beach? Most people now give an answer between 0 and 2.

I lived in Miami Beach for ten years. Before and after that I lived in Switzerland—slushy snow, occasionally icy windscreen and all. How much happier was I in Miami Beach? Answer: I wasn't.

It's called the *focusing illusion*. "Nothing in life is as important as you think it is while you are thinking about it," as Daniel Kahneman explains. The more narrowly we focus on a particular aspect of our lives, the greater its apparent influence. At the beginning of the description above, I concentrated almost entirely on the weather—ice in New York, sun in Miami Beach. This aspect was therefore dominant when I asked you to compare the satisfaction of living in New York with that of living in Miami.

We then sketched out a whole day, from morning commute to a comfy evening on the sofa, in which the weather was only one element. If we broaden that to even longer timespans— a week, a month, a year, a whole lifetime—we find that the climate suddenly becomes a negligible aspect of overall satisfaction.

Overcoming the *focusing illusion* is key to achieving a *good life*. It will enable you to avoid many stupid decisions. When you compare things (cars, careers, holiday destinations), you tend to focus on one aspect particularly closely, neglecting the hundred other factors. You assign this one aspect inordinate significance because of the *focusing illusion*. You believe this aspect is more critical than it really is.

So what can you do to combat this? You either compare all hundred factors, a labor-intensive process, or—more practically— you try to see the two things you're comparing as wholes.

Compare them from a distance to avoid overemphasizing any single factor. Easier said than done. Let me illustrate my point: a toddler thinks solely about what's currently in front of it. If I take away one of my three-year-old's toys, he shrieks like the world is coming to an end—even though he has a dozen others and has been ignoring the one I just removed. Over the course of our lives, we learn to emancipate ourselves from the momentary situation. If I feel like having a beer on a warm summer's evening, then I open the fridge to find that we've run out, I don't start screaming blue murder. I can take my focus off the beer, so the desolate emptiness of my fridge has only a minimal impact on my wellbeing. The evening isn't ruined after all.

Unfortunately, however, our development in this regard is incomplete. We find it immensely difficult to view our current situation through an ultra-wide-angle lens. Otherwise we wouldn't get upset about trivialities.

How many times have you asked yourself how much better life would be if you had a different job, lived in a different location, a different house, had a different haircut? Okay, it would be a little different. But now you know that the effect of a change is considerably less than you might think. Take the longest possible view of your life. Realize that the things that seemed so important in the moment have shrunk to the size of dots—dots that barely affect the overall picture. A *good life* is only attainable if you take the occasional peek through a wide-angle lens.

When I checked into the Shangri-La Hotel beside the Jardins du Trocadéro on my last visit to Paris, I found myself standing next to a man who started berating the receptionist—apparently because she couldn't offer him a room with a view of the Eiffel Tower. "You're ruining my whole trip to Paris!" he bawled. I shook my head. Whether or not you can see the

Eiffel Tower from your hotel bed doesn't actually matter. Far more important is how soundly you sleep. A view of the Eiffel Tower is much too small an aspect of a successful trip to Paris. In any case, you get more than enough of the tower as soon as you step outside the hotel. But the man, now beet-red, seemed about to burst with rage. The *focusing illusion* had turned a molehill into a mountain.

We're especially vulnerable to the *focusing illusion* when it comes to money. How much happier would you be as a multi-millionaire? Warren Buffett, one of the richest people in the world, once compared his own life with that of an average citizen. It didn't feel that different. Buffett spends a third of his life asleep on a normal mattress—just like you and me. Buffett buys his clothes off the rack as cheaply as mine or yours. His favorite drink is Coca-Cola. He eats no better or more healthily than a student. He works at a normal desk, on a normal chair. His office has been in the same place since 1962—in a dull building in Omaha, Nebraska. If you compare Buffett's life minute for minute with yours, the effect of his wealth is negligible.

One teeny-weeny difference: Buffett owns a private jet, while the likes of us are squeezed into Economy. After this chapter, however, we know that much worse than a narrow airline seat—where you'll spend at most 0.1 percent of your life—is a narrow mindset. By focusing on trivialities, you're wasting your *good life*.

12

THE THINGS YOU BUY LEAVE NO REAL TRACE

Why You Should Buy Less and Experience More

How much pleasure do you get from your car? Put it on a scale from 0 to 10. If you don't own a car, then do the same for your house, your flat, your laptop, anything like that. Psychologists Norbert Schwarz, Daniel Kahneman and Jing Xu asked motorists this question and compared their responses with the monetary value of the vehicle. The result? The more luxurious the car, the more pleasure it gave the owner. A BMW 7 Series generates about fifty percent more pleasure than a Ford Escort. So far, so good: when somebody sinks a load of money in a vehicle, at least they get a good return on their investment in the form of joy.

Now, let's ask a slightly different question: how happy were you during your last car trip? The researchers posed this question too, and again compared the motorists' answers with the values of their cars. The result? No correlation. No matter how luxurious or how shabby the vehicle, the owners' happiness ratings were all equally rock bottom.

The first survey revealed a correlation between the monetary value of the car and the perceived pleasure it gave its owner—the greater the luxury, the greater the pleasure. Yet the second survey revealed no such correlation—a luxury vehicle didn't make drivers any happier. How can this be? Easy: the first question makes you think about the car, while the second question makes you think about completely different things— a phone call during the journey, a situation at work, a traffic jam, the idiotic driver in front. Simply put, a car makes you happy when you're *thinking* about it but not when you're *driving* it. That's the effect of the *focusing illusion*, which we discussed in the previous chapter.

Of course, it's not just true for cars. The *focusing illusion* influences the pleasure you take in everything you buy. While you're thinking about X, you tend to grossly overestimate X's impact on your life. Whether it's a holiday home, a gigantic plasma television or a new pair of Louboutins, thinking about your purchase in a focused way makes you happy—but during daily use these things fade to the back of your mind, minimizing their effect on your happiness. When we factor in *counterproductivity*, the secret side effects and hidden costs of maintaining nice things (both time and money, as we saw in Chapter 5), we discover that these two effects often combine to leave you out of pocket—the net result being a loss in happiness.

Hard to believe? Let's take an example: you've bought a magnificent stately home outside the city. For the first three months you enjoy each of its fifteen rooms, delighting in every little detail. Yet just six months down the line, you barely notice the opulence around you. Everyday life has long since caught up with you; you're occupied with other, more urgent matters. At the same time, some things have changed—a house with fifteen rooms and a garden is different from the three-room apartment you used to rent in the city center. Now you need a cleaner and a gardener; you can't do your grocery shopping on foot any more, and your commute is an hour's drive instead of a twenty-minute bike ride. Basically, your gorgeous new home has created a net loss of happiness. Your wellbeing account is overdrawn.

This example is made up, but I've seen it happen in real life. A friend of mine owns a yacht—owned, I should say, because he sold it again almost immediately. Still, he does seem a little wiser now: the two happiest days in a yacht-owner's life, he observed laconically, are the day you buy it and the day you sell it.

As you can see, if it's the *good life* you're after then it's advisable to show restraint about what you buy. That said, there is a class of "goods" whose enjoyment is not diminished by the *focusing illusion*: experiences. When you experience something pleasurable, you're fully present in both heart and mind. So try to invest more in experiences than in physical objects. One side benefit is that most experiences cost less and are less subject to the effects of *counterproductivity*. Reading a good book, taking a trip with your family, playing cards with friends—they're all bargains. Of course, some experiences do require deep pockets, like a world tour or private space travel. But if you've got the money, they're guaranteed to be better investments than a Porsche collection.

Incidental but important: your job is an experience too. It's not simply there while you do it, the way a Porsche is simply there, fading to the back of your mind while you drive it. Your job monopolizes your thoughts; it demands constant, intensive engagement—which is great if you love it. But if you hate it, you've got a serious problem on your hands. You can't hope to be distracted from your shitty career by other thoughts.

This issue was a major part of why I decided to become a writer. I love the act of writing. It's far more important to me than the published book. Of course, I'm delighted each time I pick up the first copy of a new book. I stroke the cover tenderly, leaf through the pages, inhale the glorious scent of fresh binding glue. But the book soon disappears onto the shelf, and I hardly give it a second thought—I'm already contemplating the next one.

There's nothing more idiotic than slogging away at a job that earns you lots of money but brings you no joy—especially if you're investing that money in items rather than experiences. Warren Buffett puts it this way: "Working with people who cause your stomach to churn seems much like marrying for money—probably a bad idea under any circumstances, but absolute madness if you are already rich."

Speaking of marriage: in the end, this is also an experience. It's pointless maintaining a relationship that doesn't make you happy out of sheer loyalty or lack of other options. The *focusing illusion* won't rush to your aid. Of course, not every relationship consists exclusively of sunny days, but the darker ones shouldn't outweigh the rest. If storm clouds loom, try the art of correction (Chapter 2). If it definitely isn't working, pull the ripcord. A relationship—especially a romantic one—will never retreat into the background of your mind.

In sum? We overestimate the impact of purchases on our wellbeing and underestimate the impact of experiences. The thought of your house—even if you're currently standing in it—vanishes into the cacophony of your other daily thoughts. With experiences this isn't the case. But what if you've already bought your Louboutins? Then at least make sure you're consciously enjoying them. Ideally you want to be brushing and polishing them each morning and dreaming of nothing but bright red shoe soles each night. Make the *focusing illusion* work to your advantage for once.

13

FUCK-YOU MONEY

Saving Up Freedom

The sun is burning on your back, and the air shimmers like glass above the sand. Your gums feel like sandpaper. You drank your last drop of water two days ago and you've been on all fours ever since, crawling toward an oasis on the horizon. How much would you pay for a liter of water right now?

Let's say you've paid for and received the water. You've slaked the worst of your thirst. How much would you pay for a second liter? And for a third?

Unless you happen to be some sort of fakir blessed with superhuman powers of endurance, you'd probably give your entire savings plus pension and holiday cottage for the first liter. For the second, maybe your Breitling watch. For the third, your headphones. For the fourth, your insoles. Economists call this *diminishing marginal utility*. Each additional liter yields less marginal utility than the last, and after a certain point it yields nothing at all. This holds true for virtually all goods—water, clothing, TV channels—but above all for money. Which brings us to a question many thousands of years old: can money buy happiness? Here's a test question: how much would you have to earn per year in order to feel that additional income would no longer have any effective impact on your perceived wellbeing? Write down the figure in the margin before reading on.

Research offers clear answers. If you're living in poverty,

money plays a major role. Financial difficulties are sheer misery. If you're living on a moderate income of $38,000 per year, money plays a more moderate role. Above a household income of $75,000 per year (in San Francisco a bit more, in Cincinnati a bit less), the effect of additional income shrinks to nil—and remains there even if you reach the million mark. It's not all that surprising. Imagine the life of a billionaire from sun-up to sundown, moment by moment. Even rich people have to brush their teeth. They sleep badly sometimes. They feel like crap, argue with their families, fear age and death. On top of that they have a whole retinue of staff to manage, the media to fob off, and a flood of begging letters to work through. Does having an Olympic-sized swimming pool in your garden really cancel all that out?

In a well-known study from 1978, researchers analyzed the life satisfaction of lottery winners. The result? A few months after their big win, the brand-new millionaires were no happier in any significant sense than before.

The economist Richard Easterlin measured the life satisfaction of Americans in 1946 against that of Americans in 1970. Although living standards nearly doubled during this period (by 1970 nearly everybody had a car, a fridge, a washing machine and hot water), life satisfaction had remained fairly stable. Easterlin found similar results in the eighteen other countries whose data he compared. In other words, people were no happier with their lives in 1970 than immediately after the war. Material progress was not reflected in increased life satisfaction. This revelation has been termed the *Easterlin paradox*: once basic needs have been met, incremental financial gain contributes nothing to happiness.

Why, then, do we keep yearning to be millionaires—in the face of all scholarly consensus? The main reason is that wealth is relative, not absolute.

Let's say you and your co-worker have landed a series of very profitable contracts for your employer. Which would you prefer: a) you are given a bonus of $10,000 while your colleague gets nothing; or b) you get a bonus of $15,000 while your colleague gets $20,000? If you're like most people, you'd choose the $10,000—even though the second option would make you richer.

Imagine you've bought a nice piece of land and built a house. The house is magnificent, with at least three more bedrooms than you need. One year later, somebody else buys the neighboring plot and constructs a house so lavish it makes yours look like a garden shed. What happens? Your blood pressure rises and your life satisfaction drops—even though you're still living very well.

Money is relative. Not just in comparison to others, but in comparison to your past. If you earned $50,000 per year during the first half of your career and today you earn $75,000 you'll be happier than if you first earned $75,000 and now earn just $60,000. This is despite the fact that, averaging the figures, you come out better off overall in the second scenario.

Simply put, your level of wealth—above the poverty line—is primarily a matter of interpretation. But this is good news; it means it's up to you whether money makes you happy or not.

There a few rules of thumb for dealing with money. The first has been termed by some linguistically adventurous individuals *fuck-you money*, in reference to the last two words—ever, presumably—you will yell at your boss before storming out of the office. Basically, *fuck-you money* refers to the savings that would allow you to quit your job at a moment's notice without ending up in dire financial straits. One year's salary, say. *Fuck-you money* is freedom. More important even than material independence is that *fuck-you money* allows you to see and think objectively. So if you haven't saved up your *fuck-you money* yet, keep your fixed costs low. The lower your outgoings, the quicker you'll reach your goal. In any case, it's a nice feeling to have money without spending much of it.

Two: don't react to minor fluctuations in your income or assets. Has the value of your stock portfolio risen or dropped by one percent today? Don't let it worry you. Basically, don't think so much about money. It won't multiply more quickly the more often you think about it.

Three: don't compare yourself with the wealthy. It will make you unhappy. If you must, compare yourself with those who have less than you do—but it's better not to compare yourself with anyone at all.

Four: even if you're filthy rich, live modestly. Wealth makes people jealous. Anyone who has enough cash can buy a luxury yacht—there's no skill to that. If you're a billionaire, it's more impressive *not* to buy one, to live modestly.

Essentially, once you've left the poverty line behind you and saved up a financial safety net, money is not among the factors that contribute to a *good life*. So work on those other factors instead of hoarding money. Genuine success, as we'll see in the final chapter, is anything but financial.

14

THE CIRCLE OF COMPETENCE

Why It's Important to Know Your Limits

Nobody understands the world completely. It's far too complex for a single human brain. Even if you're highly educated, you can only understand a tiny part. Still, that's something—this minuscule patch is the runway you need for take-off, what you need to fulfill your high-flying dreams. If you don't have one, you'll never leave the ground.

Warren Buffett uses the wonderful term *circle of competence*. Inside the circle are the skills you have mastered. Beyond it are the things you understand only partially or not at all. Buffett's life motto: "Know your circle of competence, and stick within it. The size of that circle is not very important; knowing its boundaries, however, is vital." Charlie Munger adds: "Each of you will have to figure out where your talent lies. And you'll have to use your advantages. But if you try to succeed in what you're worst at, you're going to have a very lousy career. I can almost guarantee it." Tom Watson, the founder of IBM, is living proof of this thesis. As he's said of himself: "I'm no genius. I'm smart in spots—but I stay around those spots."

Be rigorous in organizing your professional life around this idea, because a radical focus on your *circle of competence* will bear more than monetary fruit. Equally important is the emotional variety. You'll gain an invaluable feeling of mastery, and you'll also be more efficient, because you won't have to decide every time whether to accept or refuse a task. With a sharply delineated *circle of competence*, unsuitable but irresistible requests suddenly become resistible.

Crucially, you should never step outside your *circle of competence*. Many years ago a wealthy entrepreneur offered me a million euros to write his biography. It was an extremely tempting offer. I turned it down. Biographies lie outside my *circle of competence*. A top-notch biography requires endless conversations and meticulous research. It demands other skills besides those needed for novels and non-fiction—skills I do not possess. I would have spun my wheels, got frustrated, and, most importantly, written at best a mediocre book.

In his far from mediocre book *Risk Intelligence*, Dylan Evans describes a professional backgammon player by the name of J.P. "He would make a few deliberate mistakes to see how well his opponent would exploit them. If the other guy played well, J.P. would stop playing. That way, he wouldn't throw good money after bad. In other words, J.P. knew something that most gamblers don't: he knew when *not* to bet." He knew which opponents would force him out of his *circle of competence*, and he learned to avoid them.

Alongside the impulse to step outside your *circle of competence* is the equally powerful temptation to broaden it. This temptation is especially great if you're successful within your current circle, if you're entirely comfortable there. Resist it. Skills don't transfer from one arena to another. In other words, skills are *domain specific*. A master chess player isn't automatically going to be a good business strategist. A heart surgeon isn't automatically a good hospital manager. A real-estate speculator isn't automatically a good president.

So how do you create a *circle of competence*? Clicking

around on Wikipedia isn't enough. Nor is a traditional degree. It takes time—lots of time. "Expect anything worthwhile to take a really long time" is the rule American designer Debbie Millman sticks to (with great success).

It also takes obsession. Obsession is a kind of addiction, which is why it's often spoken of disparagingly. We read about young people getting addicted to video games, to TV series, to model airplanes. It's high time we framed obsession more positively. Obsession drives people to invest thousands and thousands of hours into something. As a young man, Bill Gates had an obsession: programming. Steve Jobs: calligraphy and design. Warren Buffett first put his pocket money into stocks and shares as a twelve-year-old; he's been addicted to investing ever since. Nobody today would say that Gates, Jobs or Buffett wasted their youth. Quite the contrary: it's because they were so obsessed that they invested the thousands of hours it takes to achieve mastery of something. Obsession is an engine, not engine failure.

The opposite of obsession, by the way, isn't aversion but "interest"—a polite equivalent to saying "I'm not really that interested."

Why is the *circle of competence* such a powerful idea? What's its secret? Simple. A brilliant programmer isn't just twice as skilled as a good one, nor three times or even ten times; a brilliant programmer would solve the same problem in a thousandth of the time it would take a programmer who was merely "good." Ditto for lawyers, surgeons, designers, researchers, salespeople. Inside versus outside the *circle of competence*—we're talking about thousandfold differences.

Here's the other thing: the idea that you can make life stick to a plan is an illusion (Chapter 2). Chance tears through everything, sometimes with the force of a hurricane. There is only one place where it dwindles to a gentle breeze, and that's inside your *circle of competence*. You might not find it plain sailing even there, but at least the waves will allow you to navigate properly. In more prosaic terms, within your *circle of competence* you're protected to a certain extent against illusions and fallacies. You could even risk breaking with convention, because you have the necessary lie of the land and can predict roughly what's going to happen.

The upshot? Stop beating yourself up over your deficiencies. If you've got two left feet, forget the salsa lessons. If your kids can't tell whether that squiggle is supposed to be a horse or a cow, stop dreaming of a career as an artist. If you can barely cope with a visit from your aunt, drop the idea of opening your own restaurant. The truth is that it's completely irrelevant how many areas you're average or below average in. What matters is that you're far above average in at least one area—ideally, the best in the world. Once that's sorted, you'll have a solid basis for a *good life*. A single outstanding skill trumps a thousand mediocre ones. Every hour invested into your *circle of competence* is worth a thousand spent elsewhere.

15

THE SECRET OF PERSISTENCE

Why Bores Are More Successful than Adventurers

Stockbrokers—collars unbuttoned, sleeves rolled up—are yelling into several telephones at once, gesticulating as though their lives were on the line. The air crackles. Every now and again one of them slams a receiver down onto the table like he wants to break it. Then the traders start bawling at each other over their Bloomberg terminals, on which stock prices flash like carnival lights. This is how the media depicts the world of finance, relaying images from the stock-market floor or the trading area at a bank.

Scene change. A dull office on the fourteenth floor of an unassuming high-rise in sleepy Omaha, Nebraska, the most negligible state in the USA. No Bloomberg terminals, no computers, no e-mails. Just an old-fashioned desk and a telephone. There he sits, day after day, as he has done for nearly fifty years: Warren Buffett, the most successful investor of all time.

The contrast couldn't be starker. On the one hand: hyperactive, sweat-drenched, testosterone-laden stockbrokers. On the other: quiet, silver-haired Uncle Warren. Once you've grasped the difference between speculating and investing, you'll start seeing parallels everywhere—and you'll have a good mental tool to hand.

So, what exactly is the difference? The stockbrokers are

trying to make a profit through frenetically buying and selling shares. What's behind the shares—a software firm in California, a copper mine in Peru—is irrelevant. What matters is that the share prices move temporarily in the right direction.

Classic investors, however, buy shares in only a handful of companies, which they know as thoroughly as the backs of their hands. The opinion of the market means nothing to them. Their commitment is long-term. To avoid transaction costs, they buy and sell as infrequently as possible. Buffett and Charlie Munger don't even seek out new investment opportunities. They wait for opportunities to come to them. From the horse's mouth: "Charlie and I just sit around and wait for the phone to ring."

Who's more successful—speculators or investors? There are winners and losers on both sides, but the giants among the winners are to be found only on the side of the investors. Why is that? One central difference: investors take advantage of long timespans; stockbrokers don't.

Our brains love short-term, spasmodic developments. We react exaggeratedly to highs and lows, to rapid changes and jarring news—but continuous changes we barely notice. As a result, we systematically overemphasize doing above not-doing, zeal above deliberation, and action above waiting.

What are the most-purchased books of all time? Not the ones on the current bestseller lists or stacked highest on bookshop tables. I mean the ones that have remained continuously in print for decades or even hundreds of years—the Bible, Mao's *Little Red Book*, the Koran, *The Communist Manifesto*, *The Lord of the Rings*, *The Little Prince*. They're known as "longsellers," and no publisher can live without them. The same goes for Broadway shows, tourist attractions, songs and many other products. The most successful car of all time? The

Toyota Corolla, continuously available as new since 1966—now in its eleventh generation. It wasn't the first year's turnover that made the Corolla a superstar but the span of time over which it has been sold.

Such long-term successes often have inconspicuous ingredients that function like baking powder, producing incremental progress that builds up over a long period of time. Take the example of investment: if you invest $10,000 at a five percent return, after a year you'll be $500 richer. Piece of cake. But if you keep reinvesting these modest profits, after ten years you'll achieve a capital of $16,000; after twenty years an impressive $26,000; and after fifty an incredible $115,000. Your capital will accrue not linearly but exponentially. Because our brains have no instinct for duration, they also have no feel for exponential growth.

This, then, is the secret of persistence: long-term successes are like making cakes with baking powder. Slow, boring, long-winded processes lead to the best results. The same goes for your life.

There has never been a century in which activity, industry and zeal are so celebrated as in our own. The modern religion of "disruption" demands that we constantly raze and rebuild our careers, our companies and even our lives. Only by so doing, says the consensus, will we remain competitive. Similarly, many people are convinced that for a life to be *good* it must be one long highlight reel of adventures, travels and relocations. I believe the opposite is the case. The more peaceful the life, the more productive. Bertrand Russell, living in a significantly more peaceful age, agreed: "Nor have the lives of great men been exciting except at a few great moments. Socrates could enjoy a banquet now and again . . . but most of his life he lived quietly with Xanthippe, taking a constitutional in the afternoon, and perhaps meeting a few friends by the way. Kant is said never to have been more than ten miles from Konigsberg in all his life. Darwin, after going round the world, spent the whole of the rest of his life in his own house. Altogether it will be found that a quiet life is characteristic of great men, and that their pleasures have not been of the sort that would look exciting to the outward eye." Of course, the same holds true for the great female figures in history. A positive correlation between raucousness and good ideas, between restlessness and insight, between activity and results, can rarely be found.

So what does this mean for the *good life*? Less busywork, more endurance. Once you've identified your *circle of competence* (see Chapter 14), stick at it as long as possible. Likewise if you find a good spouse, a suitable place to live or a rewarding hobby. Perseverance, tenacity and long-term thinking are highly valuable yet underrated virtues. We should start fostering them again. "You don't have to be brilliant," as Charlie Munger says, "only a little bit wiser than the other guys, on average, *for a long, long time.*"

16

THE TYRANNY OF A CALLING

Do What You Can, Not What You Wish You Could

Anthony was born in 251 A.D., the son of a wealthy landowner in Egypt. When he turned eighteen his parents died, and in church he heard the following words, from the Gospel of Matthew: "If thou wilt be perfect, go and sell that thou hast, and give to the poor, and thou shalt have treasure in heaven: and come and follow me." So Anthony went and sold all his earthly possessions to go wandering along the edges of the desert, where he lived for many years as a hermit. In time, others followed. Their numbers grew and grew—young men who had also heeded God's call. A loosely affiliated band of recluses living separately from one another, they formed the core of Christian monasticism, and today Anthony is known as the Father of Monks.

A thousand years later, something similar happened to the son of a rich Italian clothier. Francis of Assisi had been living a dissolute life until he heard God calling to him in a dream. Giving away all he owned, he swapped his clothes for those of a beggar and lived as a hermit, restoring churches. Gradually other people were drawn to him, and he founded the Franciscan Order.

When we hear the word "calling" today, we think of people like Anthony or Francis of Assisi. They couldn't help but follow

God's call. We see similar moments in the lives of Paul, Augustin, Blaise Pascal and other converts in and beyond the Bible.

At the same time, however, "calling" has a decidedly contemporary ring. "How can I find my calling?" is one of the most common questions I hear from young people. Each time I have to bite my tongue, because "calling" is a relic of Christianity. For somebody who doesn't believe in God, the term sounds somewhat delusional.

Of course, people in search of a calling these days aren't interested in repudiating worldly concerns. On the contrary, they're looking to engage with the world more closely, and they cherish the Romantic notion that deep inside every human being is a bud waiting to blossom into something profound. Hence why they pay such close attention to their inner voices— they're hoping to hear the call of some fulfilling activity. But that's dangerous, because the concept of a calling is one of the greatest illusions of our age.

John Kennedy Toole considered himself born to write. When the twenty-six-year-old American submitted a manuscript to the publisher Simon & Schuster, he was convinced he'd sent off the novel of the century. But Simon & Schuster turned him down, as did all the other publishers he tried. His most deeply held conviction shaken to the core, Toole turned to booze. Six years later, in 1969, in Biloxi, Mississippi, he stuck a garden hose into the exhaust pipe of his car and fed the other end inside the vehicle, killing himself. After his suicide, his mother finally managed to find a publisher for the manuscript and *A Confederacy of Dunces* was published in 1980, hailed by critics as a masterpiece of literature from the American South. Toole was posthumously awarded the Pulitzer Prize for the best novel of the year. The book sold more than 1.5 million copies.

"One of the symptoms of approaching nervous break-down is the belief that one's work is terribly important," wrote Bertrand Russell. This is precisely the danger of a calling: that you take yourself and your work too seriously. If, like John Kennedy Toole, you pin everything on the fulfilment of your supposed vocation, you cannot live a *good life*. If Toole had viewed his writing not as his only possible calling but simply as a craft for which he happened to have a special knack, he would probably not have ended up as he did. You can pursue a craft with love, of course, and even with a touch of obsession, but your focus should always be on the activity, the work, the input—not on the success, the result, the output. Better "I'm going to do at least three pages today" than "tomorrow I've *got* to win the Nobel Prize in Literature."

The Romantic notion that a calling makes you happy is false. Those who doggedly pursue their vocation aren't happy, they're just dogged—and probably soon-to-be frustrated as well, because most callings are inextricable from unrealistic expectations. If you set out to write the novel of the century, break a world record, found a new religion or end world poverty once and for all, you have maybe a chance in a trillion of accomplishing your goal. Don't get me wrong: it's okay to set lofty goals—but only on the condition that you maintain a distanced, level-headed relationship with them. If you go blindly chasing after your calling, that's a sure-fire recipe for a miserable life.

A related pitfall is *selection bias*. We only see successful examples of people with a calling: Marie Curie, who decided to become a scientist at age fifteen and would later win two Nobel Prizes. Or Picasso, who was accepted to art school at ten and went on to revolutionize painting. Such inspiring stories have been the subject of countless biographies, interviews and documentary films. What we don't see, however, is the infinitely larger pool of failures. The frustrated scientist whose research paper is read by exactly two people: his wife and his mother. Or the unrecognized pianist who now follows her "calling" as a music teacher in some nowhere town, even though she has no gift for teaching. They all followed the siren song of their vocation—into obscurity. Yet not even local rags report on these people. Why should they?

People often claim they had no choice but to do X. It's nice Romantic rhetoric, but it's essentially nonsense. Hunters and gatherers had no choice. A slave in Egypt had no choice. A farmer's wife in the Middle Ages had no choice. But if somebody in the present day tells you his inner voice left him no choice but to dedicate his life to the guitar, you can be reasonably sure he's at least one sandwich short of a picnic.

Even if there were such a thing as a true calling, it certainly wouldn't be advisable to pursue it come what may. Hackers, fraudsters and terrorists all believe they've found their calling, and are fulfilled by their work. Hitler doubtless felt the same, as did Napoleon, Stalin and Osama bin Laden. Clearly, a calling is no guarantee of a moral compass.

So, what to do? Don't listen to your inner voice. A calling is nothing but a job you'd like to have. In the Romantic sense it doesn't exist; there is only talent and preference. Build on the skills you actually have, not on some putative sense of vocation. Luckily, the skills we've mastered are often the things we enjoy doing. One important aside: other people have also got to value your talents. You've got to put food on the table somehow. As the English philosopher John Gray put it: "Few people are as unhappy as those with a talent no one cares about."

17

THE PRISON OF A GOOD REPUTATION

How to Shift from External to Internal Validation

Which would you rather? To be the most intelligent person on Earth but considered the stupidest? Or the stupidest person on Earth but considered the most intelligent?

When Bob Dylan was awarded the Nobel Prize in Literature in 2016, he didn't acknowledge it for weeks. No statement, no interviews. He wouldn't even take the Swedish Academy's phone calls. Criticism rained down from all sides. How ungrateful can somebody be? So arrogant! So indifferent! When Dylan finally responded, speaking in an interview with a British newspaper, he dryly observed, "I appreciate the honor so much," as though the words had been forced into his mouth by a PR consultant. He did not attend the award ceremony—or rather, he was three months late. One can only assume that he couldn't care less about the world's most prestigious prize.

Grigori Perelman, born in 1966, is considered the greatest living mathematician. In 2002 he solved one of the seven mathematical "Millennium Problems." The remaining six are still unsolved. He was selected for the Fields Medal, a kind of Nobel Prize for mathematics—and declined. He even turned down the million-dollar prize money, although he could certainly use it: Perelman is unemployed, living with his mother in a high-rise block in St. Petersburg. Mathematics is all that matters to him. He's utterly indifferent to what the world thinks of him and his achievements.

When I first started writing, it was important to me to know what other people thought of my books. I delighted in positive reviews and fretted over every word of criticism. I took applause as a measure of my success. At some point during my midforties, however, I had my Bob Dylan moment: I understood that public perception has little to do with the quality of my work. It makes my books no better or worse. Having this insight felt like being released from a prison of my own making.

But back to my initial question. Warren Buffett puts it like this: "Would you rather be the world's greatest lover, but have everyone think you're the world's worst lover? Or would you rather be the world's worst lover but have everyone think you're the world's greatest lover?" In doing so, Buffett outlines one of the ideas most vital to leading a *good life*: the difference between an *inner scorecard* and an *outer scorecard*. Which matters more to you: how you evaluate yourself, or how the outside world evaluates you? "In teaching your kids, I think the lesson they're learning at a very, very early age is what their parents put the emphasis on. If all the emphasis is on what the world's going to think about you, forgetting about how you really behave, you'll wind up with an Outer Scorecard." And that, as I'm sure you've already guessed, is a pretty effective way of scuppering the *good life* from square one.

The urge to present the best possible image of ourselves is, however, an impulse that runs deep. Which do you think was more important to our hunter-gatherer ancestors, the *inner scorecard* or the *outer scorecard*? The latter, of course. Their lives depended absolutely on what other people thought of them, on whether their fellow human beings would cooperate with them or banish them from the group. Ancestors heedless of their *outer scorecards* would soon have vanished from the gene pool.

The first towns and villages were established approximately ten thousand years ago. Because it was no longer possible for everybody in these settlements to know everybody else personally, taking good care of the "reputation" that preceded you became increasingly important. Gossip assumed the function of personal acquaintance. And gossip has since conquered the world. Next time you're meeting a friend, keep track: you'll spend 90 percent of the time talking about other people.

There are understandable evolutionary reasons why we're so concerned about how we come across to others, but this doesn't mean it still makes sense today. On the contrary. The opinions of others are far less significant than you think. Your emotional response to changes in your prestige, reputation and appearance are much too highly attuned; or, to put it another way, you're still in Stone Age mode. Whether they're praising you to the skies or dragging your name through the mud, the actual impact on your life is considerably smaller than your pride or sense of shame would have you believe. So liberate yourself. Here's three reasons why you should. First, you'll be spared the emotional roller coaster. In the long run, you can't manage your reputation perfectly anyway. Warren Buffett cites Gianni Agnelli, the former boss of Fiat: "When you get old, you have the reputation you deserve." You can fool other people for a while, but not a lifetime. Second, concentrating on prestige and reputation distorts our perception of what makes us truly happy. And third, it stresses us out. It's detrimental to the *good life*.

Concentrating on your *outer scorecard* has never been more prevalent than it is today. "Social media," says David Brooks, "creates a culture in which people turn into little brand managers, using Facebook, Twitter, text messages, and Instagram to create a falsely upbeat, slightly overexuberant external self." Brooks uses the marvelous term "approval-seeking machine" to describe what people can become if they're not careful. Facebook likes, ratings, followers; they all transmute instant, quantifiable feedback into status—which isn't even your actual status. Once you're caught in this web, it's not easy to extricate yourself and lead a *good life*.

The upshot? The world is going to write, tweet and post about you whatever it damn well pleases. People will gossip and tittle-tattle behind your back. They'll heap you with praise and drag you into shitstorms. You can't control it. But, thankfully, you don't have to. If you're not a politician or a celebrity and you don't earn your money via advertising, then stop worrying about your reputation. Let go of liking and being liked. Don't Google yourself, and don't crave recognition. Instead, accomplish something. Live in such a way that you can still look at yourself in the mirror. Says Buffett: "If I do something that others don't like but I feel good about, I'm happy. If others praise something I've done, but I'm not satisfied, I feel unhappy." That's the perfect *inner scorecard*. So focus on that, and treat external praise and censure with friendly, composed disinterest.

18

THE "END OF HISTORY" ILLUSION

You Can Change Yourself—
but Not Other People

Every time I walk through Zurich airport, I notice slight changes. A new shop here, a new coffee place there, a gigantic billboard displayed overhead, gleaming new check-in desks arrayed like soldiers. Now and again I drive into a new parking structure; sometimes I find myself frantically scanning a renovated terminal wing for electricity sockets. I traverse the labyrinth of the airport about once a month, on average—and I've done so for thirty years. Each time my brain accustoms itself to the fractionally different infrastructure, so next time I find my way to the gate without issue. When I think back to my first visit, however, as a small boy holding my mother's hand, waiting to welcome my father back from a business trip—I saw him coming down the airplane steps, waving at us across the runway—it strikes me that *that* airport has virtually nothing in common with the one that exists today. In those days Zurich-Kloten Airport had a single chilly hall through which a monotone voice announced every departure and called every late passenger over the loudspeakers (in German, English, and French). You could hear the periodic rustling of the letters and numbers on the destination board being turned. Today, Zurich International Airport is essentially a bustling shopping center with three runways. I'm sure you can also think of places—train stations, cities, universities—that have changed completely over long periods without you really noticing it on all your visits.

But what about you? How much have you changed over time? Try to imagine who you were twenty years ago. Don't think about external things (job, home, appearance), but your personality, your character, your temperament, your values and predilections. Compare that person with your current self. How would you rate the amount you've changed on a scale from 0 (no change) to 10 (complete change; I'm a totally different person)?

Most people I ask identify several differences in their personality, values and likes and dislikes over the last twenty years. They usually come up with a figure between 2 and 4. Not the drastic remodeling of Zurich airport, but still—they've changed a little.

Now for my follow-up question: how much do you think you'll change over the *next* twenty years? The usual answers are now much lower—between 0 and 1. In other words, most people don't believe they will change in the future, not deep down, and if so, it will only be a tiny bit. Unlike airports, train stations and cities. Funny, isn't it? Can it really be true that today is the day our personalities stop developing? Of course not. Harvard psychologist Daniel Gilbert calls this the *end of history illusion*. The reality is that we'll change almost as much in the future as we have in the past. In what direction? Well, that's unclear, but it's safe to say you'll have a different personality with different values. The research is unambiguous.

But let's put big concepts like "personality" and "values" on the back burner for a moment. Let's just take the things you like. Think back twenty years. What was your favorite film? What is it today? Who were your idols? Who are they today?

Who were your most important friends? Who are they today? Take a minute to answer these questions.

Gilbert had an ingenious idea about how to measure these changes in people's likes and dislikes. He asked people two questions: a) What was your favorite band *ten years ago*, and how much would you pay *today* for a ticket to one of their concerts; and b) What is your favorite band *today*, and how much would you pay for a ticket to one of their concerts *in ten years*? The difference is remarkable. People are willing to pay an average of 61 percent more to hear their current favorite band play in ten years' time than their former favorite band today. Proof of the *end of history illusion* and the instability of our preferences.

I have good news and bad news. First, the good: you can exercise some influence over changes in your personality. Not much—the vast majority of these developments will unfold according to the interplay between a genetic program and its environment—but nonetheless you ought to seize your chance. The most efficient way to steer your development is to use your idols. So be careful how you choose the people you admire.

The bad news: you can't change other people—no, not even your partner or your children. Motivation for personal change must come from within. Neither external pressure nor rational argument will work.

That's why one of my golden rules for leading a *good life* is as follows: "Avoid situations in which you have to change other people." This simple strategy has already spared me a good deal of misery, expense and disappointment. In practical terms, I never employ anybody whose character I have to change—because I know I can't. I don't do business with people whose disposition doesn't suit me—no matter how profitable it might potentially be. And I would never take on leadership of an organization if I had to alter the mindset of the people in it.

Smart businesspeople have always taken that tack. One of Southwest Airlines' guiding principles since its inception has been "Hire for attitude, train for skill." Attitudes cannot be altered, at least not in a reasonable amount of time, and certainly not by external pressures. Skills can.

I'm constantly surprised to see how many people disregard this simple rule. A friend of mine—a party animal and social butterfly—married a beautiful, introverted woman and assumed he'd be able to turn this quiet soul into an outgoing party-lover. He failed, of course, and the result was a quick and expensive divorce.

A related life rule is "Only work with people you like and trust." As Charlie Munger says, "Oh, it's just so useful dealing with people you can trust and getting all the others the hell out of your life...But wise people want to avoid other people who are just total rat poison, and there are a lot of them." So how do you rid yourself of these poisonous individuals? One recommendation: every year on December 31 my wife and I write down on slips of paper the names of people who aren't good for us and whom we no longer want in our lives. Then we cast them solemnly into the fire, one by one. It's a therapeutic and salutary ritual.

19

THE SMALLER MEANING OF LIFE

Which Goals You Can Achieve—and
Which You Can't

When the author Terry Pearce tried to call his friend Gary, he heard the following message: "Hi, this is Gary, and this is not an answering machine, it is a questioning machine! The two questions are, 'Who are you?' and 'What do you want?'" There was a pause, then the voice continued, "And if you think those are trivial questions, consider that 95 percent of the population goes through life and never answers either one!"

How would you answer the question "Who are you?" Most people give their name and say what they do for a living, sometimes followed up with a brief snippet of information about their family ("I'm the mother of two children") or a personality trait ("I like people"). But what use is a response like that? None. You can't hold it against them, though, because there is no single-sentence answer to a question about your own identity. Nor a single-paragraph one, for that matter. Nor ten pages. Regardless of who you are, you'd need a novel of Proustian depth to do justice to your life and being.

Because our lives consist of infinitely many facets, any one-line answer is by definition inaccurate. Yet we're constantly reducing ourselves to that—not only when we call Gary but, interestingly, with ourselves, as part of our own self-conception. We construct an image of ourselves that's like a comic-book drawing: absurdly oversimplified, completely without contradiction—and entirely too positive. As we'll see in Chapter 22, we fabricate all the stories we tell ourselves about our lives, but here's a sneak preview: you're better off not answering the question of who you are. You'll only be wasting your time.

On to the second question: What do you want? Unlike the first, this question is eminently answerable. Indeed, it's crucial you should reply. It's asking about your purpose in life, sometimes also referred to as the "meaning of life." Now, the word "meaning" is somewhat confusing, so I recommend distinguishing more precisely between the "larger meaning of life" and the "smaller meaning of life."

If you're trying to find the larger meaning of life, you're looking for answers to questions like: Why are we on this Earth? Why does the universe exist? And what does it all mean? So far every culture has responded with its own mythology. Particularly lovely is the notion that the Earth is the shell of an enormous tortoise—a myth that can be found in both China and South America. Or the Christian mythos: God created everything in six days, and on the Day of Judgment He will wipe the slate clean. Unlike the writers of mythology, science has found no answer to the "larger meaning of life" question. All it knows about life is that it will continue to develop aimlessly as long as there's sufficient material and energy available. There is no discernable overarching purpose—not for humanity, life or the universe. The world is fundamentally meaningless. So stop looking for the "larger meaning of life." You're only wasting your time.

The question of the "smaller meaning of life," however, is crucial. It's about your personal goals, your ambitions, your mission—it's about the second question on Gary's answering machine. There can be no *good life* without personal goals.

Seneca figured that out two thousand years ago: "Let all your efforts be directed to something, let it keep that end in mind." There's no guarantee of achieving your end, but if you don't have one, you're guaranteed to achieve nothing.

Life goals are massively important. An example: researchers in the USA surveyed seventeen- and eighteen-year-old students about the importance of financial success, asking them to rate it on a scale where 1 meant unimportant, 2 somewhat important, 3 very important and 4 indispensable. Many years later they surveyed the same people about their actual income, and about how happy they were with their lives in general. The first result: the greater people's financial ambitions in their younger years, the more they earned by middle age. Turns out goals work! That only came as a surprise to the psychologists, who had believed for a very long time that people merely reacted to external stimuli, like Pavlov's dogs.

The second result: all the students who had set their sights on a high-income job after finishing their education—and who had achieved that goal—tended to be deeply satisfied with their lives. By contrast, those for whom money was important but who had failed to achieve their financial goals were deeply unsatisfied. Sure, you may be thinking. Money makes you happy. But that's not it, because a higher income had no effect on the satisfaction of people for whom wealth was *not* a life goal. It's not money that makes you happy or unhappy, it's whether or not you realize your ambitions. The equivalent holds true for other life goals, too.

Why do goals work? Because goal-orientated people put more effort into accomplishing them. And because goals make decisions easier. Life consists of endless forks in the road. You could make each choice on a whim—or refer to your goals. No wonder students who described financial success as "indispensable" in the study chose well-paying jobs (doctor, lawyer, consultant).

Life goals, then, are recommended. Yet there are two potential problems. "One recipe for a dissatisfied adulthood is setting goals that are especially difficult to attain," as Daniel Kahneman has observed. In other words, you need to make sure your goals are realistic. If you're short and squat and dreaming of becoming a basketball star, you've stymied yourself right off the bat. Ditto if you want to be the first person on Mars. Or the president. Or a billionaire. You can't really aim for goals like that, because 99 percent of the various things that have to fall into place are beyond your control. Unrealistic goals are killjoys. My recommendation? Leave your goals deliberately a little vague ("well-off" instead of "billionaire," for instance). If you achieve them, wonderful. If you don't, you can still interpret your situation as though you had (at least in part). It doesn't even have to be a conscious process. Your brain will do it for you automatically.

The upshot? Goals work. Goals are important. Yet most people don't think clearly enough about the "smaller meaning of life." Either they have no goals or they merely accept the ones currently in fashion. Sometimes, however, the path to a *good life* means adjusting the bar and setting achievable goals. What matters is to know where you're going, not to get to any old place quickly.

20

YOUR TWO SELVES

Why Your Life Isn't a Photo Album

I'd like to introduce you to two people you know very well, although not by name: your *experiencing self* and your *remembering self*.

Your *experiencing self* is the part of your conscious mind that experiences the present moment. In your case, it's reading these words right now. In a while it will experience you shutting the book, putting it down, maybe getting to your feet and brewing a cup of tea. Your *experiencing self* experiences not only what you're currently doing but also what you're thinking and feeling as you do it. It perceives physical conditions like tiredness, toothache or tension, mixing it all together into a single experienced moment.

How long does a moment last? Psychologists estimate three seconds, give or take. That's the span of time we perceive as the present. Basically, it's all the experienced things we condense into "now." Longer periods are perceived as a series of individual moments. Discounting time spent asleep, this adds up to approximately twenty thousand moments per day—about half a billion moments over an average lifespan.

What happens to all the impressions hurtling through your brain every second? The vast majority are irretrievably lost. Test yourself: what exactly did you experience twenty-four hours, ten minutes and three seconds ago? Maybe you had to sneeze. Or you looked out of the window. Brushed a crumb off your trousers. Whatever it was, it's gone now. We retain less than a millionth of our experiences. We're gigantic experience-vanishing machines.

That was your *experiencing self.* The second person I'd like to introduce is your *remembering self.* This is the part of your conscious mind that gathers, evaluates and organizes the few things your experiencing self hasn't thrown away. If, twenty-four hours, ten minutes and three seconds ago, you were putting the best praline you've ever tasted into your mouth, then perhaps your *remembering self* does in fact still know that.

The difference between your two selves can be amply illustrated with a simple question. Are you happy? Take a little time to answer the question.

Okay. How did you get on? If you consulted your *experiencing self,* it will have replied with your currently experienced condition, your mental state during that exact three-second interval. As the author of the words you're reading, I naturally hope the response was positive. If, however, you asked your *remembering self,* it will have given you a broad assessment of your overall mood—roughly how you've been feeling recently, and how generally satisfied you are with your life.

Unfortunately, the two selves rarely give the same reply. Researchers studied happiness among students during the holidays. With some they randomly surveyed their momentary state, texting them questions several times a day. With others, they questioned the students at the end of the holiday. The result? The *experiencing self* was less happy than the *remembering self.* Not surprising, really. I'm sure you've heard of rose-tinted glasses: lots of things seem better in retrospect. But this also means we shouldn't trust our powers of recall, because they're prone to systematic errors.

The magnitude of these errors is revealed by the following experiment. Students held their hand in cold 14-degree water for one minute—a rather unpleasant experience. In a second test, they held their hand in cold 14-degree water for one minute, then cold 15-degree water for thirty seconds. Immediately afterward they were asked which version they'd like to repeat. Eighty percent opted for the second. That makes no sense, because viewed objectively the second version was worse—all the pain of the first go-round *plus* the relative unpleasantness of the second.

What's going on here? Daniel Kahneman calls it the *peak–end rule*, which we encountered in Chapter 1. He realized that we remember most clearly the peak of an episode, i.e., the moment of greatest intensity, and the end. Hardly anything else filters through into our memories. In the case of the water experiment, the peak experience was identical in both versions—the cold 14-degree water. The ends, however, were different. The end of the first version (14 degrees) was more unpleasant than the end of the second (15 degrees), which is why the test subjects' brains recorded the latter as more pleasant, even though from the perspective of the *experiencing self* (and objectively speaking) it was less so.

Not even duration matters. The students didn't factor in the length of the experiment at all, whether it lasted sixty or ninety seconds. This holds true more generally: whether you're on holiday for one week or three, your memory of it will be roughly the same. Likewise, whether you're in prison for a month or a year, it makes no difference to your memory—the specific amount of time spent behind bars will be forgotten. This cognitive bias is called *duration neglect*, and apart from the *peak–end rule* it's the most serious error your *remembering self* can commit.

While the *experiencing self* is profligate (it throws almost everything away), the *remembering self* is remarkably error-prone—and it leads us to make the wrong decisions. Because of our *remembering self*'s miscalculations, we tend to prize brief, intense pleasures too highly and quiet, lasting, tranquil joys too little: bungee jumping instead of long hikes, thrilling one-night-stands instead of regular sex with your partner, attention-grabbing YouTube videos instead of a good book.

There is a whole genre of books on "extreme living." Their authors are almost exclusively war reporters, extreme mountain climbers, start-up entrepreneurs or performance artists. They preach that life is too short for moderate pleasures. Only in extreme highs and lows can you really "feel" anything. A calm, unspectacular life is a failed life. These authors—and their readers—have fallen into the trap of the *remembering self*. Running barefoot across the USA or conquering Everest in record time can only be considered wonderful experiences in retrospect. At the time, they're torture. Extreme sports feed memory at the cost of moment-by-moment happiness.

So which one matters, your *experiencing self* or your *remembering self*? Both, of course. Nobody wants to miss out on great memories. Yet we tend to overvalue the *remembering self*, living with one eye on the aggregation of future memories, instead of focusing on the present. Guard against this impulse. Decide what's more important to you: a fulfilled moment-to-moment life or a full photo album?

21

THE MEMORY BANK

Experience Trumps Memory

Picture your best possible experience—a ten-year cruise through the Caribbean, maybe, or traveling across the galaxy, or dinner with God himself and a 1947 Cheval Blanc Vandermeulen. How much would you be prepared to pay for this ideal experience?

Take a moment to jot down a few key words describing the most wonderful experience you can imagine, and what your highest bid would be.

A follow-up question: how much would you be willing to pay if you weren't able to remember it afterward? If you had no idea what your Caribbean yacht even looked like. If you climbed out of your space capsule back on Earth and didn't know whether the planets in faraway solar systems were green, blue, or red. If you couldn't recall whether God was a man or a woman, let alone the taste of the wine. If you could rack your brains as long as you liked—and find nothing left, not even a trace. Most people I ask reply that such an experience is not worth having.

You probably feel the same. But how much would you be willing to pay for the experience if you could remember it afterward for one day? One year? One decade?

Sadly there are no scientific studies on this question that was originally posited by Daniel Kahneman. The responses I've gathered are anecdotal, but the general consensus is that experiences only count if you remember them. Let's call this phenomenon the *memory bank*. The longer we live with a memory, the greater the value it accrues. If a (positive) memory remains in the bank until the day you die, it will in retrospect be highly valued. If it only lasts for half that time, its value is halved—and so on, until its value reaches zero. Without memory, the experience is perceived as entirely valueless. This is surprising, and it makes no sense. Surely it's better to experience something wonderful than not—regardless of whether you remember it. After all, in the moment you'll be having a fabulous time! And once we're dead, you and I will forget everything anyway—because there'll no longer be any "you" or any "I." If death is going to erase your memories, how important is it to schlep them with you until your very final moment?

It would be interesting to explore the emotional world of dementia patients, because that's precisely what they experience: a series of transitory events, moment by moment, without any subsequent memory of them. As far as we can tell, this also describes the emotional life of most animals. They have moments, but few or no memories. You sometimes find carers in old folks' homes treating their dementia patients harshly and arguing that "they won't remember it anyway." This may be true, but the patients will certainly experience it in the moment. Their *experiencing self* is operating just fine—and the same goes for you.

Studies show that people feel happier while remembering positive experiences, especially when viewing them through the rose-tinted glasses of nostalgia. Many psychologists have concluded from this that we should take time to deliberately recall happy moments from the past. A dubious proposition. Why shouldn't we put this time toward creating wonderful experiences for ourselves in the here and now? The effort of consciously experiencing the present moment seems to me no greater than that of dusting off old memories. On the contrary. The things we experience in the present are also much more forceful, more intensely flavored and colorful than our fogged-up recollections. You don't have to experience a parachute jump or the perfect sunset to enjoy the moment. Even if, like now, you're sitting on a chair reading this chapter, you will (I hope, anyway) experience a series of enjoyable chunks of time. Be consciously aware of these moments, physically perceive them, instead of scrabbling for memories. You won't dig up much anyway. Of a holiday, for instance, we only remember the high (or low) and the final part. That's Kahneman's *peak–end rule*, as we learned in Chapter 20. We may also recall two or three other scenes, but that's the lot. Yet people still think they can replay their memories like watching a film. No. Memories are one-dimensional, shallow, abstract, frequently mistaken, partially fabricated and ultimately unproductive. In short, we overvalue memory and undervalue the experienced moment.

Finally, in the 1960s, the awareness of the "here and now" came into the spotlight and young people started experimenting with LSD, free sex and "happenings." In 1971, the celebrated Harvard professor Richard Alpert (known by his Indian guru name Ram Dass) published his bestselling *Be Here Now*. You couldn't come up with a better motto for this approach to life. Ram Dass mainly propagated ancient Buddhist teachings, adapting them for the West. Today, the 1960s "feeling of being in the moment" is back in fashion, now labeled as "mindfulness." An elite group of urban hipsters, yoga teachers and lifestyle coaches is utterly obsessed with it.

That's all well and good, except that mindfulness is often confused with "not thinking about the future." A mistake. The beloved platitude "live each day as if it were your last," ever popular on calendars, is an idiotic piece of advice that will send you catapulted into hospital, prison or the grave in next to no time. Part of the *good life* is making provision for the future, recognizing dangers early and giving them a wide berth.

The takeaway? Our brains cope automatically with all three layers of time—past, present and future. The issue is which one we concentrate on. My suggestion is not to avoid making long-term plans, but once they're in place to focus wholly on the now. Make the most of your present experiences instead of worrying about future memories. Savor the sunset instead of photographing it. A life of wondrous yet forgotten moments is still a wondrous life, so stop thinking of experiences as deposits for your *memory bank*. One day you'll be on your death-bed, and your account will be permanently closed.

22

LIFE STORIES ARE LIES

Why We Go Through the World
with a False Self-Image

What do you know about the First World War? Correct: in 1914 a Serbian freedom fighter shot the successor to the Austro-Hungarian throne in Sarajevo, whereupon Austria-Hungary declared war on Serbia. Because nearly all the European states were bound by treaties, within a few days they'd all been dragged into the war. None of the allied blocs were dominant, so the front soon froze solid. It was a war of attrition that resulted in unparalleled loss of life, and Verdun became a symbol of punishing trench warfare. Four years and eighteen million deaths later, it was all over.

That's probably more or less how you'd summarize the First World War. Unless you're a historian—in which case you'll know, of course, that it wasn't like that. The events of the war were much more complex, intricate and riddled with chance than the story in our heads would have us believe. In truth we still don't understand why the war began in Serbia, specifically. There were numerous assassinations in those days (more than there are today). Germany could just as easily have declared war on France, or vice versa. We also don't know why there was such drawn-out trench warfare. The various innovations in weapons technology that had appeared shortly beforehand (machine guns, tanks, poison gas, submarines and a nascent air force) seem, in retrospect, like they should have led to a much more fluid battle line.

The human brain is often compared to a computer. The comparison doesn't work. Computers store raw data using bits, the smallest unit of information. Brains store not raw but processed data. Their preferred format is not the bit but the story. Why? Because our storage space is limited to our skulls. Eighty billion brain cells sounds like a lot, but it's a far cry from what we'd need to store everything we see, read, hear, smell, taste, think and feel. So the brain has developed a data-compression trick: the story.

The real world has no stories. You could trudge through all seven continents for ten years with a magnifying glass, turning over every stone, and you wouldn't find a single story. You'd fine stones, animals, plants, fungi . . . with a powerful microscope even cells, then molecules, then atoms and finally elementary particles. But no stories. Even if you'd been alive during the First World War, objectively speaking you wouldn't have seen a world war—you'd have seen trenches filled with people wearing strange steel hats, forests consisting of nothing but tree stumps, bullets whistling through the air, and countless dead bodies, both human and horse.

How does the brain weave facts into memories? By binding them into a compact, consistent and causal story. Compact, consistent, causal—the three Cs. Compact: the stories are short, simplified and devoid of holes. Consistent: they're contradiction-free. Causal: there's a clear connection of cause to effect—A leads to B leads to C, and the developments make sense.

Our brains do this automatically. Not just with facts about wars, changes in the stock market or fashion trends, but also with our own lives. Constructing stories is the primary task of your *remembering self*, which you'll recall from the previous chapter. Your life story tells you who you are, where you come from, where you're going, what matters to you. It's also called your "self" or your "self-image." Your life story is compact: if somebody asks who you are, you'll have a brief, succinct answer ready. It's consistent: things that don't fit are comfortably forgotten, and you plug gaps in your memory with astonishing inventive skill (a skill you don't even know you have). It's causal: your actions make sense—there's a reason behind everything that happens in your life. Compact, consistent, causal.

Yet how realistic is the life story you carry around in your head? About as realistic as the portraits of me my three-year-old son does in chalk on the living-room wall. Perhaps now you're saying: Okay, fine, but is that actually a problem? Too right it's a problem! There are four reasons for this:

First: we change more rapidly than we think. This is true not just of our likes and dislikes (hobbies, favorite music, favorite food) but also of such supposedly inalterable things as personality traits and values. The person we'll be in twenty or forty years, for whose future wellbeing we're working so hard today—toiling seventy hours per week, bringing up children, buying a vacation home—is guaranteed to be a different person from the one we imagine. Perhaps this person won't want a holiday home any more, and will look back uncomprehendingly at your heart attack and the seventy-hour weeks you spent working for anonymous taskmasters and shareholders.

Second: our life seems more amenable to planning than it actually is. Chance plays a far greater role than we'd like to think. The notion of fate, of Fortuna, the goddess of luck—an intellectual tool tried and tested over millennia—has been almost entirely expunged in the past hundred years. This is why we're so devastated when something bad strikes out of the blue. Accidents, cancer, war, death. Until the previous century, such catastrophes were more readily accepted. People were mentally prepared for Fortuna's visit. Today, fate signifies a "failure of the system." Part of the *good life*, however, is putting the mental tool of Fortuna back in its rightful place.

Third: our fabricated life story makes it difficult to judge individual facts plainly—without interpretation, without context, without excuse. Excuses are brake pads that stop us learning from our mistakes.

Fourth: we see ourselves as better—more good-looking, more successful and more intelligent—than we really are. This *self-serving bias* leads us to run more risks than we would otherwise do. It leads us to think too highly of ourselves.

The end result is that we're walking around with a false self-image, believing we're less multi-layered, conflicted and paradoxical than we truly are. So don't be surprised when somebody else judges you "incorrectly." You do the same yourself. A realistic self-image can only be gleaned from someone who's known you well for years and who's not afraid to be honest—your partner or an old friend. Even better, keep a diary and dip back into it every now and again. You'll be amazed at the things you used to write. Part of the *good life* is seeing yourself as realistically as possible—contradictions, shortcomings, dark sides and all. If you see yourself realistically, you've got a much better chance of becoming who you want to be.

23

THE "GOOD DEATH" FALLACY

Why Your Final Moments Shouldn't Worry You

I'm sure you recognize the sentiment: "When I'm on my death-bed, looking back on my life…" A magnificently lofty idea, but rather nonsensical in practice. For a start, almost no one is that lucid when they're on their deathbed. The three main doors into the afterlife are heart attack, stroke and cancer. In the first two cases, you won't have time for philosophical reflection. In most cases of cancer, you'll be so stuffed to the gunnels with painkillers that you won't be able to think straight. Nor do those afflicted with dementia or Alzheimer's achieve any new insights on their deathbeds. And even if you do have the time and wherewithal in your final moments to reminisce, your memories won't (as we saw in the previous three chapters) correspond fully to reality. Your *remembering self* produces systematic errors. It tells tall tales.

Basically, it's not worth coming up with hypotheses about the moment of your death or your final hours. Trust me, it won't be like you picture it today. More crucial still is that the way you feel in your final moments is totally irrelevant in the context of your whole life. Contemplating your hour of death is unproductive, and will only distract you from the *good life*.

Daniel Kahneman has systematically uncovered various

flaws in our memories. One of these is *duration neglect*: the duration of an episode is not reflected in your memory of it. Your brain retrospectively judges a three-week holiday no more or less positively or negatively than a one-week holiday. In terms of your overall assessment, only the peak and end of the holiday matter (the *peak–end rule* familiar from Chapter 20). You will remember a film that's exciting throughout but which ends unsatisfactorily as a bad film. Ditto for parties, concerts, books, lectures, homes and relationships.

Does the same go for judging a whole life? Let's find out. We'll evaluate Anna's life: "Anna was never married and had no children. She was extremely happy, enjoyed her work, loved her holidays, her free time and her many friends. At the age of thirty she died suddenly and painlessly in a car accident." Rate the attractiveness of Anna's life on a scale from 1 (terrible) to 9 (fantastic), with 5 as the midpoint (so-so).

Now evaluate Berta's life: "Berta was never married and had no children. She was extremely happy, enjoyed her work, loved her holidays, her free time and her many friends. The last five years of her life weren't as great as the previous ones, but still enjoyable. At the age of thirty-five she died suddenly and painlessly in a car accident." Rate this life on a scale from 1 to 9 too.

Researchers in the USA confronted students with similar life stories. The result? Lives like Anna's were rated significantly better than Berta's. That's illogical, because both women led extremely happy lives for their first thirty years. Berta had an extra five years of life, admittedly not as good but on the whole pleasant. Viewed rationally, we have to rate Berta's life more highly. Yet Anna's life ended on a high, and Berta's on a relative low. The *peak–end rule* comes into play here, but it still seems remarkable that the extra five pleasant years weren't counted. The researchers termed this the *James Dean effect*. Dean died in a road accident at the peak of his glittering career—at the tender age of twenty-four. If he'd lived further years or decades as a moderately successful and moderately happy actor, many people would doubtless rate his life as less attractive.

Now I'd like you to rate Anna's and Berta's lives once more, this time supposing that the accidents took place when Anna was sixty and Berta sixty-five. Everything else remains unchanged. How would you rate them now? Take a moment before you read on.

The test subjects were asked the same in the study. The result? Anna's life was rated significantly better than Berta's again (as you'd expect from the *peak–end rule*). What's astonishing is that the thirty extremely happy additional years Anna experienced had hardly any bearing on the ratings. It made no difference whether Anna died at thirty or sixty. Ditto for Berta. Now, that really is illogical—and a classic example of *duration neglect*.

All in all, we have terrible trouble evaluating the attractiveness of other people's lives. We commit systematic errors in reasoning. That's forgivable in the case of fictional people like Anna and Berta, but not when it comes to your own actual life. Bear in mind that you almost certainly won't die in your prime, like James Dean—but after a protracted and gradual decline in your physical and mental capacities. Depending on the extent of your afflictions, your level of moment-by-moment happiness will on average be lower than in earlier, complaint-free decades. So what conclusions should you draw? Don't let those afflictions cloud your judgment of your *whole* life. Better a life well lived and a few painful days on your deathbed than a shoddy life and a good death. Age and death are the price we pay for a *good life*—like a hefty bill after a meal. I'm not willing to pay that price for a fast-food burger. Give me a six-course dinner in a Michelin-starred restaurant with first-class wine and good company every time.

24

THE SPIRAL OF SELF-PITY

Why It Makes No Sense to Wallow in the Past

Canio, a clown, discovers shortly before he's due to perform that his beautiful wife, whom he loves above all else, is betraying him with another man. He sits alone behind the circus tent, fighting back tears and trying to put on his stage makeup. Inside, the audience is eagerly waiting for him to appear. In a few minutes he'll have to act the fool—after all, the show must go on—but first he launches into the gloriously tragic and beautiful aria "Vesti la giubba" ("Put on your costume") as tears roll down his cheeks.

Thus ends the first act of Leoncavallo's opera *Pagliacci*, premiered in 1892. "Vesti la giubba" is one of the most emotional arias ever composed, and all the greatest tenors in the world have wailed their way through it—Enrico Caruso, Plácido Domingo, José Carreras. Type "Pavarotti" and "Vesti la giubba" into YouTube. The music will break your heart, while Pavarotti, playing Canio the clown, wallows in self-pity.

The second (and final) act sees the customary stabbings, and all those involved die. Yet after the true climax of the opera, none of this seems particularly moving. Since its first performance, the image of the teary clown has been lodged in our cultural memory, long since finding its way into popular culture: in the Miracles' song "The Tears of a Clown," for instance, one of the most-purchased singles of the 1960s—with approximately one percent of the original aria's musical complexity and half a percent of its emotional charge.

If you don't get a little misty-eyed while listening to "Vesti la giubba," then I can't help you. Yet we know that Canio's behavior is, in the long-term, counterproductive. Self-pity is one of the most useless responses to life's trials. Self-pity doesn't change anything. It does the opposite, in fact, because self-pity is an emotional whirlpool, a spiral that sucks you deeper down the longer you're bobbing around in it. Trapped, people rapidly fall victim to paranoia. They feel as if a group of people, the whole of humanity or even the universe has turned against them. It's a vicious circle for the person in question, but also for those around them, who at some point will understandably start to keep their distance. The moment I notice the first hints of self-pity in myself, I do my best to swim away from its dangerous pull, holding true to the adage "If you find yourself in a hole, stop digging."

Charlie Munger tells the story of a friend who always carried with him a stack of printed cards. When he met someone who showed even a trace of self-pity, he would remove the top card with a theatrical gesture and hand it to the person. On the card was written: "Your story has touched my heart. Never have I heard of anyone with as many misfortunes as you." A witty, refreshing, but also slightly callous way of confronting someone with their own self-pity. Yet Munger is right: self-pity is a disastrously wrong-headed pattern of thought.

Even more surprising, then, that self-pity has flourished over the past decades, particularly in the form of "facing up to" or "working through" things. There's the social version of this, in which large groups of people feel themselves to be the victims of events that happened over centuries in the past. Whole university departments are dedicated to exposing the historical roots of this victimization and analyzing them down to the tiniest filament. All of it absolutely justified: even today, African Americans are still experiencing the effects of slavery and segregation, and colonialism still casts a long shadow across the African continent. The same goes for women, indigenous peoples, Jews, gay men and women, immigrants... of which exposition and analysis are understandable and justified.

Yet this way of thinking is unproductive, and even toxic. Moreover, how many centuries should you go back in order to "face up to" the past? One hundred, two hundred, five hundred years? Five hundred years ago, a million of your direct, blood-related ancestors were alive on Earth. Your grandparents' grandparents' grandparents' and so forth. Major branches of your family tree will inevitably have been brutally oppressed. You could face up to all of it, but what for? Accept the wrongs of the past and try to either manage or endure the hardships of the present. Collective self-pity is as unproductive as the individual kind.

A second form of "facing up to things" takes place in the private sphere. On the therapist's couch, the patient digs around in his own childhood and comes up with all sorts of things he'd rather forget—but which can easily be made responsible for his current, probably sub-optimal situation. This is problematic in two respects. One: blaming other people, especially your parents, has an expiry date. If you're still holding your parents liable for your problems at the age of forty, then one can argue that you're so immature you practically deserve them.

Two: studies show that even undeniably awful childhood events (the death of a parent, divorce, neglect, sexual abuse) are minimally correlated with success or satisfaction in adult life. The former president of the American Psychological

Association, Martin Seligman, analyzed hundreds of these studies and concluded that "It has turned out to be difficult to find even small effects of childhood events on adult personality, and there is no evidence at all of large—to say nothing of determining—effects." Far more decisive than our history are our genes—and their distribution is sheer chance. Sure, you could blame your genes for your situation and complain about the ovarian lottery (see Chapter 7), but what would that achieve?

Not getting bogged down in self-pity is a golden rule of mental health. Accept the fact that life isn't perfect—yours or anyone else's. As the Roman philosopher Seneca said, "Things will get thrown at you and things will hit you. Life's no soft affair." What point is there in "being unhappy, just because once you were unhappy"? If you can do something to mitigate the current problems in your life, then do it. If you can't, then put up with the situation. Complaining is a waste of time, and self-pity is doubly counterproductive: first, you're doing nothing to overcome your unhappiness; and two, you're adding to your original unhappiness the further misery of being self-destructive. Or, to quote Charlie Munger's "iron prescription": "Whenever you think that some situation or some person is ruining your life, it is actually you who are ruining your life... Feeling like a victim is a perfectly disastrous way to go through life."

25

HEDONISM AND EUDEMONIA

How Meaning Can Compensate for Enjoyment—and the Other Way Around

How *enjoyable* are the following activities for you? Put them on a scale from 0 (totally unenjoyable, you aren't interested) to 10 (extremely enjoyable, you can't imagine anything better). Eating your favorite chocolate, fighting for your country in a war, spending time on your hobby, raising children, funding hospitals in Africa, preventing global warming, sex, watching the World Cup, helping an old lady across the street, taking a spa holiday to the Caribbean. Give yourself a few seconds.

Most people rate sex, chocolate, TV and spa holidays at 9 or 10, while raising children is a 2 or a 3.

Another question: how *meaningful* are the aforementioned activities? Put them on a scale from 0 (completely meaningless) to 10 (deeply meaningful). Give yourself another moment to think.

Most people come up with a totally different order. Raising children is rated significantly higher than a spa holiday. Helping an old lady across the street is more meaningful than stuffing your face with chocolate.

Hmm. What really matters? What should we be focusing on? Which activities contribute to a *good life*—the "enjoyable" ones or the "meaningful" ones?

As early as the fifth century B.C., Greek thinkers were pondering these issues. A minority of philosophers, known as hedonists, believed that a *good life* consisted of consuming the maximum possible number of immediate pleasures. The word hedonistic originates from the Ancient Greek "hedoné," which means delight, pleasure, enjoyment, gratification and sensual desire. Basically, why help an old lady cross the street when you could be watching a funny YouTube video on your mobile phone?

Most philosophers, however, believed that instant gratification was base, decadent, even animalistic. A *good life* was made up of the "higher pleasures." Striving for these was called *eudemonia*. As soon as the term had been coined, however, people started wrangling about what it meant. Many philosophers concluded that "higher pleasures" meant virtues: only an honest life could be a *good life*. Hospitals in Africa, basically, instead of the World Cup. Some virtues were considered especially conducive to happiness: Plato and Aristotle both believed that people should be as temperate, courageous, just and prudent as possible. These four new catchwords were gratefully adopted several centuries later by the Catholic Church and repurposed (now in Version 2.0) into what became known as the cardinal virtues: prudence, temperance, fortitude and justice. Following this logic consequentially, you reach absurd conclusions—things like "a Nazi war criminal who is basking on an Argentinean beach is not really happy, whereas the pious missionary who is being eaten alive by cannibals is," as the Harvard psychologist Dan Gilbert has laconically remarked.

So it's all a bit of a muddle. The psychologist Paul Dolan at the London School of Economics has tried to disentangle it. Just as every musical note has two qualities—pitch and volume—every experienced moment has two components: a pleasurable (or hedonistic) component and a meaningful component. The hedonistic component is the instant gratification. The meaningful component, on the other hand, refers to our perception of how purposeful a moment is. Eating chocolate, for instance, has a greater hedonistic but a smaller meaningful component, at least for most people. The ratio between the two components is reversed, however, if you're helping an old lady cross the street.

Paul Dolan's refusal to define more precisely "meaningfulness," or "purposefulness," as he puts it, means he can abandon the whole 2,500-year-old "virtues" house of cards to collapse behind his back. True to the motto "I know it when I see it," everybody knows instantly how meaningful or meaningless an experienced moment is. Right now you're reading this paragraph. The pleasurable component is probably smaller than a sip of Château Pétrus, but hopefully the meaningful component is bigger. Your author's experience is yet more extreme. Writing this chapter is, admittedly, unenjoyable; I'm struggling, but the attempt to get my thoughts down on paper in an intelligible form feels highly meaningful. Purpose and pleasure as the two cornerstones of happiness—it's "a bold and original move," as Daniel Kahneman has observed.

Every year, Hollywood produces four hundred to five hundred films—a billion-dollar industry. No wonder researchers are trying to figure out why people go to the cinema, hoping to create a recipe for a surefire blockbuster. For a long time the hedonistic film theory reigned supreme: give audiences just enough excitement—not too boring, not too stressful—to transport them away from their banal realities. Offer them beautiful actors and entertaining stories with a happy ending. Yet blockbusters keep being produced whose success doesn't rely on this recipe, and thus cannot be explained hedonistically—*Life Is Beautiful*, for instance, or *A Beautiful Mind*. Only recently have film scholars confirmed what good directors and writers have known from the beginning: there's got to be a meaningful component, something besides sheer gratification. Even a sad movie filmed on a shoestring budget can be good—if there's enough meaning in it.

Meaningfulness also plays a role on the job market. Young employees, in particular, are willing to accept a salary below market standards to participate in "meaningful" projects. This is good for idealistic start-ups and bad for major corporations—the latter have to compensate for their deficit in meaning by upping the hedonistic component (read: money). Artists, of course, have always had to consider this trade-off: is it better to die in a blaze of artistic glory or sell out to a mass audience for hard cash?

I recommend you strike a balance between enjoyment and meaning. Avoid the extremes. Why? Because your marginal utility decreases the further you wander toward the fringe. Chocolate, TV and sex become ineffectual after—at the most—the second kilogram of chocolate, the twenty-fourth hour of binge-watching or the fifth orgasm. Equally, it won't make you happy to spend all day and night saving the world while denying yourself any pleasure. It's best to switch between meaningfulness and enjoyment. So if you've saved a small piece of the world, then I think you deserve a glass of fine red wine.

26

THE CIRCLE OF DIGNITY—PART I

But If Not

In 1939, shortly after Germany invaded Poland and set in motion the Second World War, England began sending soldiers across the English Channel. They were intended to support the French in the imminent battle with the Germans. One year later, in May 1940, 300,000 British troops were stationed in and around Dunkirk, a port town in northern France. That same month, German forces attacked Belgium and Holland and marched into France. A few days later, the British found themselves surrounded. It was only a question of time before the Germans slaughtered them. The situation was hopeless. A British officer telegraphed three words to London: "But if not." Question: how would you interpret those three words?

A person familiar with the Bible—something taken for granted in those days—would have realized in a flash what those words meant. They come from the Old Testament (Daniel 3:18). The Babylonian king, Nebuchadnezzar, announces to three god-fearing Jews, "If ye worship not [the image of my god], ye shall be cast the same hour into the midst of a burning fiery furnace." The king gives the three men time to consider. They reply, "O Nebuchadnezzar, we are not careful to answer thee in this matter. If it be so, our God whom we serve is able to deliver us from the burning fiery furnace, and he will deliver us out of thine hand, O king. *But if not*, be it known unto thee,

O king, that we will not serve thy gods, nor worship the golden image which thou hast set up."

The message that reached London in May 1940 said: The situation here in Dunkirk is bleak. We're surrounded. It would take a miracle to get us out of this, but we're determined not to give up—come what may. All that was contained in the three words *but if not*. It was an expression of total commitment.

A few days later, the British evacuated 338,000 French and British troops in a chaotic operation that incorporated eight hundred destroyers, fishing boats, merchant ships, leisure craft and Thames ferries. Even today, people talk about the Miracle of Dunkirk.

Because few people are so conversant with the Bible today, hardly anybody understands the significance of *but if not*. A modern equivalent might be "over my dead body."

This attitude has defined a sharply delineated area of my life that encompasses everything not up for negotiation. It contains preferences and principles that need no justification. For example, I never do anything for money that I wouldn't do for a tenth the offered sum; in other words, I never let money be the decisive factor. I never put photos of our children online. I would never badmouth my family or friends to anybody, even if I had a reason to—which has never happened. Analogously to the *circle of competence*, I've dubbed this the *circle of dignity*. The idea connects back to Chapter 3, where we encountered the *pledge*. The *circle of dignity* draws together your individual *pledges* and protects them from three forms of attack: a) better arguments; b) mortal danger; and c) deals with the Devil. This brings me to the first part of my trilogy about the *circle of dignity*: the threat of better arguments. We'll take a closer look at the second and third threats in the following two chapters.

As with the *circle of competence*, the size of your *circle of dignity* doesn't really matter—what's vital is that you know exactly where its boundaries lie.

Establishing a *circle of dignity* has little to do with the Enlightenment spirit. It conflicts with everything I otherwise hold sacred—clear thinking, rationality and the supremacy of "better arguments." Is that allowed? Isn't progress based on consistently calling everything into question? The answer: Yes, but. A small, inviolable, clearly demarcated *circle of dignity* is essential to the *good life*. In fact, I'd go so far as to say that it's imperative the things within your circle aren't rationally justifiable. If they were, you'd never get any peace. Your life would have no solid ground. You'd always have to be prepared for a better argument to come along and toss all your preferences, principles and commitments overboard.

How do you establish a *circle of dignity*? Not through deliberation. Rather, it's something that crystallizes with time—for most people, by middle age. This process of crystallization is an indispensable step toward becoming a mature adult. You need to have experienced certain things—wrong decisions, disappointments, failures, crises. And you need to be self-aware enough to know which principles you're ready to defend and which you're prepared to give up. Some people never develop a *circle of dignity*. Such people lack a foundation, so they're perpetually vulnerable to cunning arguments.

Keep your *circle of dignity* tight. A small circle is more powerful than a large one, for two reasons. First, the more you pack into your circle, the more these things are in conflict. You can't satisfy a dozen priorities. Second, the less you pack into your circle, the more seriously you can commit to your beliefs and the better you can defend them. "Commitments are so sacred that by nature they should be rare," warns Warren Buffett.

That's true not only for promises made to other people, but also to promises made to yourself. So be highly selective in your choice of non-negotiables—the principles you refuse to abandon.

So far so clear. But be prepared for one thing: you'll disappoint some people by defending your principles—especially people you care about. You'll hurt people. You'll snub people. You'll be disappointed, hurt and offended in turn. It's critical you be prepared to deal with all these emotions, because that's the price you pay for a *circle of dignity*. Only puppets live free of conflict. The *circle of competence*—that's ten thousand hours. The *circle of dignity*—that's ten thousand wounds.

Is it worth the price? That's the wrong question. By definition, things that are invaluable have no price. "If an individual has not discovered something that he will die for, he isn't fit to live," said Martin Luther King. Certainly not to live the *good life*.

27

THE CIRCLE OF DIGNITY—PART II

If You Break on the Outside

On 9 September 1965, the young American Marine pilot James Stockdale set off in his fighter jet from the aircraft carrier USS *Oriskany*, bound for North Vietnam. Returning from a successful routine attack on Communist emplacements, he flew inadvertently into anti-aircraft fire. The ejector seat catapulted him out of the plane. "I was below a thousand feet, I had about twenty seconds in the parachute, and I looked down and I was going to land right over the main street of a little town... [T]hey were firing guns at me, holding up their fists." Stockdale was promptly captured and thrown into the infamous Hanoi Hilton, where other American prisoners of war were already being held. He was interrogated. He was beaten. He was tortured. Stockdale spent seven and a half years in prison, four of them in solitary confinement—until the end of the Vietnam War.

Stockdale could have avoided this abuse by cozying up to his tormentors somewhat. The occasional anti-American statement and they would have treated him like an ordinary inmate. No torture. Yet it never crossed his mind. He willingly gave himself up to his tormentors. As he later explained, it was the only way he could maintain his self-respect. He didn't do it for love of his country. Nor was it about the war, which he no longer believed in. It was purely about not breaking down inside. He did it solely for himself.

At one point they were planning to transfer him to another prison. He was due to be marched through the city, paraded before the international media clean and well nourished. Before leaving the prison, however, Stockdale grabbed a stool and bashed it into his own face until blood ran down his body and his eyes swelled shut. They could hardly present him to the world in that condition. "I laid down and I cried that night, right on that floor. I was so happy that I had had the guts to get it all together and make it impossible for them to do what they were going to try to do."

Viewed from the outside, it sounds absurd. In Stockdale's situation, it would have been sensible to do as his tormentors instructed. Take orders. Go with the flow. Not stand out. Question the American invasion. After his release he could believably have claimed that otherwise they would have tortured him to death. Everybody would have understood why he acted as he did, and nobody would have blamed him. But would Stockdale have had the strength to withstand seven and a half years? And if so, looking back, would he have described his time in prison as "priceless beyond measure"?

If you don't make it clear on the outside what you believe deep down, you gradually turn into a puppet. Other people exploit you for their own purposes, and sooner or later, you give up. You don't fight any more. You don't hold up to stresses. Your willpower atrophies. If you break on the outside, at some point you'll break on the inside too.

There's a whole genre of prison literature, from Solzhenitsyn's *Gulag Archipelago* to Elie Wiesel's *Song of the Dead*, from to Primo Levi's *If This Is a Man* to Viktor Frankl's *Man's Search for Meaning*. These books are frequently misread. People scan them for survival tips in horrendous situations, even though survival is largely a matter of chance. In Auschwitz there were no survival strategies. If you were interned toward the end of the war, you had a higher probability of making it out than if you'd been brought there in 1942. It's that simple. Then there's the fact that only survivors can write about being a POW. The dead don't write books. Stockdale was lucky he wasn't hit by a bullet as he seesawed down into the enemy village in his parachute. And yet!

And yet one fundamental principle does emerge from all this literature. Those who braced themselves to make it through the day—and the next, and the next—increased their chances of survival step by step. Eventually Auschwitz was liberated. At some point every imprisonment is ended. You just have to persevere, assuming that's possible. And only someone who refuses to break, within or without, will be able to do that. Someone who never gives up, who cherishes their own will, no matter how tiny their leeway.

All of this, as I said above, can only be understood as subject to chance. Personal stories from extreme situations are relevant even to ordinary citizens like us. We're unlikely to be tortured, thankfully; nor do we have to endure solitary confinement or freezing ice in Siberia's gulag. But we are assailed every day by attacks on our wills, our principles, our preferences—on our *circle of dignity*. These attacks aren't as overt as torture. Rather, they're so subtle that often we don't even notice them: advertising, social pressure, unsolicited advice from all angles, soft propaganda, fashion trends, media hype and laws. It's as though arrows are being shot every day into your *circle of dignity*. Sharp, poisoned arrows—none of them fatal, but each keen enough to injure your self-esteem and weaken your emotional immune system.

Why is society bombarding you with arrows? Because its concerns are not your concerns. Society cares about cohesion, not about the private interests of a single member. Individuals are dispensable, and quickly perceived as threats to the collective—especially if they hold divergent principles. Society only leaves people in peace if they conform. So brace yourself for those arrows and shore up your *circle of dignity*.

Your *circle of dignity*, the protective wall that surrounds your *pledges*, can only be tested under fire. You might lay claim to high ideals, noble principles and distinctive preferences, but it's not until you come to defend them that you will "cry with happiness," to paraphrase Stockdale.

The worst attacks—you'll know this from experience—are often not physical but verbal. So let me give you a defensive tactic. Say you're in a meeting and somebody starts going for you, really getting vitriolic. Ask them to repeat what they've said word for word. You'll soon see that, most of the time, your attacker will fold. The Serbian president Aleksandar Vučić once asked a journalist who'd insulted him on his website to read his own words aloud during an interview—the journalist, ashamed, cut the meeting short.

People with a clear *circle of dignity* fascinate us, in literature as in film—like Todd Anderson in *Dead Poets Society*, who stood on a desk to defend his teacher. Or think of Socrates, who refused to recant his teachings. He was sentenced to death, and drank his cup of hemlock in utter serenity.

For most people, the *circle of dignity* is not a matter of life and death but a battle to maintain the upper hand. Make it as hard as possible for your assailants. Keep the reins in your hand as long as possible when it comes to the things you hold sacred. If you have to give up, then do so in a way that makes your opponent pay the highest practicable price for your capitulation. There's tremendous power in this commitment. It's one of the keys to a *good life*.

28

THE CIRCLE OF DIGNITY—PART III

The Devil's Bargain

The Alps. An enormous obstacle in the middle of Europe. For centuries they've blocked the transport of people and goods between North and South, and those of an adventurous spirit have tried numerous times to cross them. The most promising path was the Gotthard Pass—it cuts through the middle of the Alps, between the Swiss cantons of Uri and Ticino. Yet in the middle was the wild, deep-set Schöllenen Gorge that leads to the pass from the north. How to cross this vast fissure? The answer, in the thirteenth century, was to build a bridge—the Devil's Bridge.

The locals had tried and failed many times to build one. At last, the head of the regional assembly, the Landammann, cried in desperation: "Do sell der Tyfel e Brigg bue!" (Urner German dialect for "Then let the Devil build a bridge there!"). Hardly were the words spoken before the Devil appeared to the baffled locals and offered them a pact. He would be happy to build the bridge, on one condition: that the soul of the first creature to cross the finished structure would belong to him—to the Devil.

The wily locals accepted, and secretly came up with a plan. After the Devil built the bridge, they sent a goat to cross it first. The Devil, understandably annoyed, picked up a boulder the size of a house and was about to smash the bridge. Just then, however, he was confronted by a pious woman, who scratched a cross into the stone. Distracted, the Devil let the boulder drop. It thundered down into the gorge, narrowly missing the bridge, and didn't stop until it had passed the village of Göschenen. You can still see it there today, a few meters from the Autobahn—it's been called the "Devil's stone" ever since.

The people of Uri had sold their souls but wriggled out of it without a scratch—and come away with a revolutionary transport bridge. Similar tales can be found in all cultures, though most of them are less mild. In Oscar Wilde's novel *The Picture of Dorian Gray*, the hero sells his soul to the Devil in exchange for remaining permanently young and beautiful while his portrait ages instead. Gray spirals into debauchery as his portrait grows ever more hideous; eventually he can bear it no longer and destroys it—thereby killing himself. More famous still is the pact of Faustian legend, in which the alchemist Johann Georg Faust sold his soul to acquire all the world's knowledge and indulge in all its possible and impossible pleasures. Goethe turned the story into a classic, and it's now required reading at German schools.

To sell your soul—what does that mean? Evidently, in financial transactions, certain things are considered taboo across all ages and cultures. No deals. No trades. No money changing hands. These things are *sacred*—they are priceless. For an economist, of course, nothing is priceless. Sacred things are just "massively overvalued," the economist would say—offer enough money and the owner weakens. This is what makes narratives like Friedrich Dürrenmatt's *The Visit* so compelling. In Dürrenmatt's play, Claire Zachanassian offers the inhabitants of an impoverished town a billion Swiss francs if they kill her former lover—and she gets what she wants.

Ask yourself the following question: are there things you hold so sacred that you wouldn't sell them for any price, even a billion dollars? Write down your answer in the margin.

What's on your list? The obvious candidates are your life, the lives of your immediate and extended family, of your friends, perhaps any human life. What about your health? Would you accept being ill, say with leukemia or depression, for a billion pounds? What about your opinions? Do your opinions have a price? Some politicians are willing to sell their vote to whichever company has the biggest budget. Would you consider doing the same? Would you reconsider if you were living on the breadline? What about your time? Your attention? Your principles? Are there some you would never throw overboard, even to become a billionaire?

A few of these decisions may be black and white, but others are not. My point is that, as we have seen elsewhere, part of a *good life* is having a small but clearly delineated *circle of dignity*—which brings me now to the third part of my trilogy. We've got to defend our circle from three types of attack: a) better arguments; b) mortal danger; and c) the "deal with the devil." I'm now talking about the third type. If you don't outline your *circle of dignity* clearly enough, you'll have to rethink every time a new deal or tempting offer comes along. Not only is this a huge waste of time but it also erodes your self-respect and reputation, making you yet more vulnerable to future offers. It's a vicious circle.

I'm sure you're not short of offers in your own life. In his book *What Money Can't Buy*, Harvard professor Michael Sandel reveals how the "deal" has increasingly infiltrated new areas of life over the last fifty years. Things that were formerly non-negotiable are now open to discussion. One woman in America, for instance, accepted $10,000 to get the name of an online casino tattooed on her forehead, so that she could finance her son's education. This is a voluntary transaction, of course, but it involves something that was once sacrosanct: the human body, now degraded into a billboard. Meanwhile, banks routinely invest in pensioners' life insurance. The earlier the pensioners die, the more money the banks earn. Hundreds of similar examples show that the monetary economy is expanding its assault on formerly *sacred* subjects. You can't expect legislators to prevent the encroachment of financial logic. It's up to you to repel these attacks on your own *circle of dignity*.

The upshot? Define your *circle of dignity* sharply. Don't let yourself be infected when the financial virus tries to penetrate your values' immune system. The things inside your *circle of dignity* are non-negotiable, always—no matter how much cash is offered in return. Anything else would be a devil's bargain, and you're not likely to escape as unscathed as the people of Uri.

29

THE BOOK OF WORRIES

How to Switch Off the Loudspeaker
in Your Head

Suppose you're God and you're creating a new species. You've already chosen the hardware—the new animal is going to resemble a chimpanzee. Now you're wondering about the software: how strongly, quickly and sensitively should it react to dangers, especially to the indistinct, purely conjectural kind?

If you set your creation's "danger sensor" too low, the species will soon fall off a cliff or be eaten by its natural enemies. It will die out in two seconds flat. But if you set the danger sensor too high, your new species will be perpetually rooted to the spot in terror. It will starve to death before it has the chance to reproduce, giving you the same result: extinction.

So you need the right amount of anxiety—the right setting on the "worry detector." Yet what is the "right" amount? Precisely in the middle between the two fatal extremes? No. You program your species to err on the side of caution. Better to run from a moving shadow once too often than the other way around. So you give your species a hefty dose of anxiety, concern and fear—just not so much that it won't seek food.

This is precisely what evolution has done with every species on Earth. Including us. That's why we're plagued by anxiety morning till night. This unease is a totally normal software component of our brains, biologically hardwired and virtually impossible to switch off. Without the burden of worry, neither you, dear reader, nor I, nor any other human being would exist. Over millions of years, constant anxiety has proved itself an excellent survival strategy.

Let's be glad it has! But there's a catch: our level of anxiety is no longer proportional to the actual dangers of living. You're not on the savannah any more, where there's a saber-toothed tiger lurking around every waterhole. In fact, ninety percent of your worries are superfluous—either because the problems you're turning over in your mind aren't really dangerous or because you can't do anything about them anyway. Lying in bed panicking about global warming, market sentiment or life after death isn't going to accomplish anything. It's just going to keep you awake.

Perpetual anxiety leads to chronic stress, which can take years off your life. A memorable example from the animal kingdom illustrates the problem. Sparrows have a variety of natural predators—racoons, owls, falcons. Canadian researchers decided to block off a whole area of forest with nets, shutting out the sparrows' natural enemies. Never before had the sparrows been safer. Then the researchers dotted the forest with hidden loudspeakers. In one area of the woods they played the noises of predators, and in the other unthreatening natural sounds. The sparrows exposed to the "bad" noises laid forty percent fewer eggs, the eggs they did lay were smaller, and fewer of them hatched. Many of the chicks starved to death because their parents were too afraid to forage for food, and the surviving chicks were weaker. The experiment clearly showed that it doesn't even take a real threat to influence a whole ecosystem—fear is enough.

What goes for sparrows also goes for human beings. Worse still, we're afraid not just of predators but also of all sorts of different things. Moreover, fretting has become a popular diversionary tactic, because it's easier to deal with abstract questions than to engage with actual problems. This is where fretting becomes procrastination. The resultant chronic anxiety leads to bad decisions and can make you ill—even if, viewed objectively, you're not in any danger.

At this point it would be nice if I could point you to the switch that turns off the loudspeaker in your head. Unfortunately, however, there isn't one.

The Greek and Roman philosophers known as the Stoics recommended the following trick to sweep away worry: determine what you can influence and what you can't. Address the former. Don't let the latter prey on your mind. Two thousand years later, the American theologian Reinhold Niebuhr put it this way: "God, grant me the serenity to accept the things I cannot change, courage to change the things I can, and wisdom to know the difference." Sounds easy, but it isn't, because "serenity" can't be conjured at the push of a button.

More recently, meditation has been extolled as a remedy for all that ails you—especially for unease and lingering anxiety. The reality? Meditation does work, but only while you're meditating. As soon as you resurface, the thoughts and feelings return, just as strong as before.

With all due respect to philosophy and meditation, concrete strategies are more helpful. Here are three that, in my experience, work.

One: fetch a notebook and title it *My Big Book of Worries*. Set aside a fixed time to dedicate to your anxieties. In practical terms, this means reserving ten minutes a day to jot down everything that's worrying you—no matter how justified, idiotic or vague. Once you've done so, the rest of the day will be relatively worry-free. Your brain knows its concerns have been recorded and not simply ignored. Do this every day, turning to a fresh page each time. You'll realize, incidentally, that it's always the same dozen or so worries tormenting you. At the weekend, read through the week's notes and follow the advice of Bertrand Russell: "When you find yourself inclined to brood on anything, no matter what, the best plan always is to think about it even more than you naturally would, until at last its morbid fascination is worn off." In practical terms, this means imagining the worst possible consequences and forcing yourself to think beyond them. You'll discover that most concerns are overblown. The rest are genuine dangers, and those must be confronted.

Two: take out insurance. Insurance policies are a marvelous invention. They're among the most elegant worry-killers. Their true value is not the monetary pay-out when there's a problem but the reduced anxiety beforehand.

Three: focused work is the best therapy against brooding. Focused, fulfilling work is better than meditation. It's a better distraction than anything else.

If you use these three strategies, you'll have a real chance of living a carefree life—a *good life*. Then perhaps even in your younger years or, at least, in middle age, you'll be able to chuckle over Mark Twain's late-in-life insight: "I am an old man and have known a great many troubles, but most of them have never happened."

30

THE OPINION VOLCANO

Why You're Better Off
Without Opinions

Should the minimum wage be increased? Should shops be allowed to sell genetically modified foods? Is it a fact that global warming is caused by human activity or is it the hysterical fantasy of environmentalist politicians? Should advocates of Sharia law be deported from Europe? I'm sure you have an answer at the ready for all these questions. As politically interested people, you don't need more than a second to decide. In reality, however, these questions are far too complicated to be settled in the blink of an eye. Each of them demands at least an hour's concentrated deliberation for a sensible resolution to be reached.

The human brain is a volcano of opinions. It spews out viewpoints and ideas nonstop. No matter whether the questions are relevant or irrelevant, answerable or unanswerable, complex or simple—the brain tosses out answers like confetti.

In doing so it makes three mistakes. The first: we express opinions on topics in which we have no interest. In a recent discussion with friends, I caught myself professing a heated opinion on a doping scandal, even though I'm not remotely interested in elite sports. You can open any popular newspaper and your opinion volcano will begin to seethe. Keep a lid on it—as I should have done.

The second mistake: we spew out opinions on unanswerable questions. When can we expect the next stock market crash? Is there more than one universe? What will the weather be like next summer? Nobody can say for sure, not even experts. So here, too: be wary of blurting out opinions.

The third mistake: we tend to give over-hasty answers to complex questions—like those at the beginning of this chapter. This mistake is the most serious of the three. The American psychologist Jonathan Haidt has done extensive studies into what happens inside our brains when we do this, revealing that we tend—especially with difficult questions—to instantly pick a side. Only then do we consult our rational mind, looking to justify and shore up our position. This has to do with the *affect heuristic*. An affect is an instantaneous, one-dimensional emotion. It's superficial and has only two settings: positive or negative, "I like" or "I don't like." We see a face—"I like." We hear about a murder—"I don't like." Affects are entirely legitimate—just not in responding to difficult questions, where we confuse them with the right answer. An affect appears at lightning speed, we hurriedly ransack our brains for reasons, examples and anecdotes to back it up—and there we have our opinion. It's a pretty inadequate process when it comes to complex topics.

Poor decisions based on half-baked opinions can be disastrous, but there's another good reason to prevent opinion incontinence. Not always feeling like you *need* to have an opinion calms the mind and makes you more relaxed—an ingredient vital to a *good life*.

My suggestion? Get yourself a "too complicated" bucket. Throw in all the questions that don't interest you, that are unanswerable or too much hard work. Don't worry, you'll still be left with a handful of topics every day on which you can or must offer an opinion.

Recently a journalist asked me about my political beliefs. Apparently being a writer qualifies you to answer all the major world questions. Was I in favor of more or less state interference? Did I think a consumption tax was fairer than income tax? I looked him in the eye and said, "I don't know." He lowered his pen. His expression twisted into a pained smile, as though he didn't understand the meaning of this simple sentence. "What do you mean, you don't know?" "I haven't thought it through," I said. "But you must have an opinion!" "No, I don't. That topic is in my 'too complicated' bucket."

It's immensely liberating not having to hold an opinion on all and sundry. And there's no need to worry that opinionlessness is a sign of intellectual weakness. It isn't. it's a sign of intelligence. Opinionlessness is an asset. It's not information overload besetting our era—it's opinion overload.

Select your topics of interest very carefully. Why should you let journalists, bloggers or tweeters dictate what's on your mind? They're not the boss of you! Be extremely selective. Dump everything else into your "too complicated" bucket. When you're asked to pass judgment on this or that, refrain. You'll find, astonishingly, that the world keeps spinning even without your commentary.

But when you do want to form an opinion, how should you do it? Set aside some time to write about it in peace. Writing is the ideal way to organize your thoughts. A diffuse thought automatically becomes clearer when you have to pour it into sentence form. Finally, get external viewpoints, preferably from people who think differently from you. When you're sure of your opinion, question it. Try to poke holes in your argument—that's the only way to find out whether it holds up.

All in all, the fewer hasty opinions you hold, the better your life will be. I'd go so far as to say that ninety-nine percent of your opinions are simply unnecessary. Only one percent are truly relevant for you—for your personal or work life. Even when it comes to this small group of topics, don't just seize the first opinion your volcano spits out. Imagine you're invited onto a TV talk show with five other guests, all of whom are committed to the opposite standpoint from yours. Only when you can argue their views at least as eloquently as your own will you truly have earned your opinion.

31

YOUR MENTAL FORTRESS

The Wheel of Fortune

One morning in the year 523 A.D., there was a knock at Boethius's front gate. The forty-year-old Boethius was a successful, celebrated, if somewhat over-confident intellectual. Born into an aristocratic family, he had received the best education. Under King Theodoric he occupied the highest offices in Rome. He had the perfect marriage and wonderful children. And he could dedicate himself day in, day out to his greatest passion, translating books from Greek into Latin (in those days hardly anybody could still read the Greek classics in the original). Boethius's wealth, reputation, social status and creative energies were at their peak when the aforementioned knock came at his door, and Boethius was promptly arrested. Accused of having supported a conspiracy against Theodoric, he had been sentenced to death in his absence. His assets, his money, his library, his houses, his pictures and his beautiful clothes—all were confiscated. He wrote his final book, *The Consolation of Philosophy*, in jail. One year after his arrest he was executed—by the sword, as was the custom. Today Boethius's grave can be visited at the Church of San Pietro in Ciel d'Oro in Pavia (about thirty miles southwest of Milan).

The Consolation of Philosophy became one of the most-read books of the Middle Ages, although unlike nearly all successful medieval books it has nothing to do with the Christian faith. What's the book about? As Boethius sits in jail—fearful, desperate, awaiting execution—a striking, somewhat older female figure appears: "Philosophy." She explains the world to him, providing him with some mental tools (in this regard it's not dissimilar to the aspirations of this book) to help him cope with his new, inescapable situation. The following is a summary of Philosophy's recommendations, which are of course Boethius's.

First: accept the existence of fate. In Boethius's day, people liked to personify fate as Fortuna, a goddess who turned the Wheel of Fortune, in which highs and lows were endlessly rotated. Those who played along, hoping to catch the wheel as it rose, had to accept that eventually they would come down once more. So don't be too concerned about whether you're ascending or descending. It could all be turned on its head.

Second: everything you own, value and love is ephemeral—your health, your partner, your children, your friends, your house, your money, your homeland, your reputation, your status. Don't set your heart on those things. Relax, be glad if fate grants them to you, but always be aware that they are fleeting, fragile and temporary. The best attitude to have is that all of them are on loan to you, and may be taken away at any time. By death, if nothing else.

Third: if you, like Boethius, have lost many things or even everything, remember that the positive has outweighed the negative in your life (or you wouldn't be complaining) and that all sweet things are tinged with bitterness. Whining is misplaced.

Four: what can't be taken from you are your thoughts, your mental tools, the way you interpret bad luck, loss and setbacks. You can call this space your *mental fortress*—a piece of freedom that can never be assailed.

I'm sure you've read and heard all this before, and even for

Boethius they weren't new ideas. They are the fundamental principles of Stoicism, an ancient, highly practical philosophy of life that originated in the fourth century B.C., i.e., a millennium before Boethius, in Athens. In the first two centuries A.D., it underwent a revival in Rome. Famous Stoics include Seneca (a multi-millionaire), Epictetus (a slave), and Marcus Aurelius (a Roman emperor). Remarkably, Stoicism is still the only branch of philosophy that offers practical answers to life's everyday questions. The other twigs and branches are intellectually stimulating, but offer little help dealing with life.

Boethius was one of the last Stoics, before Christianity thoroughly befogged the European mind and delegated responsibility for one's own life to a fiction (God). Not for another thousand years did the fog lift. Yet even after the glorious sunrise of the Enlightenment, Stoicism was sorely neglected—and remains essentially insider's knowledge even today. Flashes of Stoic thinking have emerged here and there, as when the Holocaust survivor Victor Frankl wrote: "the last of the human freedoms is to choose one's attitude to things"—perfectly describing the *mental fortress*. If you read Primo Levi, you'll be amazed how stoically he recounts his experiences in the concentration camp. And in Chapter 27 we met fighter pilot and Stoic James Stockdale, who spent seven years as a prisoner of war, four of them in solitary confinement. On the whole, however, the Stoics' ideas are alien to us these days. If you use the word "fate," you probably mean a systemic failure rather than the Wheel of Fortune. Unemployment, hunger, war, sickness, even death itself—we blame the system for everything. We assume we've fallen through the cracks.

But that's the wrong way of thinking about it. Precisely because fate strikes more rarely—in our neck of the woods, at least—it hits us harder emotionally. Moreover, the more complex and interconnected the world becomes, the greater the likelihood of radically new and totally unexpected blows of fate. In short, it's more worthwhile than ever to invest in an intellectual toolkit that emotionally prepares you for loss.

You don't have to be Boethius, Jews under the Third Reich or ordinary people caught up in the Syrian civil war to be struck by fate. An internet shitstorm can wipe you out. A global financial crisis can decimate your savings. Your partner falls in love with a Facebook friend and throws you out of the house. All of that's bad, but none of it's deadly. The greatest trials of fate you've already overcome. Think of the improbability of your conception, of the thousands of agonizing births your mother, your two grandmothers, your grandmothers' grandmothers and so forth had to endure (some of them bleeding to death) just to bring you into the world. And now you're moaning about your stock portfolio halving in value?

Simply put, the world is full of unrest and chance, and every so often your life will be upturned. You won't find happiness in status, in expensive cars, in your bank account or in social success. All of it could be taken from you in a split second— as it was with Boethius. Happiness can be found only in your *mental fortress*. So invest in that, not in a Porsche collection.

32

ENVY

Mirror, Mirror, on the Wall

"Whenever a friend succeeds a little something in me dies," confessed the acid-tongued American writer Gore Vidal in an interview. In doing so he expressed an emotion that nobody likes to admit to, even though it overcomes all of us from time to time. It's the most pointless, useless and toxic of all emotions. It's envy.

Not that the pointlessness of envy is a fresh insight. Even the Greek philosophers warned against it. The Bible illustrates its destructive power with dozens of stories, above all in the parable of Cain and Abel. *Snow White*, that criminological fairytale, is an exemplary tale of envy.

Nobel Prize winner Bertrand Russell likewise considered envy one of the most important sources of unhappiness. Envy has a bigger impact on your life satisfaction then physical affliction or financial ruin, and the ability to manage it is fundamental to the *good life*. If you can pull that off, that's a major breakthrough. Unfortunately, we're dealing with an evolutionary program that's tough to outwit.

Envy is not only a human emotion; it's actually an animal instinct. The primate researchers Frans de Waal and Sarah Brosnan rewarded two capuchins for simple tasks with a piece of cucumber each. Seemingly satisfied, the monkeys gratefully accepted their pieces of cucumber. Next time, however, the researchers rewarded one capuchin with another piece of cucumber but the other with a sweet grape. When the first monkey saw that, it threw its piece of cucumber out of its cage and refused to cooperate.

This is the interesting thing about envy: the more we compare ourselves with others, the greater the danger of jealousy. Above all, we envy those who are similar to us in terms of age, career, environment and lifestyle. Tennis pros compare themselves with tennis pros, top executives with top executives, writers with writers. You're not comparing yourself with the Pope, so you're not jealous of him. Ditto for Alexander the Great or a super-successful Stone Age human from your part of the world. Ditto for someone on another planet, a majestic great white shark, or a gigantic Redwood tree. None of them—magnificent beings though they may be—is a suitable object of envy.

And here we have the solution to the problem. Stop comparing yourself to other people and you'll enjoy an envy-free existence. Steer well clear of all comparisons. That's the golden rule.

Easier said than done. Sometimes comparisons are practically shoved down your throat. The University of California, for instance, is obliged by law to make the salaries of its researchers public. There's a website where researchers can see what their colleagues earn. If you're in the bottom half, you'll be less satisfied with your job than before you were given that information. In other words, transparency has squashed happiness.

Another much larger, frankly enormous experiment in comparison is social media. By now it's common knowledge that Facebook leaves many users frustrated and tired. In a study at Humboldt University, researchers decided to find out why. Top of the list? You guessed it: envy. Understandably so,

because Facebook is practically designed to make similar people compare themselves with each other—it's a perfect breed-
ing ground for resentment. I'd recommend giving social media
a wide berth. All those silly statistics (likes, followers, friends,
etc.) generate a hyper-propensity for comparison that begets
unhappiness. And not only that. The images uploaded have
nothing to do with your friends' normal lives. They've been
meticulously curated, giving the (fake) impression that others
in your social circle are doing better than they really are.

Never before have so many people compared themselves
with so many others. The internet has turned jealousy into
a modern-day epidemic. So after you withdraw from social
media, you should try to minimize the urge to compare yourself with others in everyday life, too. Avoid school reunions,
for example. Unless you're top dog in all possible respects—
income, status, health, family wellbeing. Yet how will you
know that unless you attend? You can't—that's why you don't
go in the first place.

Choose a place to live, a city, a neighborhood where you're
in the "local elite." The same goes for your peer group. Don't
join a rotary club full of millionaires unless you're also wealthy.
You might be better off with the volunteer fire service—and
you'll be doing something meaningful.

Above all, however, be aware of the *focusing illusion*,
which we discussed in Chapter 11. Let's say you're envious of
your neighbor because he's inherited a glossy silver Porsche
911 Turbo. You can see the "silver kitten," as your neighbor
affectionately calls his vehicle, neatly parked outside from
your living-room window. Every time he revs the engine it's
like a tiny knife to the heart. Yet this is purely because you're
focusing on the wrong thing. In comparing your neighbor's life
with your own, you focus automatically on the aspects that

are different—his Porsche 911 compared to your VW Golf. In doing so you're overestimating their importance on your life satisfaction. You believe your neighbor is significantly happier than you, but viewed objectively a car contributes very little (if anything) to overall wellbeing as we saw in Chapter 12. If you're aware of the *focusing illusion*, you can lessen jealousy's sting. Remember, the things you envy are all far less important than you think.

If none of that works and you're still seething with jealousy, it's time to bring out the big guns: deliberately identifying the worst aspects of the person's life and imagining them struggling with those problems. It'll make you feel instantly better. Admittedly, it's not a very noble solution, but it's something to fall back on in an emergency.

If your own life happens to be especially enviable, stay modest. That way you'll be doing your bit to protect others from the worst pangs of jealousy. Modesty is your contribution to the greater good. The greatest challenge of success is keeping quiet about it, as they say. If you're going to be proud of anything, be proud of that.

So what should you take away from all this? That there's always going to be someone in your neighborhood, your social circle or your field of work who's doing better than you. Accept it. The sooner you can wipe envy from your repertoire of emotions, the better.

33

PREVENTION

Avoid Problems Before You Have to Solve Them

Before you read this chapter, take a moment to answer the following question: what is wisdom?

Maybe you're getting spontaneous images of wise old ladies and wise old men popping into your head—people who have vast reservoirs of experience. Maybe you're thinking of professors whose books could fill a small library. Or you're picturing honest, natural-living folk, herdsmen in the Swiss Alps or simple fishermen in the Amazon Delta. Perhaps you're imagining a hermit meditating cross-legged on a mountaintop.

Enough imagining; back to the question. What is wisdom? Someone on a TV quiz show who can list the names and star signs of all the winners of the Eurovision Song Contest might be a wise person, but they probably aren't, or they wouldn't have filled their brain with a load of guff. Even being in the heart of your *circle of competence* (see Chapter 14)—which presumes specialized knowledge—is no guarantee of wisdom. So wisdom isn't identical with the accumulation of knowledge.

Wisdom is a *practical* ability. It's a measure of the skill with which we navigate life. Once you've come to realize that virtually all difficulties are easier to avoid than to solve, the following simple definition will be self-evident: "Wisdom is prevention."

The fact is, life is hard. Problems rain down on all sides. Fate opens pitfalls beneath your feet and throws up barriers to block your path. You can't change that. But if you know where danger lurks, you can ward it off. You can evade all sorts of obstacles. Einstein put it this way: "A clever person solves a problem. A wise person avoids it."

The trouble is that avoidance isn't sexy. Imagine two film plots, A and B. In Film A, a ship runs into an iceberg. The ship sinks. The noble captain selflessly, heart-wrenchingly rescues all the passengers from drowning. He's the last person to leave the ship and clamber into a lifeboat—just moments before it disappears forever into a spout of foam. In Film B, the captain steers the ship around the iceberg, keeping a sensible distance. Which film would you pay to watch? A, of course. But which situation would you prefer as an actual passenger on the ship? That's equally obvious: B.

Let's say the examples are real. What would happen next? Captain A would be invited onto talk shows. He'd get a six-figure book contract. He'd hang up his captain's hat and earn a living as a motivational speaker at client events and team meetings for major corporations. His home town would name a street after him and his children, for the first time ever, would feel something like pride in their father. Captain B, on the other hand, would keep avoiding obstacles until his retirement many years later, sticking to Charlie Munger's maxim: "I have a rule in life, if there is a big whirlpool you don't want to miss it with 20 feet—you round it with 500 feet." Although B is demonstrably the better captain, A is the one we celebrate. Why? Because successes achieved through prevention (i.e., failures successfully dodged) are invisible to the outside world.

The financial press loves nothing better than a turnaround manager, and that's all well and good, but they should applaud managers who prevent companies needing a turnaround in the first place even louder. Yet because preventative successes aren't externally apparent, they fly under the media's radar. Only the individual manager and his or her team know how wisely they acted—and even then to a limited degree.

As a result, we systematically overemphasize the role of successful generals, politicians, emergency surgeons and therapists while underemphasizing the role of people who help society and individuals from veering into catastrophe. They are the true heroes, the truly wise: competent GPs, good teachers, sensible legislators, skillful diplomats.

What about your own life? Even if you don't believe it, the reality is that at least half your successes are preventative. I'm sure you botch things occasionally, as we all do, but more often you *evade* stupid mistakes. Think of the dangers you've steered around using the wisdom of foresight—in terms of your health, career, finances and relationships.

Prevention isn't trivial. In his book *The Most Important Thing*, the American hedge-fund manager Howard Marks tells a story about a gambler. "One day he heard about a race with only one horse in it, so he bet the rent money. Halfway around the track, the horse jumped over the fence and ran away." Henry Kissinger referred to these mistakes as a "lack of imagination." Prevention requires more than just knowledge; it requires imagination, and imagination, sadly, is frequently misunderstood. Many people assume it means letting your mind wander while you're drinking a glass of wine. Unfortunately, this is unlikely to produce any new ideas. Imagination means forcing yourself to think possibilities and consequences all the way through—until the last drops of juice have been squeezed out. Yeah, imagination is hard work.

Especially so, you might be thinking, when it comes to

looming problems! Do you really have to keep harping on potential disasters? Won't that just get you down? Experience says no. According to Charlie Munger: "All my life I've gone through life anticipating trouble...It didn't make me unhappy to anticipate trouble all the time and be ready to perform adequately if trouble came."

I recommend spending fifteen minutes a week focusing intently on the potential catastrophic risks in your life. Then forget all about it and spend the rest of the week happy and carefree. What you're doing in those fifteen minutes is called a pre-mortem. Imagine, for example, that your marriage is on the rocks, you've suddenly gone bankrupt or you've had a heart attack. Now track back, analyzing what led to this (imagined) catastrophe—right down to the underlying causes. As a final step, try to address these issues so that the worst never actually happens.

Of course, even if you do all this regularly and conscientiously, you'll still overlook dangers and make the wrong decisions. Those unavoidable disasters can be mitigated by facing up to reality and tackling problems straight away. But in terms of foreseeable difficulties, it's easier to avoid them than to resolve them. Wisdom is prevention. It's invisible, so you can't show it off—but preening isn't conducive to a *good life* anyway. You know that already.

34

MENTAL RELIEF WORK

Why You're Not Responsible for the State of the World

In Syria, combat aircraft deliberately target hospitals and aid convoys. ISIS thugs behead people on camera. In Libya, gangs of smugglers enslave men, women and children, work them until they're exhausted, then float them across the Mediterranean on rubber dinghies, where half of them drown. In East Africa, one famine after another has brought devastation to millions of people. Across the world, babies are born with AIDS, condemned to a brief and bitter life. Domestic violence rages behind countless closed doors. The world is full of atrocities. And you're reading a book about the *good life*. How does that fit together?

Anyone with a modicum of empathy will react to these horrors with outrage. Yet few people have a plan to deal with that outrage. Every story is a cry for help. We feel like traveling to Ethiopia with an enormous supply of water and personally giving it to the people there dying of thirst. But then it occurs to us that our kids haven't done their homework, someone needs to descale the showerhead, and we've run out of butter.

Yet we're bothered by the injustices of the world. We need a personal strategy—a mental toolkit—to cope with its calamities without losing our inner equanimity. Here are five recommendations.

One: there's not much you can do personally, unless your name happens to be Augustus, Caesar, Charlemagne or John F. Kennedy. Bear that in mind. Most manmade catastrophes (conflicts, wars, terrorism) are far more complex than they appear, which is why no one can foresee how they will turn out. It's also why they always last longer than predicted. You don't need a doctorate in military leadership to understand that most conflicts cannot be resolved by purely military means. Nearly all the inhabitants of Libya and Iraq were better off before the Western powers' well-intentioned intervention—an unplanned side effect. Even as president of the USA, with the best possible team of advisers, you would overestimate yourself, make mistakes and get your fingers burned—not because of a lack of empathy, firepower or intelligence but because of the escalating complexity of such hostilities. Even an organization like the World Economic Forum (the WEF), whose stated aim is to "make the world a better place," has thus far failed to accomplish its mission. Despite forging many close relationships with the rich and powerful, the WEF has, viewed objectively, achieved nothing since its foundation. So don't overestimate yourself. You can't resolve this or that crisis all on your own. And if you think you've found the magic bullet that will bring an end to some war or other, think again. In all likelihood, somebody closer to the situation and professionally concerned with the issues will already have rejected your solution long ago, for good reason.

Two: if you want to help reduce suffering on the planet, donate money. Just money. Not time. Money. Don't travel to conflict zones unless you're an emergency doctor, bomb-disposal expert or diplomat. Many people fall for the *volunteer's folly*—they believe there's a point to voluntary work. In reality, it's a waste. Your time is more meaningfully invested in your *circle of competence* (Chapter 14), because it's there that you'll generate the most value per day. If you're installing water pumps in the Sahara, you're doing work that local well-diggers could carry out for a fraction of the cost. Plus, you're taking work away from them. Let's say you could dig one well per day as a volunteer. If you spent that day working at your office and used the money you earned to pay local well-diggers, by the end of the day you'd have a hundred new wells. Sure, volunteering makes you feel good, but it shouldn't be about that. And that warm Good Samaritan glow is based on a fallacy. The first-rate specialists on site (Médecins Sans Frontières, the Red Cross, UNICEF, etc.) will put your donations to more effective use than you could yourself. So work hard and put your money in the hands of professionals.

Three: drastically restrict your news consumption—especially when it comes to humanitarian catastrophes. Sitting in front of your television, watching images of disasters and wringing your hands isn't going to help anyone. Not the victims, not you. Being "interested" in global tragedies is nothing more than voyeurism. "Staying informed" may make you feel more humane, but the truth is you're deluding yourself. And the victims. If you really want to understand a conflict, war or catastrophe you're better off reading a book, even if it isn't published for another year. You can't change anything as the drama unfolds anyway (except through donations).

Four: you can reasonably assume that the universe is teeming with life, and that similar crises, disasters and suffering are rife on countless planets besides our own. This idea helps us to get some perspective. In other words, evil is all around us, always; it's universal and cannot be stamped out. Since your personal resources are limited, you've got to focus. Choose two or three relief organizations and donate generously. The other atrocities—in your city, your country, on this planet or on other stars—you'll just have to stoically accept.

Five: you're not responsible for the state of the world. It sounds harsh and unsympathetic, but it's the truth. Nobel Prize winner in physics Richard Feynman was told much the same thing by John von Neumann, the brilliant mathematician and "father of computing": "[John] von Neumann gave me an interesting idea: that you don't have to be responsible for the world that you're in. So I have developed a very powerful sense of social irresponsibility as a result of von Neumann's advice. It's made me a very happy man ever since." What Feynman means by "social irresponsibility" is this: don't feel bad for concentrating on your work instead of building hospitals in Africa. There's no reason to feel guilty that you happen to be better off than a bombing victim in Aleppo—your situations could easily be reversed. Lead an upright, productive life, and don't be a monster. Follow that advice and you'll already be contributing to a better world.

The upshot? Find a strategy to help you cope with global atrocities. It doesn't have to be one I've suggested here, but it is important to have a plan. Otherwise getting through life will be tough. You'll be constantly torn between the things that *still* have to be done, you'll feel guilty—and ultimately you'll accomplish nothing with that burden.

35

THE FOCUS TRAP

How to Manage Your Most
Important Resource

You're sitting in a restaurant, your eyes scanning the menu. The choice is between a set "menu dégustation surprise" or the à la carte selection. You soon see that every individual combination of appetizers and mains comes out more expensive than the tasting menu, which also includes wine—so that's what you order. "Good choice," smiles the waiter. "Most people order that."

One course after the next is dished up—amuse-bouches, four types of foie gras, pickled trout with asparagus, chocolate savarin with strawberries, roebuck, a cheese board with fig mustard, wild-garlic ricotta ravioli, a lemon sorbet to cleanse the palate, then duck breast, aubergine gnocchi and sweetbreads; all sorts of things, in an endless stream. Then the various wines, in an equally random sequence. After about twenty courses, you ask for the bill. You've never been so stuffed, never eaten such a melee of different things, and you've never felt so sick.

Cut to a dinner that actually took place. More on the traditional side, culinarily speaking, but highly exclusive when it came to the guests—billionaires, every last one, including Warren Buffett and Bill Gates. Gates asked the group what they felt was the most important factor in their success.

Buffett said: "Focus." Gates agreed. Evidently focus is vital, but equally crucial is where you direct it. What's remarkable, then, is that instead of choosing our objects of focus "à la carte" we stuff our faces morning to night with an "informational tasting menu" that others have selected for us. E-mails, Facebook updates, texts, tweets, alerts, news items from across the world, document hyperlinks, video clips on websites, and screens as far as the eye can see, in airports, train stations and trams—all of them vying for our attention. We're ceaselessly entertained with sometimes banal, sometimes thrilling stories. We're flattered, wooed and offered suggestions. And so we feel a little like kings, when in reality we should feel like spoon-fed slaves.

All these offerings are thefts not gifts, losses not wins, debits not credits. An Instagram post, no matter how beautifully designed, is a debit. Breaking news is a debit. An e-mail is (in most cases) a debit. The moment we read it, we pay—in focus, time or even money.

Focus, time and money are our three most important resources. The latter two are most familiar. There's even a science devoted to time and money—referred to in that context as "work" and "capital." Focus, however, is little understood, although today it's the most valuable of these three resources, the most crucial to our success and our wellbeing. Unfortunately, when it comes to focus we tend to commit systematic errors. Here are several key ways you can avoid them.

One: don't confuse what's new with what's relevant. Every novelty—product, opinion, news item—wants an audience. The louder the world, the louder the novelty must shout in order to be heard. Don't take this noise too seriously. Most of what's hailed as revolutionary is irrelevant.

Two: avoid content or technology that's "free." They're the

definition of focus traps, because they're financed by advertising. Why would you voluntarily walk into a trap?

Three: give everything "multimedia" a wide berth. Images, moving images and—in the future—virtual reality accelerate your emotions above a safe speed, markedly worsening the quality of your decision-making. Information is best absorbed in written form, from documents with the fewest possible hyperlinks—books, ideally.

Four: be aware that focus cannot be divided. It's not like time and money. The attention you're giving your Facebook stream on your mobile phone is attention you're taking away from the person sitting opposite.

Five: act from a position of strength, not weakness. When people bring things to your attention unasked, you're automatically in a position of weakness. Why should an advertiser, a journalist or a Facebook friend decide where you direct your focus? That Porsche advert, article about the latest Trump tweet or video clip of hilariously adorable puppies is probably not something that's going to make you happy or move you forwards. Even without an Instagram account, the philosopher Epictetus came to a similar conclusion two thousand years ago: 'If a person gave your body to any stranger he met on his way, you would certainly be angry. And do you feel no shame in handing over your own mind to be confused and mystified by anyone who happens to verbally attack you?'

Unfortunately, our brains are evolutionarily predisposed to respond straight away to the minutest of changes: a spider here, a snake there. This sensitivity was once critical to survival, but today it makes withstanding the crossfire of modern stimuli a formidable task. Dealing correctly with contemporary media isn't an innate skill, nor is it one you learn by simply hanging about on the internet. Hence, according to the technology journalist Kevin Kelly, why we've got to deliberately learn how to handle it. How did you learn to read and do arithmetic? By hanging out with people who could read and do arithmetic? No. You spent years deliberately practicing those skills. Now you need similarly intensive training in how to manage information, the internet and the news. Focus must be learned.

Another aspect: focus and happiness. What does focus have to do with happiness? Everything. "Your happiness is determined by how you allocate your attention," wrote Paul Dolan. The same life events (positive or negative) can influence your happiness strongly, weakly or not at all—depending on how much attention you give them.

Essentially, you always live where your focus is directed, no matter where the atoms of your body are located. Each moment comes only once. If you deliberately focus your attention, you'll get more out of life. Be critical, strict and careful when it comes to your intake of information—no less critical, strict and careful than you are with your food or medication.

36

READ LESS, BUT TWICE—ON PRINCIPLE

We're Reading Wrong

A multi-trip ticket on the Swiss national railway has room for six stamps. Before each journey you stick the ticket into an orange machine that validates it by stamping the date and time and cutting off a tiny notch along the left edge. Once it has six stamps, the ticket is worthless.

Imagine a book-reading ticket with fifty spaces. The system is otherwise the same: before you read a book, you've got to stamp your ticket. Yet unlike the train ticket, this is the only one you'll ever have. You can't buy a new one. Once the ticket has been used up, you can't open any more new books—and there's no fare-dodging allowed. Fifty books across a whole lifetime? For many people that's a non-issue, but for you as the reader of this book it's a horrifying thought. How are you supposed to get through life in a half-civilized manner with so few books?

My personal library consists of three thousand books—about one third read, one third skimmed, and one third unread. I regularly add new ones, and I have an annual clear-out when I chuck the old ones away. Three thousand books. It's a modest library in comparison to that of, say, the deceased Umberto Eco (thirty thousand books). Yet often I can only faintly recall its contents. As I let my gaze wander over the spines, my mind is filled with wispy shreds of memory mixed with vague emotions and the occasional flashes of a particular scene. Sometimes a sentence will drift by, like an abandoned rowboat in the silent fog. Rarely do I remember a compact précis. There are a couple of books I can't even say with certainty I've actually read—I have to open them and hunt for crinkled pages or notes in the margin. At such moments I don't know what's more shameful, my Swiss-cheese memory or the apparently negligible impact of so many of these books, though I do find it reassuring that lots of my friends have had the same experience. For me it happens not just with books but also with essays, articles, analyses and all kinds of texts I have read and enjoyed. Little of them has stuck. Dismally little.

What's the point of reading a book when the content largely seeps away? The felt experience at the moment of reading matters, of course, no question. But so does the felt experience of crème brûlée, and you don't expect it to shape the character of the person gobbling it down. Why is it we retain so little of what we read?

We're reading wrong. We're reading neither selectively nor thoroughly enough. We let our attention off the leash as though it were a dog we're happy to let roam, instead of directing it toward its splendid quarry. We fritter our most valuable resource on things that don't deserve them.

Today I read differently than I did a few years ago. Just as much, but fewer books—only I read them better, and twice. I've become radically selective. A book earns ten minutes of my time, maximum, then I give my verdict—to read or not to read. The multi-trip ticket metaphor helps me be more drastic. Is the book I'm holding in my hands a book for which I'd be willing to sacrifice a space on my ticket? Few are. Those that do make the cut I read twice in direct succession. On principle.

Read a book twice? Why not? In music we're used to listening to a track more than once. And if you play an instrument, you'll know you can't master a score on the first attempt. It takes several concentrated iterations before you can hurry on to the next piece. Why shouldn't the same go for books?

The effect of reading twice isn't twice the effect of reading once. It's much greater—judging by my own experience, I'd put it at a factor of ten. If I retain three percent of the content after one reading, after two readings it's up to thirty percent.

I'm continually astonished by how much you can absorb during slow, focused reading, how many new things you discover on a second pass, and how greatly your understanding deepens through this measured approach. When Dostoyevsky saw Holbein's *The Body of the Dead Christ in the Tomb* in Basel in 1867, he was so captivated by the painting that his wife had to drag him away after half an hour. Two years later he could describe it in near-photographic detail in *The Idiot*. Would a snapshot on your iPhone have the same degree of effectiveness? Hardly. The great novelist needed to be immersed in the painting in order to make productive use of it. "Immersed" is the key word here. Immersion—the opposite of surfing.

Let's refine this a little. One: *degree of effectiveness*—that sounds technical. Can you make that sort of judgment about books? Yes, this type of reading is use-orientated and unromantic. Leave Romanticism for other activities. If a book leaves no trace in your brain—because it was a bad book or you read it badly—I'd count that as a waste of time. A book is something qualitatively different from crème brûlée, a scenic flight over the Alps or sex.

Two: crime novels and thrillers are excluded from the ticketing system, because with few exceptions you can't read them twice. Who wants to re-identify a killer?

Three: you've got to decide how many spaces your personal reading ticket should have. I've limited mine to one hundred for the next ten years. That's an average of ten books per year—criminally few for a writer. Yet, as I said, I read these excellent books twice or even three times, with great enjoyment and ten times the effectiveness.

Four: if you're still young, say in the first third of your active reading life, you should devour as many books as possible—novels, short stories, poetry, non-fiction of all stripes. Go nuts. Pay no attention to quality. Read your fill. Why? The answer has to do with a kind of mathematical optimization called the *secretary problem* (see Chapter 48). In the classic formulation, you're trying to select the best secretary from a pool of applicants. The solution is to establish the basic distribution by interviewing and rejecting the first thirty-seven percent of applicants. Through indiscriminate reading, or—in statistical terms—by taking multiple samples in the first third of your reading life, you'll get a representative picture of the literary landscape. You'll sharpen your powers of judgment, too, which will enable you to be drastically selective later. So don't start stamping your reading ticket until you're about thirty, but be ruthless thereafter. Once you hit thirty, life's too short for bad books.

37

THE DOGMA TRAP

Why Ideologues Oversimplify Things

How does a zipper work? Rate your understanding on a scale from 0 (no clue) to 10 (easy-peasy). Write the number down. Now sketch out on a piece of paper how a zipper actually works. Add a brief description, as though you were trying to explain it very precisely to someone who'd never seen a zipper before. Give yourself a couple of minutes. Finished? Now reassess your understanding of zippers on the same scale.

Leonid Rozenblit and Frank Keil, researchers at Yale University, confronted hundreds of people with equally simple questions. How does a toilet work? How does a battery work? The results were always the same: we think we understand these things reasonably well until we're forced to explain them. Only then do we appreciate how many gaps there are in our knowledge. You're probably similar. You were convinced you understood more than you actually did. That's the *knowledge illusion*.

If we mess up with such simple contraptions as zippers and toilets, imagine how ignorant we much be when it comes to the really big questions. Questions like: how much immigration is good for society in the long term? Or: should gene therapy be allowed? Or: does private gun ownership make societies safer?

Even with these unwieldy questions—interestingly, *especially* with these unwieldy questions—answers come shooting out like bullets from a pistol. But let's be honest: we haven't thought them through. Not even on a superficial level. Social issues are far more complex than zippers, toilets and batteries. Why? Because any intervention into social structures has consequences infinitely more far-reaching than flushing the loo. It's not enough to consider the first wave of effects. You've got to account for the effects of the effects of the effects. Thinking through the chain reaction properly would take days, weeks, even months, and who's got the time or the energy for that?

So we take comfortable shortcuts. At this point something peculiar happens: instead of reading books on the topic or consulting experts, we merely adopt the opinions of our peers. This may be a political party, a profession, a social group, a sports club or a street gang. Our opinions are therefore much less objective than we'd like to believe, being sourced primarily from a "community of knowledge," as Steven Sloman and Philip Fernbach call it in their book *The Knowledge Illusion*. Sadly we're not the independent thinkers we'd like to imagine we are. Instead, we treat our opinions rather like our clothes. We'll wear whatever's in fashion—or, more specifically, whatever's in fashion among our peers.

When this inclination to toe the party line spreads beyond individual topics and starts constituting a whole worldview, it can spell disaster. That's when we start talking about ideologies. Ideologies are party lines raised to the power of ten, and they come with a pre-packaged set of opinions.

Ideologies are highly dangerous. Their effect on the brain is like a high-voltage current, causing an array of rash decisions and blowing all kinds of fuses. It's like, for example, when young European men with a university education swear loyalty to ISIS and fight to reintroduce the medieval teachings of Islam.

THE ART OF THE GOOD LIFE

Avoid ideologies and dogmas at all cost—especially if you're sympathetic to them. Ideologies are guaranteed to be wrong. They narrow your worldview and prompt you to make appalling decisions. I don't know of a single dogmatist with anything approaching a *good life*.

So far so clear. The problem, however, is that many people don't notice that they're falling for an ideology. How do you recognize one? Here are three red flags: a) they explain everything, b) they're irrefutable, and c) they're obscure.

An excellent example of an irrefutable ideology with an explanation for everything is Marxism. If the concentration of wealth in a society increases, the faithful will immediately attribute it to the fundamental evil of capitalism—as described by Marx. If inequality decreases, however, they will explain it as the development of history toward a classless society—as predicted by Marx.

At first glance, such irrefutability appears to be an advantage. Who wouldn't want a theory on hand that's so powerful it means you're always right? In reality, however, irrefutable theories are anything but invulnerable—in fact, they're very easily exposed. When you meet someone showing signs of a dogmatic infection, ask them this question: "Tell me what specific facts you'd need in order to give up your worldview." If they don't have an answer, keep that person at arm's length. You should ask yourself the same question, for that matter, if you suspect you've strayed too far into dogma territory.

To be as unassailable as possible, ideologies often hide behind a smokescreen of obscurantism. That's the third red flag by which to recognize an ideology. Here's an example: the ordinarily clear and articulate theologian Hans Küng describes God as "the absolute-relative, here-hereafter, transcendent-immanent, all-embracing and all-permeating most real reality in the heart of things, in man, in the history of mankind, in the world." All-explaining, irrefutable and utterly obscure!

This type of language is a sure sign of ideological gibberish. Watch out for it—including in your own speech. Try to find your own words to express things. Don't just mindlessly adopt the formulations and imagery of your peer group. An example: don't talk about "the people" when your party means only one specific social group. Avoid slogans.

Be especially wary when speaking in public. Defending a dogmatic position in public has been shown to beat it even deeper into your brain. It becomes virtually ineradicable.

Start looking for counterarguments. You could even do as I suggested in Chapter 30 and imagine you're on a TV talk show with five other guests, all of whom hold the opposite conviction from yours. Only when you can argue their views at least as eloquently as your own will you truly have earned your opinion.

In sum: think independently, don't be too faithful to the party line, and above all give dogmas a wide berth. The quicker you understand that you don't understand the world, the better you'll understand the world.

38

MENTAL SUBTRACTION

How to Realize That You're Happy

On Christmas Eve in the small American town of Bedford Falls, George Bailey is about to take his own life. Bailey, the head of a small savings and loan association, an upstanding man with a wife and four children, is facing bankruptcy because his uncle has gambled away all his money. He's standing on a bridge, about to jump into the river. In the nick of time, an old man falls into the water and cries for help. Bailey saves him, and the old man tells him he's an angel. Naturally Bailey doesn't believe him. Instead, he wishes he'd never been born. The angel grants his wish, transforming Bedford Falls into the miserable place it would have been if George Bailey had never existed. When he wakes up again on Christmas Eve, George Bailey has been liberated from his depression. Overjoyed that he's still alive, he runs down the main street of the snowy town, laughing and shouting "Merry Christmas! Merry Christmas!"

The tragi-comedy *It's a Wonderful Life*, released in 1946 and starring James Stewart, has since become a Christmas classic. Less familiar, however, is the strategy the angel uses in the film. In psychology it's known as *mental subtraction*, and it should definitely be in your *good life* toolkit. Let's do a quick run through. First, answer me one question: how generally happy are you with your life? Put it on a scale from 0 (deeply unhappy) to 10 (ecstatic) and jot down the number in the margin of this page. Now read the next paragraph (but no further). Then close your eyes and follow the instructions you've just read.

Close your eyes. Imagine you've lost your right arm. There's nothing but a stump hanging from your shoulder. How does it feel? How much more difficult is your life with only one arm? What about eating? Typing? Cycling? Hugging someone? Now imagine you've lost your left arm too. No hands. No picking anything up, no touching, no caressing. How does it feel? Finally, imagine you've also lost your sight. You can still hear, but you'll never see another landscape, never see the faces of your partner, your children, your friends. How does it feel? Okay, now open your eyes. Take at least two minutes to play through the three situations—to "feel" through them—before reading on.

How happy are you now, after the exercise, with your life? Put it on a scale from 0 (deeply unhappy) to 10 (ecstatic). If you're anything like most people, your perception of your own happiness has just skyrocketed. When I did this exercise for the first time, it felt like I was a ball being held underwater and someone had just let me go—I shot upward like a fountain. That's the dramatic effect of *mental subtraction*.

Of course, you don't have to pretend you've lost any limbs to boost your sense of wellbeing. Just think about how you would feel if you'd never met your partner, if you'd lost your kids in an accident, if you were standing in a trench or lying on your deathbed. It's crucial not to think in the abstract but to really *feel* the situation.

Gratitude, as we saw in Chapter 7, is a very appropriate emotion given all the lucky coincidences in our lives—and especially given the lucky coincidences that made our lives possible in the first place. There's scarcely a single self-help book that doesn't exhort its readers to reflect on the positives in their lives every night and feel grateful.

But there are two problems with gratitude. First, who do you thank? If you're not religious, there's nobody to feel grateful to. Second, habituation. The human brain reacts violently to change but adapts rapidly to situations. This is an advantage when disaster strikes—our grief at being abandoned or at being stuck in a wheelchair after an accident will fade more swiftly than we think, thanks to habituation. Dan Gilbert calls this our *psychological immune system*. Unfortunately, however, the effects of the *psychological immune system* are not limited to disasters. Six months after we win millions on the lottery, for instance, the effect on our happiness will have dissipated. The same goes for the birth of our children or the purchase of a new home. Because ninety-nine percent of the positive aspects of our lives didn't just crop up today but are of long standing, the power of habituation has negated the joy we originally felt about them. Gratitude is an explicit attempt to fight this process by deliberately naming and emphasizing the positive things we have going for us. Sadly, however, we grow accustomed to this tactic too. People who make a mental "gratitude" checklist each evening find it weakens the effect on their wellbeing compared to people who do it less frequently. A paradoxical result—yet one explained by the leveling power of habituation.

These, then, are the downsides of the much-vaunted practice of gratitude—the question of who to thank and the issue of habituation. Now the good news: *mental subtraction* brings none of these disadvantages. It's such an unexpected move that your brain never sees it coming. In several studies, Dan Gilbert, Timothy Wilson and their research colleagues have shown that *mental subtraction* increases happiness significantly more markedly than simply focusing on the positives. The Stoics figured this out two thousand years ago: instead of thinking about all the things you don't yet have, consider how much you'd miss the things you do have if you didn't have them any longer.

Say you're an athlete taking part in the Olympics. You're in peak condition, even winning a medal. Which would make you happier, silver or bronze? Silver, of course, you reply. Yet a survey of medalists during the 1992 Olympic Games in Barcelona revealed that silver medalists were less happy than bronze medalists. Why? Because silver medalists measured themselves against gold, while bronze medalists measured themselves against the runners-up. *Mental subtraction* could have forestalled this adverse effect. With *mental subtraction*, you're always comparing yourself against non-medalists—and of course you can substitute "non-medalists" with whatever you like.

All in all, *mental subtraction* is an effective way of tricking your brain into valuing the positive aspects of your life more highly. Because it makes you happy, it also contributes to the *good life*.

"Our happiness is sometimes not very salient," wrote Paul Dolan. "We need to do what we can to make it more so. Imagine playing a piano and not being able to hear what it sounds like. Many activities in life are like playing a piano that you do not hear." With *mental subtraction*, you'll finally experience the music's true sonority.

39

THE POINT OF MAXIMUM DELIBERATION

Thinking Is to Acting Like a Torch Is to a Floodlight

Psst! I'm about to let you in on the biggest secret in writing: the best ideas come to you while you're writing, not while you're mulling things over. Even if you're not a writer, this insight may prove useful, because it holds true for all spheres of human activity. An entrepreneur won't know whether a product will be successful until she produces it and launches it onto the market—no matter how much consumer research she's done. A salesman develops a killer pitch by making countless refinements and experiencing numerous rebuffs—not by studying sales manuals. Parents become proficient at childrearing by dealing with their own kids on a daily basis—not by reading handbooks. And musicians develop mastery through practice—not by debating the potential of their instruments.

Why should this be? Because the world is opaque to us—non-transparent, cloudy as frosted glass. Reality is never fully illuminated; even the most erudite among us can see only a few meters in a particular direction. If we want to go beyond the limits of our knowledge, we've got to forge ahead instead of standing still—we've got to act, not agonize.

I have a friend, an intelligent man with an MBA (but let's not hold that against him) and a good middle-management job at a pharmaceutical company, who has spent more than ten years setting up his own firm. He's devoured hundreds of books about entrepreneurship, spent thousands of hours considering his product offering, pored over stacks of market research and written two dozen business plans. The upshot? So far, nothing. He always reaches a point at which his deliberations tell him: Your idea's got a lot of promise, but so much depends on how well you implement it and how your competitors behave. And no amount of contemplation will take him a millimeter beyond this point. This is the moment at which the amount of additional information that can be gleaned by pondering an issue drops to zero. This is the moment I like to call the *point of maximum deliberation*.

Not that I've got any objection to mulling things over! Even brief periods spent considering an idea can produce tremendous insights. Yet this process gives rapidly diminishing returns, and it's astonishing how quickly the *point of maximum deliberation* is reached. Take investment decisions, for instance: once you've got all the available facts on the table, you need at most three days to chew them over. Decisions about your private life? Perhaps a week. A career change? Five days, max. You might give yourself a bit of extra time so that passing mood swings don't have an undue impact on your decision. But after that, meditation won't get you any further—if you want new information, you've got to act.

Compared with the pocket torch of deliberation, action is a veritable floodlight. Its beam carries far further into the unfathomable world beyond. And once you've reached a place that's new and interesting, you can always switch your torch back on.

The following question illustrates the importance of enterprise. Whom would you choose to keep you company on a desert island in the middle of the ocean? Take a moment to think about it before you read on. Your partner? Your boyfriend or girlfriend? A consultant? The cleverest professor you know? Or an entertainer? Of course not! You'd choose a boatbuilder.

Theorists, professors, consultants, writers, bloggers and journalists like to imagine that the world reveals itself to them through contemplation. Sadly, this is rarely the case. Thinkers like Newton, Einstein and Feynman are exceptions. Nearly all progress toward greater understanding—whether in the sciences, the economy or everyday life—is achieved through physical interaction with the invisible world. Through exposure to the unknown.

This is easier said than done. Even I tend to give things far too much thought, going well beyond the *point of maximum deliberation*. Why? Because it's more comfortable. It's much nicer to mull things over than to seize the initiative. Speculation is more agreeable than realization. As long as you're still weighing up your options, the risk of failure is nil; once you take action, however, that risk is always greater than zero. This is why reflection and commentary are so popular. If you're simply thinking something over, you'll never bump up against reality, which means you can never fail. Act, however, and suddenly failure is back on the cards—but you'll gain new experiences. "Experience is what you get when you didn't get what you wanted," as the saying goes.

Pablo Picasso knew how valuable it was to be bold, to experiment. "To know what you want to draw," he said, "you must begin to draw." And it's exactly the same with life. To know what you want, it's best to just embark on something. This chapter may give you a prod in the right direction, but be warned: you won't find the *good life* by thinking about it.

Psychologists call it the *introspection illusion*: the mistaken notion that contemplation by itself can allow us to identify our true desires, our purpose in life, the golden core of personal happiness (see Chapter 8). It's more likely that self-inquiry will get you bogged down in moodiness, vague thoughts and diffuse emotional impulses.

So the next time you're about to make an important decision, mull it over carefully—but only to the *point of maximum deliberation*. You'll be surprised how quickly you reach it. Once you're there, flick off your torch and switch on your floodlight. It's as useful in the workplace as it is in the home, whether you're investing in your career or in your love life.

40

OTHER PEOPLE'S SHOES

Role Reversal

The entrepreneur Ben Horowitz, cofounder of Opsware and currently a venture capitalist, found himself confronted several years ago with a management problem. Two outstanding departments at a company he managed—Customer Support and Sales Engineering—were at loggerheads. Sales Engineering accused Customer Support of not responding promptly enough to customers, thereby hampering sales. Customer Support accused Sales Engineering of writing defective code and ignoring their suggestions for improvement. Obviously it was essential the two departments work closely together. Considered separately, both were well managed and superbly staffed. Appealing to them to try and see things from each other's perspective accomplished little, but then Horowitz had an idea. He made the head of Customer Support the head of Sales Engineering—and vice versa. Not temporarily, mind you. Permanently. Both were initially horrified, but a week after stepping into their antagonist's shoes they had got to the bottom of the conflict. Over the following weeks they adjusted their operations, and from then on the two departments cooperated better than any others at the firm.

Thinking yourself into your opponent's position seldom works. The requisite mental leap is too great, the motivation lacking. In order to genuinely understand someone, you have to adopt their position—not intellectually but in actual fact. You have to step into their shoes and experience your opponent's situation first-hand.

I never took mothers' work seriously until we had children of our own and I occasionally looked after the babies (twins) by myself. After half a day I was more exhausted than after a ten-day business trip. Of course, various mothers had already told me that, and it's also in countless parenting books. Yet all that had left me cold. Only by doing could I begin to understand.

It's surprising how rarely we use this simple trick. "We've got to see things from the customer's perspective," is a platitude of every corporate mission statement. It's a noble idea, but it's not enough. Really, it should be "We've got to be customers." There are firms that have understood that. Schindler is the leading worldwide supplier of lifts and escalators. In their first year, every Schindler employee—from secretary to CEO—has to spend three weeks on site. He or she climbs into blue overalls and helps install lifts or escalators. This is how novices not only learn about the complicated inner life of their products but also experience what it's like to work on a building site. It also makes a statement: "Look, I'm not too good to get my hands dirty." This alone fosters deep goodwill between the individual departments.

Companies love pretending they're in touch with their workforce. You know the kind of thing I mean: hardly a company report gets published without photos of the ladies and gentlemen in senior management posing in front of an assembly line. Only one in every hundred reports features images of top executives actually *working* on the factory floor, dressed in work clothes and hardhats. Evidently they're not too good to ruin their hairdo for at least one photograph. Those are the firms whose stock I tend to buy.

Thinking and doing are two fundamentally different ways of comprehending the world, although many people confuse the two. Business Studies is an ideal degree if you want to obtain a Business Studies professorship, but not if you want to work in business. Studying literature is perfect if you want to be a literature professor, but don't imagine it's going to make you a good writer.

Does thinking at least translate into doing when it comes to abstract areas like morality? Eric Schwitzgebel and Joshua Rust tested precisely this question. Are professors of ethics, who are occupied day in and day out with moral questions, better people? It seems a reasonable assumption. The researchers compared ethicists with other professors across seventeen categories of behavior, from how often they gave blood to whether they slammed doors or cleared up after themselves at conferences. The result? The moral philosophers behaved no more morally than anyone else.

Once you've accepted that thinking and doing are separate spheres, you can put this knowledge to good use. Churches, armies and universities are among the most stable organizations in the world. They've outlasted several centuries and survived dozens of wars. What's the secret of their stability? They recruit from within. Each level of management possesses intimate, practical knowledge about how it feels to be below that level. To become a bishop, you have to start at the very bottom, as a priest. Every general was once a soldier. And you won't be head of a university unless you were once a lowly assistant professor. Do you think the CEO of, say, Walmart—a man who leads two million employees—would make a suitable general, commanding two million troops? Clearly not. No army in the world would consider recruiting him.

The upshot? It's worth slipping into other people's shoes and actually walking around in them. Do it with the most important relationships in your life—your partner, your clients, your employees, your voters (if you're a politician). Role reversal is by far the most efficient, quick and cost-effective way of building mutual understanding. Be the proverbial king who dressed as a beggar to mingle among his subjects. And because that's not always possible, here's another recommendation: read novels. Being immersed in a good novel, accompanying the protagonist throughout both highs and lows, is an efficient workaround that sits somewhere between thinking and doing.

41

THE ILLUSION OF CHANGING
THE WORLD—PART I

Don't Fall for the "Great Men" Theory

"We can change the world and make it a better place. It is in your hands to make a difference" (Nelson Mandela). "The people who are crazy enough to think they can change the world are the ones who do" (Steve Jobs). These are powerful words. Words that spark our imaginations. Words that communicate a sense of meaning, vitality and hope.

But can we really change the world? Despite the doomsday tenor that newspapers love to evoke (or perhaps precisely *because* of it), today such messages are repeated mantrastyle. Never before has such optimism about the influence of the individual been so widespread. To people in the Middle Ages, Classical Antiquity or the Stone Age, the two quotations above would probably have been incomprehensible. For them, the world was as it had always been. When there were upheavals, it was because kings were waging war or sullen gods were exacting revenge by making the earth tremble. That an individual citizen, an individual farmer, an individual slave might change the world—such an absurd notion never entered their heads.

Not so with Earth's contemporary inhabitants. We see ourselves not merely as citizens of the world but as its engineers. We're obsessed with the idea that we can reshape it through start-ups, crowdfunding and charity projects, just as the fabulously successful entrepreneurs of Silicon Valley or the inventive geniuses of world history have done before us. It's no longer enough to change our lives; we want to change the world. We work for organizations committed to this goal, and—grateful for a sense of "purpose"—we're even willing to do it for half the salary.

The notion that an individual can change the world is one of the greatest ideologies of our century—and one of its grandest illusions. In it, two cognitive biases are intertwined. One is the *focusing illusion*, which we saw Daniel Kahneman explain in Chapter 11: "Nothing in life is as important as you think it is while you are thinking about it." When you peer at a map through a magnifying glass, the areas you're looking at are enlarged. Our attention functions in much the same way: when we're engrossed in our campaign to change the world, its significance appears much greater than it actually is. We systematically overestimate the importance of our projects.

The second cognitive bias is known as the *intentional stance*, a term coined by the American philosopher Daniel Dennett. Under the *intentional stance* we assume an intention behind every change—regardless of whether or not it was actually intentional. So when the Iron Curtain fell in 1989, it was because somebody had deliberately brought about its collapse. The end of apartheid in South Africa would not have been possible without a campaigner like Nelson Mandela. India needed Gandhi to gain independence. Smartphones needed Steve Jobs. Without Oppenheimer, no atomic bomb. Without Einstein, no relativity theory. Without Benz, no cars. Without Tim Berners-Lee, no World Wide Web. Behind every global development we posit a human being willing it into existence.

This supposition of intent is rooted in our evolutionary past.

Better to assume too much than too little. Better, if you hear a rustle in the bushes, to imagine the source is a hungry saber-toothed tiger or an enemy warrior than the wind. There must have been a few people who regularly assumed it was the wind, saving themselves the energy of running away—but sooner or later they would have been abruptly and messily removed from the gene pool. Human beings today are the biological descendants of the hominids with a hyperactive *intentional stance*. It's hardwired into our brains. That's why we see intention and active agents even where there are none. Yet how could something like the dissolution of apartheid have happened without Nelson Mandela? How could someone other than the visionary Steve Jobs have come up with something like the iPhone?

The *intentional stance* leads us to interpret the history of the world as the history of "great men" (sadly, they were predominantly men). In his excellent book *The Evolution of Everything*, the brilliant British polymath Matt Ridley proposes a radical rejection of the "great men" theory: "We tend to give too much credit to whichever clever person is standing nearby at the right moment." Enlightenment philosophers had come to the same conclusion long before. Montesquieu wrote: "Martin Luther has been credited with the Reformation...But it had to happen. If it had not been Luther, it would have been someone else."

In the years around 1500, a handful of Portuguese and Spanish conquerors subdued the whole of Central and South America. The empires of the Aztecs, Maya and Incas crumbled with remarkable speed. Why? Not because "great men" like Cortés were especially cunning or talented, but because the foolhardy adventurers had unknowingly brought with them illnesses from Europe—illnesses to which they were immune but which proved deadly to the indigenous population. These viruses and bacteria are the reason why today half the continent speaks Spanish or Portuguese, and why they pray to a Catholic God.

But if it wasn't "great men" who wrote the story of the world, then who was it? The answer: nobody. Events are the accidental by-product of an infinite number of trends and influences. It works like traffic, not like cars. There's nobody directing it. World history is fundamentally disorderly, fortuitous and unpredictable. If you study historical documents for long enough, you'll come to see that all major developments have a touch of the coincidental about them, and that even the most prominent figures in world history were simply puppets of their age. Key to the *good life* is not idolizing "great men"— and not clinging to the illusion that you can be one yourself.

42

THE ILLUSION OF CHANGING THE WORLD—PART II

Why You Shouldn't Put Anyone on a Pedestal—Least of All Yourself

In the previous chapter we exposed the "great men" theory as a fallacy. Yet there have been some "great men," you might object—a few have shaped the fate of whole continents! One example would be Deng Xiaoping. In 1978 he introduced China to a free-market economy, liberating several hundred million people from poverty—the most successful development project of all time. Without Deng Xiaoping, China would not be a world power today.

Wouldn't it? The analysis of British author Matt Ridley offers a different picture. The introduction of a market economy was never Deng Xiaoping's intention. It was a development from below. In the remote village of Xiaogang, eighteen desperate farmers decided to share state land among themselves. Each one would be allowed to farm for himself. Only by this criminal act, they believed, could they make the land productive enough to feed their families. In fact, in the first year alone they produced more than in the previous five years combined. The generous harvest attracted the attention of the local party functionary, who suggested expanding the experiment to other farms. Eventually the proposal landed in the hands of Deng Xiaoping, who decided to let the experiment run its course. A less pragmatic party boss than Deng "might have delayed the reform, but surely one day it would have come," wrote Ridley.

Fine, you may be thinking, but there are exceptions. Without Gutenberg, no books. Without Edison, no lightbulbs. Without the Wright brothers, no plane trips.

But not even that's true, because those three were also products of their age. If Gutenberg hadn't figured it out, someone else would have developed printing technology—or sooner or later the technology would have found its way from China (where it had long been known) to Europe. The same goes for the lightbulb: after the discovery of electricity, it was only a matter of time before the first artificial light was switched on. It wasn't even Edison who got there first. Twenty-three other tinkerers are known to have made wires glow before he did. Ridley explains: "For all his brilliance, Edison was wholly dispensable and unnecessary. Consider the fact that Elisha Gray and Alexander Graham Bell filed for a patent on the telephone on the very same day. If one of them had been trampled by a horse en route to the patent office, history would have been much the same." Similarly, the Wright brothers were just one team of many worldwide to combine gliders with an engine. If the Wrights had never existed, that wouldn't mean you'd have to take the ferry to Mallorca. Somebody else would have developed motorized air travel. Ditto for virtually all inventions and discoveries. "Technology will find its inventors," argues Ridley, "not vice versa."

Even highly scientific breakthroughs are independent of specific people. As soon as measuring instruments achieve the necessary precision, eventually the discoveries will happen of their own accord. That's the curse of science: individual researchers are fundamentally irrelevant. Everything there is to discover will, at some point, be discovered by someone.

The same goes for entrepreneurs and captains of industry. When the home computer was launched onto the market in the eighties, somebody urgently needed to design an operating system for it. That person happened to be Bill Gates. Somebody else might not have met with quite the same success, but we would have similar software solutions today. Our smartphones might not look as elegant without Steve Jobs, but they would function in more or less the same way.

My circle of friends includes a number of CEOs. Some lead major corporations with hundreds of thousands of employees. They take their jobs seriously, some working themselves into the ground and earning plenty of money in recompense. Yet they're fundamentally interchangeable. A few short years after their retirement, nobody even remembers their names. Huge firms like General Electric, Siemens or Volkswagen must have had outstanding CEOs. But who knows their names today? It's not just that they're interchangeable; even their companies' strong results have less to do with their decisions than with market trends as a whole. Warren Buffett puts it like this: "[A] good managerial record (measured by economic returns) is far more a function of what business boat you get into than it is of how effectively you row." Ridley is a little blunter: "Most CEOs are along for the ride, paid well to surf on the waves their employees create. [...] The illusion that they are feudal kings is maintained by the media as much as anything. But it is an illusion."

Mandela, Jobs, Gorbachev, Gandhi, Luther, the famous inventors and the great CEOs—all were children of their age, not its parents. Each guided important processes using their own tactics, of course, but if it hadn't been them it would have been somebody else. So we should be hesitant about putting "great men" or "great women" on a pedestal—and modest about our own achievements.

No matter how extraordinary your accomplishments might be, the truth is that they would have happened without you. Your personal impact on the world is minute. It doesn't matter how brilliant you are—as a businessperson, an academic, a CEO, a general or a president; in the great scheme of things you're insignificant, unnecessary and interchangeable. The only place where you can really make a difference is in your own life. Focus on your own surroundings. You'll soon see that getting to grips with that is ambitious enough. Why take it upon yourself to change the world? Spare yourself the disappointment.

Okay, so maybe chance occasionally sweeps you into a position of great responsibility and you rise to the challenge masterfully. You're the best entrepreneur, the wisest politician, the most capable CEO and the most brilliant scholar you can be. But don't make the mistake of thinking that the whole of humanity has been waiting for you.

I don't doubt for a moment that my books will vanish like stones dropped into the ocean of world history. After my death, my sons will probably still talk about me for a while. Hopefully so will my wife, and maybe even my grandchildren. But then that's it. Rolf Dobelli will be forgotten—and that's exactly as it should be. Not believing too much in your own self-importance is one of the most valuable strategies for a *good life*.

43

THE "JUST WORLD" FALLACY

Why Our Lives Aren't Like Classic Crime

Let's consider two crime novels. In the first one, after a thrilling search, the detective finally identifies and arrests the killer. The murderer is taken to court and sentenced. In the second novel, after a thrilling search, the detective doesn't find the killer. The detective closes the file and turns to his next case. Which novel is more satisfying for the audience? The first, obviously. Our desire for justice is so great that we can hardly bear the thought of injustice.

Yet this is no ordinary desire, because it's one we assume will be fulfilled. If not now, then in the future. Most people are deeply convinced that the world is fundamentally just. That good deeds will be rewarded and bad deeds punished. That evil people will eventually be called to account and that murderers will end up behind bars.

Reality, I'm afraid, is not like that. The world isn't actually just; it's immensely unjust. What should we do with this disagreeable fact? It's my belief that you'll have a better life if you simply accept the unfairness of the world as fact and endure it with stoicism. In doing so you'll spare yourself a lot of disappointments along the way.

One of the most powerful and complex stories in the Bible is that of Job. Job is a much-loved, successful, pious businessman who leads an upstanding life, a man of character with a stable marriage and ten wonderful children—in short, he's the kind of enviable person for whom things always run smoothly. The Devil says to God: "No wonder Job's so pious. Everything's going swimmingly. If he had more problems, his faith would soon be shaken."

God is offended. Intending to refute the Devil's claim, he allows him to bring a little disorder into Job's life. At a single stroke, Job loses all his money. The Devil kills all his children—seven sons and three daughters. Even his slaves die. Finally, for good measure, the Devil afflicts Job with an illness, making agonizing sores erupt all over his body. He's mocked and cast out. Job is at the end of his rope. As he sits in the ashes of his burned-out house, his wife gives him the following piece of advice: "Curse God and die." Yet Job continues to praise the Lord. He is eager to die, if only to deaden the pain—but God won't permit even that. Finally a storm approaches and God speaks to Job out of a whirlwind, explaining that His actions are incomprehensible to human beings and will always be incomprehensible; He, God, cannot be understood. Because Job has remained faithful, because not even the cruelest punishments led him to doubt God, he is given everything back—his health, his riches, his whole family, brood of children included. He's overwhelmed with joy and lives to a ripe old age.

Compared with a standard crime novel, in which the killer is caught and brought to justice, the story of Job is rather more knotty. In the end he comes full circle. He experiences profound injustice, but ultimately everything comes out all right. The message is that the world can sometimes *appear* unjust—but only because we don't understand how God operates. You've got to put up with unfairness, says the Bible. It won't last forever. Behind it all is a just plan, which you humans, limited as you are, simply don't understand.

In psychological terms, this is a perfect coping strategy for dealing with the slings and arrows of fate. Getting fired, being diagnosed with cancer, experiencing the death of a child—they're tragic, but in the grand scheme of things they will make some kind of sense, and it's not for me to understand how it all fits together. God's only testing me, and if I continue to believe in Him unshakeably he'll reward me for it down the line.

So far, so comforting—but who seriously believes in a God who allows such hair-raising atrocities even though He could easily sort things out? More and more people are shaking their heads in disbelief. And yet, secretly, we're still clinging to the notion of a just plan for the world. We're desperate to believe in karma of some kind, that we'll be rewarded for good deeds and punished for bad ones—if not in this life, then in the next.

The English philosopher John Gray wrote that in ancient Greece, "it was taken for granted that everyone's life is ruled by fate and chance...Ethics was about virtues such as courage and wisdom; but even the bravest and wisest of men go down to defeat and ruin. We prefer to found our lives—in public, at least—on the pretense that 'morality' wins out in the end. Yet we do not really believe it. At bottom, we know that nothing can make us proof against fate and chance."

Here's the truth: there is no just plan for the world. There isn't even an unjust plan. There's no plan at all. The world is fundamentally amoral. We find this information so difficult to accept that science has come up with its own term for the phenomenon: the *"just world" fallacy*. This certainly doesn't mean that we shouldn't mitigate unfairness—through insurance or social welfare, for example. It's just that there are plenty of things that can't be insured or redistributed.

One of my teachers in high school assigned grades randomly, without the slightest relationship to achievement. These haphazard grades, picked out of a hat, went directly into our reports. The students protested vehemently. When this proved useless, we ran to the headmaster—who respected our teacher's decision and did nothing. It was completely unfair, we cried. But the teacher remained calm: "Life is unfair. The sooner you learn that, the better!" We could have wrung his neck. In retrospect, however, this was one of the most important lessons I learned in my seven years of high school.

When the German philosopher Leibniz claimed three hundred years ago that we were living in the best of all possible worlds (because, of course, God wouldn't have deliberately built a bad one), Voltaire countered this a few years later by writing the satirical novel *Candide*. After the brutal Lisbon earthquake of 1755, which razed the whole city, no reasonable person could continue to believe in a just plan for the world. The utopian dream of a carefree life for all was over. Candide, the main character, leads a life beset with disaster, and ends up realizing that "we must take care of our garden."

The upshot? There is no just plan for the world. Part of the *good life* is to radically accept that. Focus on your garden—on your own everyday life—and you'll find enough weeds to keep you busy. The things that happen to you across the course of your life, especially the more serious blows of fate, have little to do with whether you're a good or a bad person. So accept unhappiness and misfortune with stoicism and calm. Treat incredible success and strokes of luck exactly the same.

44

CARGO CULTS

Don't Build Planes out of Straw

In the Second World War, a few tiny islands in the Pacific played host to one of the fiercest battles between Japanese and American troops. The local people, who had never seen soldiers before—to say nothing of jeeps and walkie-talkies— watched the violent spectacle unfolding outside their straw huts in astonishment. People in strange uniforms held bones to their faces and spoke into them. Enormous birds circled the skies, dropping packages that floated down to earth on billowing pieces of cloth. The packages were full of tin cans.

Nothing seemed to approximate more closely the idea of paradise than nourishment falling from the sky. The soldiers shared the tinned food with the locals. Nobody had ever seen the strangers hunt or gather. Evidently they were doing something right. But how were they managing to lure these cargo birds?

After the war, when the troops had withdrawn and the locals were alone again, something peculiar happened. A new cult sprang up on many of the islands—a *cargo cult*. The locals had taken to burning down the foliage on hilltops and encircling the cleared area with stones. They built full-scale planes out of straw and placed them on the artificial runways. Then they constructed radio towers out of bamboo, carved headphones out of wood, and mimicked the movements of the soldiers they'd seen during the war. They lit fires to imitate signal lights and tattooed emblems on their skin like the ones they'd seen on the troops' uniforms. Basically, they were mocking up an airport, hoping to attract the enormous birds that had dropped so much food during the war.

Richard Feynman described *cargo cults* in one of his talks: "In the South Seas there is a Cargo Cult of people. [...] They're doing everything right. The form is perfect. It looks exactly the way it looked before. But it doesn't work. No airplanes land." Feynman was pillorying a tendency that was encroaching even into the sciences: the adherence to form without a real understanding of content.

It's not just indigenous peoples and scientists who fall for *cargo cults*. I had a friend who dreamed of becoming a great novelist. Ever since studying English at university, he'd spoken of nothing else. Hemingway was his idol. Not a bad example to follow: Hemingway looked fantastic, he had all sorts of women, and his books sold millions of copies. Hemingway was the first superstar author of international fame. What did my friend do? He grew a mustache, wore his shirts unironed and unbuttoned, and experimented liberally with cocktails. He stocked up on Moleskine notebooks, because apparently Hemingway used them (which isn't actually true). Tragically, none of those habits had any impact whatsoever on his success, or lack thereof. My friend had fallen victim to the *cargo cult*.

You might be laughing at *cargo cults*, but they're astonishingly widespread. Even in the world of finance. How many businesses kit out their offices in imitation of Google—complete with slides, massage rooms, and free food—in the hope of attracting brilliant employees? How many ambitious entrepreneurs attend meetings with investors clad in hoodies, hoping to become the next Mark Zuckerberg?

One particularly well-established *cargo cult ritual* can be found among financial auditors. They have a strict checklist to go through during annual audits. Is there a signed record of every board meeting? Has every expenses receipt been correctly entered? Has revenue been recognized during the proper accounting periods? All the forms have been adhered to, so when the companies collapse a few months later or get into trouble—like Enron, Lehman Brothers, AIG or UBS—the financial auditors are blindsided. Evidently they're very good at identifying areas where companies have fallen short of the forms, just not at finding the actual risks.

One particularly lovely example comes from the world of music. After navigating the intrigues of the French court and rising to become *"compositeur de la musique instrumentale du Roi"* (chief composer and later director of music) for the Sun King at Versailles, Jean-Baptiste Lully defined down to the smallest detail how music for the court should be composed. For instance, opera overtures had to follow a very particular structure—progressions had to be repeated in a certain way, the rhythm of the first phrase had to be dotted ("ta-daa"), a fugue had to follow next, and so on and so forth. In time Lully convinced the king to give him a monopoly over all opera, not just in Paris but across the whole of France. He made eager use of this power, ruthlessly disposing of the competition. Lully gradually became "the most hated musician of all time" (Robert Greenberg), yet suddenly all the courts of Europe were demanding music à la Lully. Even in the shabbiest, most secluded castles in the Swiss Alps, courts adopted the conventions of Paris—*cargo cultism* in its purest form, because it allowed the aristocrats to feel a bit like they were at Versailles.

A side note: at the height of his power, on 8 January 1687, Lully was conducting a concert using a heavy staff to beat the rhythm on the ground, as was customary at the time. In a moment of clumsiness, he crushed one of his toes. It became inflamed and turned gangrenous, and Lully died three months later, much to the relief of the French music scene.

What should you learn from this story? Don't copy Lully. Stay far away from any type of *cargo cult*. And be on your guard: the substanceless imitation of form is more common than we think. See it for what it is, and banish it from your life; otherwise it will waste your time and narrow your perspective. Give a wide berth to people and organizations that have fallen for *cargo cults*. Avoid companies that reward pomp and ceremony instead of achievement. And, above all, don't mimic the behavior of successful people without truly understanding what made them successful in the first place.

45

IF YOU RUN YOUR OWN RACE, YOU CAN'T LOSE

Why General Knowledge Is Only Useful as a Hobby

How much do you know if you're a graphic designer, airline pilot, heart surgeon or personnel manager? A whole lot. Your brain is humming with facts about your area of expertise. Even if you're still in the early stages of your career, you probably already know more than your predecessors ever did. Pilots no longer simply have to master aerodynamics and a range of analog instruments. Every year they're confronted with new technologies and aviation rules with which they have to be familiar—in addition to the old ones. Graphic designers must be conversant not only with software packages like Photoshop and InDesign but also with the last fifty years of esthetics in advertising. Otherwise they run the risk of recycling old ideas or, worse still, of not being able to keep up. New software comes onto the market annually and is adopted in offices, as clients become increasingly demanding, requiring designers to produce videos and master social media, videos, and virtual reality.

What about outside your area of expertise? Do you know more or less than your predecessors? Less, I'd imagine. How could it be otherwise? Your brain has only limited capacity, and the more you fill it with things from your specialist area the less space remains for general knowledge. Perhaps you're protesting indignantly. Me, a one-trick pony? Nobody wants to be one of those. We'd rather call ourselves generalists, curators (the author's description of choice) or networkers. We gush about how wide-ranging our job is, how diverse our portfolio of clients, how exciting every new project. We all see ourselves as versatile, not as blinkered specialists.

Yet when you look at the infinite number of specialized fields—from designing computer chips to trading in cocoa beans—our presumed universe of knowledge suddenly shrinks to a tiny niche. We know more and more about less and less. To put it another way, as our expertise gradually increases, our general ignorance practically explodes. In order to survive, we're reliant on countless other niche workers, who rely in their turn on other niche workers. Or do you think you'd be able to quickly cobble yourself together a new mobile phone?

These niches are sprouting out of the ground like mushrooms. The inordinate speed at which they multiply is a first in human history. The only division of labor that has existed for millions of years is between men and women, and then merely because of the plain biological circumstance that men are generally bigger and stronger—and that women have to go through pregnancy. If we could observe our ancient forebears living and working fifty thousand years ago, we'd be surprised by how good nearly all of them were at nearly everything. There were no specialists in stone ax design, stone ax production, stone ax marketing, stone ax customer support, stone ax training or stone ax community management. There weren't even people who focused on brandishing them. They all produced their own axes, and they all knew how to use them. Hunters and gatherers didn't have "professions."

This didn't change until around ten thousand years ago, when communities became increasingly settled. Suddenly specialized roles emerged: breeders of livestock, crop farmers, potters, surveyors, kings, soldiers, water-carriers, cooks and scribes. The profession was invented, the career, the field of expertise—and with it, the blinkered nerd.

A Stone Age person could only survive as a generalist. As a specialist they'd have no chance. Now, 10,000 years later, the situation is precisely reversed: people can only survive as specialists, and as generalists they'd have no chance. The remaining generalists—the jacks of all trades, the hack writers among journalists—have seen the value of their craft fall off a cliff. It's astounding how rapidly a general education has become unusable.

Ten thousand years—from an evolutionary perspective, it's the blink of an eye. That's why we still don't feel fully comfortable in our niches. As the specialists we are now, we feel incomplete and vulnerable, open to attack. As proud as a person might feel of being a call center manager, for instance, he will sometimes feel embarrassed, even ashamed, of the job. He thinks he has to apologize if he doesn't understand something outside his field of expertise. Yet that's the most natural thing in the world.

It's time we stopped romanticizing being a generalist. For ten thousand years the only path to professional success—and to social prosperity—has been through specialization. During that time, however, two things have happened that no one could have foreseen. Globalization fused niches that previously had been geographically separate. A tenor in one city and a tenor in the neighboring city, both of whom had formerly earned a comfortable income and never got in each other's way, abruptly found themselves in the same—now global—niche, thanks to the advent of recorded disks. All at once, the world no longer needed ten thousand tenors. Three was enough. The *"winner takes it all" effect* led to stark income inequality. A few victors dominated almost the entire market, while the remaining majority were relegated to scavenging on the periphery.

Something else happened, too. The niches began to subdivide endlessly into sub-niches and sub-sub-niches. The number of specialisms exploded. What previously was regionally separate but professionally integrated is now globally integrated but professionally separate. The competition within fields is huge, the number of those fields equally so. "There's an infinite number of winners," Kevin Kelly has said, "as long as you're not trying to win somebody else's race."

What does this mean for you and me? First: often we don't specialize radically enough, then we react with surprise when other people overtake us. Becoming a radiologist in a hospital, for example, is really only useful these days if you're going to specialize—as a nuclear radiologist, interventional radiologist, neuroradiologist or the like. So don't just stick to your field; ask yourself what exactly that field is. This doesn't mean you can't occasionally poke your head out of your silo—you can import plenty of useful stuff from other fields by analogy. Just make sure you're doing it with an eye to your niche, to your own *circle of competence* (see Chapter 14).

Second: the *"winner takes it all" effect* will help you out if you're the best in your niche—and I mean worldwide. If that's not the case, you'll have to specialize further. You've got to run your own race if you want to emerge the victor.

And, finally, third: stop hoarding all the knowledge you possibly can in the hopes of improving your job prospects. Financially speaking, there's no longer any benefit to that. These days "accumulating general knowledge" makes sense only as a hobby. So relax and read a book about Stone Age humans, if you're genuinely interested. Just be careful you don't become one yourself.

46

THE ARMS RACE

Why You Should Avoid
the Field of Battle

Do you remember the kind of copy shops that were around ten or twenty years ago? They were simple places with a couple of photocopiers. In some of them you could use the machines yourself by inserting a coin into a slot. Copy shops today are a very different proposition. They're more like small printing houses, offering full color and a hundred different types of paper. Sheets are automatically bound in high-tech machines—hardback and jacketed, if that's what you want. Now, you might assume that this technological wizardry has done wonders for copy shop owners' profit margins, but sadly not. Their margins, already low, have actually worsened. So where did the value of these expensive machines go?

Many young people believe that going to university is a prerequisite for a glittering career, and starting salaries do tend to be higher for graduates than for those without a degree. Yet on balance, after discounting the costs and time invested, many students are no better off or even worse off than their less educated peers. So what kind of value does this expensive and time-consuming process add?

After his bestselling children's book *Alice's Adventures in Wonderland*, Lewis Carroll wrote the sequel, *Through the Looking Glass*, in 1871. In it, the Red Queen (a chess piece) says to little Alice: "Now, here, you see, it takes all the running you can do, to stay in the same place." In doing so she describes precisely the dynamic that has trapped copy shops and students. Both cases involve a kind of *arms race*. Originally a military term, its treacherous underlying dynamic can be seen everywhere: people are forced to arm themselves because others are doing the same—even if, taken as a whole, the process makes no sense.

Let's get back to the two examples and the question at hand: what happens to the value of the invested money? Well, partly it goes to the customers, but mainly it goes to photocopier suppliers and universities. "If almost everybody has a college degree, getting one doesn't differentiate you from the pack. To get the job you want, you might have to go to a fancy (and expensive) college, or get a higher degree. Education turns into an arms race, which primarily benefits the arms manufacturers—in this case, colleges and universities," wrote John Cassidy in the *New Yorker*.

People who find themselves caught up in an *arms race* seldom realize it. The insidious thing is that each step and each investment appears sensible when considered on its own, but the overall balance comes out nil or negative. So take a good look around you. If, contrary to expectation, you find yourself in an *arms race*, get out of it. You won't find the *good life* there, I guarantee you that.

But how do you get out? Try to find a field of activity not beset by *arms races*. When I set up the company getAbstract with some friends, one of our criteria was to avoid the *arms race* dynamic. In practical terms, this meant finding a niche where there was no competition, and for more than ten years we ended up being the only supplier of book abstracts—a fantastic situation.

In Chapter 45 we discussed the importance of specialization.

Yet specialization alone is not enough, because even in tiny niches you can often uncover a hidden *arms race*. You need a niche in which you can operate smoothly and confidently, but also one that's free of the *arms race* dynamic.

You can see the dynamic play out in many people's working lives. The longer your colleagues work, the longer you have to work in order not to fall behind, so you end up wasting time far beyond the point of reasonable productivity. If we compare ourselves to our hunter-gatherer forebears, we find that they worked between fifteen and twenty hours per week. The rest was leisure time. Sounds like paradise—and, without the *arms race*, we could do the same. No wonder anthropologists call the age of hunting and gathering "the original affluent society." The competition for goods and possessions could never really get off the ground, because people in those days weren't settled. Being nomads, they already had plenty to lug around—arrows, bows, furs, small children. Did they feel like burdening themselves still further? No thank you. There simply wasn't the necessary reward system in place for an *arms race*.

Things are different today, and not just in the workplace. Even in your personal life, you can end up in the stranglehold of an *arms race* if you're not careful. The more other people tweet, the more often you've got to tweet in order to stay relevant on Twitter. The more effort other people put into their Facebook pages, the more you've got to make, so that you don't fade into social media irrelevance. If more of your friends are getting plastic surgery, you too will soon feel pressured to go under the knife. The same goes for clothing trends, accessories, the size of your apartment, fitness and sporting pursuits (marathons, triathlons, gigathlons), the horsepower of your car and other social yardsticks.

Two million scientific studies are published every year. A

hundred years ago (in Einstein's time), the figure wasn't even one percent of that. Yet the frequency of scientific break-throughs has remained roughly constant. Even in the sciences, the perverse dynamic of the *arms race* has taken hold. Academics are paid and promoted on the basis of the number of papers they have published and the frequency with which those papers are cited. The more other scholars publish and the more frequently they're cited, the more everyone has to publish in order to keep pace. This competition is only loosely connected to the pursuit of knowledge. The profiteers are the academic journals.

If you're keen on a career as a musician, don't under any circumstances choose the piano or the violin. Pianists and violinists are the unhappiest musicians on the planet, because the pressure of competition is at its most brutal for those instruments. Moreover, it's continually ratcheting up, because concert halls across the world are flooded every year with thousands of brand-new piano and violin virtuosos from Asia. You're better off choosing a niche instrument. That way it will be much easier to find a spot in an orchestra, and people will be much more impressed by your ability even if you're not world class. As a pianist or a violinist, you'll perpetually be compared with Lang Lang or Ann-Sophie Mutter. You'll compare yourself, too, sapping your spirit further.

The upshot? Try to escape the *arms race* dynamic. It's difficult to recognize, because each individual step seems reasonable when considered on its own. So retreat every so often from the field of battle and observe it from above. Don't fall victim to the madness. An *arms race* is a succession of Pyrrhic victories, and your best bet is to steer clear. You'll only find the *good life* where people aren't fighting over it.

47

MAKING FRIENDS WITH WEIRDOS

Get to Know Outsiders but
Don't Be One Yourself

"By the decree of the angels, and by the command of the holy men, we excommunicate, expel, curse and damn Baruch de Espinoza [...]. Cursed be he by day and cursed be he by night; cursed be he when he lies down, and cursed be he when he rises up; cursed be he when he goes out, and cursed be he when he comes in. The Lord will not spare him [...]. We order that no one should communicate with him orally or in writing, or show him any favor, or stay with him under the same roof, or within four ells of him, or read anything composed or written by him."

With this writ of excommunication—published in 1656 and in the un-abbreviated version approximately four times as long and five times as harsh—the twenty-three-year-old, highly strung Spinoza was cast out of the Jewish community in Amsterdam. He had been denounced at the highest official level as *persona non grata*, as an outsider. Although Spinoza hadn't published anything by that point, the young intellectual's freethinking views had put him on a collision course with the establishment. Today, Spinoza is considered one of the greatest philosophers of all time.

We might chuckle about the excommunication, but poor Baruch probably didn't find it so amusing. Imagine if the authorities cursed you in all the newspapers, on billboards, and on every single social media platform, and if agents were posted everywhere to make sure that nobody approached you or spoke to you. It must have stunned him.

If you're a member of a business club, you'll know all about the advantages of membership. You'll have free access to club facilities, where the plush armchairs are comfortable enough to sleep in, the tables are spread with the latest magazines, and you can always find someone for a congenial chat. Basically, the whole infrastructure is set up to cater to your needs.

Most people are members of one or more "clubs"—as employees at a company, pupils at a school, professors at a university, citizens of a city, members of an association and so on. All these groups meet our needs; we've grown comfortable in them. We feel looked after.

Yet there are always people who are not members of any club. Either they avoid them on purpose, they were never let in in the first place, or they were kicked out, like Spinoza. Most of these outsiders are crazy people, but not all. Occasionally one of them turns out to be somebody who pushes the world one step forward, all by themselves. The number of breakthroughs in science, economics and culture that can be attributed to outsiders is astonishing. Einstein, for example, couldn't find a job at a university, so he eked out a badly paid living as a third-class patent officer in Bern and revolutionized physics in his spare time. Two hundred years earlier, Newton developed the law of gravity and invented a whole branch of mathematics, even though his club (Trinity College, Cambridge) had been forced to close due to rampant bubonic plague and he'd spent two years living in the country. Charles Darwin was an independent researcher, never salaried at an institution and never employed as a professor. Margaret Thatcher, one of the strongest British prime ministers, was a housewife who exploded onto the political scene out of nowhere. Jazz is a musical genre created entirely by outsiders. So is rap. The list of great writers, thinkers and artists includes countless non-conformists: Kleist, Nietzsche, Wilde, Tolstoy, Solzhenitsyn, Gaugin. And let's not forget that the founders of all religions, without exception, were outsiders. Of course, we don't want to overestimate the impact of "great women" and "great men" (see Chapter 41). If they'd never existed, other women and men would have stepped into their place to similarly stellar effect. The point, however, is this: outsiders tend to be quicker and therefore earlier to make an impact than insiders.

Outsiders enjoy a tactical advantage. They don't have to adhere to establishment protocols, which would slow them down. They don't have to play along with the bullshit that's a permanent fixture in most clubs. They don't have to dumb down their ideas with visually snazzy but ridiculous Power-Point slides. They can sidestep the kind of nerve-wracking power plays you get in meetings. They can happily ignore convention, and are under no pressure to accept invitations or take part in events simply to "show their face"—because they were never invited in the first place. They don't have to be politically correct for fear of expulsion, because they're already on the outside.

Another advantage: their position off the intellectual beaten track sharpens their perception of the contradictions and shortcomings of the prevailing system, to which members of the club are blind. Outsiders look more deeply, meaning that their critique of the status quo is not cosmetic but fundamental.

There's a certain romance about the idea of living as an outsider—but don't make the mistake of becoming one yourself. The forces of society will be arrayed against you. The headwinds will be pitiless and sharp. Virtually all outsiders are broken by the world, which opposes them with all its might. Only a few shine as bright as comets. No, the life of an outsider is the stuff of movies, not of the *good life*.

So what to do? Keep one foot firmly planted in the establishment. That way you'll secure all the advantages of club membership. But let your other foot wander. I know that sounds like a bit of a challenge, flexibility-wise; in practice, however, it works well. Make friends with outsiders. It's easier said than done. Here are the rules for getting along with them: 1) No flattery. Just be genuinely interested in their work. 2) Don't stand on your dignity. Outsiders couldn't care less whether you've got a PhD or are president of the Rotary Club. 3) Be tolerant. Outsiders are rarely on time. Sometimes they're unwashed or wearing colorful shirts. 4) Reciprocity. Give them something back: ideas, money, connections.

Once you've perfected this balancing act, it's possible you might even become a connective piece, as Steve Jobs and Bill Gates managed to be—both were members of the establishment with strong connections in the community of crazy technology freaks. These days hardly any CEOs are in contact with outsiders. No wonder so many companies are running out of ideas.

At the end of the day, it's better to have a Van Gogh on your wall than to be Van Gogh. Best of all is to surround yourself with as many living Van Goghs as possible. Their fresh perspective will rub off on you—and help you on your way to the *good life*.

48

THE SECRETARY PROBLEM

Why Our Sample Sizes Are Too Small

Let's say you want to hire a secretary (sorry: a PA). A hundred women have applied for the role, and you're interviewing them one by one in random order. After each interview, you have to make a decision: will I hire or reject this candidate? No sleeping on it, no putting it off until you've seen all the applicants. The decision you make straight after the interview cannot be overridden. How do you proceed?

Do you take the first candidate who makes a decent impression? If so, then you run the risk of missing out on the best candidates, because you'd probably meet applicants who are just as good or even better further down the line. Or do you interview the first ninety-five to get a feel for the quality of the pool, then choose the one from the final five who's most similar to the best candidate you've seen so far? And what if the final five are all disappointments?

This question is known among mathematicians by a politically incorrect label: the *secretary problem*. Surprisingly, there is only one optimal solution. You should interview the first thirty-seven candidates and reject them all; meanwhile, however, you should be monitoring their quality. Then keep interviewing until you find someone who is better than the top applicant out of the previous thirty-seven. Hire her. You'll be making an excellent decision. She may not be the very *best* of the hundred applicants, but she's sure to be a solid choice. Every other approach has been shown to produce statistically worse results.

What is it about the number thirty-seven? Thirty-seven is 100 divided by the mathematical constant e (2.718). If you had only fifty applicants, you would turn down the first eighteen (50/e) then hire the first candidate who was better than anyone out of the previous eighteen.

Originally, the *secretary problem* was also known as the *marriage problem*, and the question was this: how many potential partners should I "try out" before I marry one? But because the total number of possible life partners can't be known in advance, the approach described above isn't ideal. Hence why the mathematicians renamed the problem.

Now, the *good life* isn't a question of mathematical exactness. As Warren Buffett says, "It's better to be approximately right than precisely wrong." This is how Buffett makes investment decisions; you should take the same tack in your personal life. So why is the *secretary problem* still relevant? Because it gives us some guidelines about how long we should spend testing things out before we make a final decision on important issues. Experiments with the *secretary problem* have shown that most people plump for a candidate too soon. Try to resist this impulse. When it comes time to pick a career, a job, an industry, a partner, a place to live, a favorite author, a musical instrument, a preferred sport or an ideal holiday destination, it's worthwhile quickly trying out many different options at first—more options than you'd like—before making a firm decision. Choosing before you have a strong sense of what's out there is not a sensible idea.

Why do we tend to make decisions too soon? Where does our impatience come from? Random sampling is time-intensive.

Doing a hundred job interviews when we could be done in five? Going through ten different application procedures before picking a place to work? It's a lot of effort—much more than we'd like. Plus, sampling is gluey. It's easy to get stuck in an industry simply because you poked around in it a bit when you were young. You might have built a career in it, of course, but you almost certainly would have met with the same success elsewhere, or perhaps with more success and greater enjoyment—if only you'd been a little more willing to experiment. The third reason why we tend to make choices too quickly is that we prefer to keep our minds clear. We like ticking stuff off and moving onto the next item on the list. That's fine for inconsequential decisions, but counterproductive for the important ones.

Our nanny (aged twenty) knocked on our door a few months ago looking rather dispirited. Her first and thus far only boyfriend had dumped her. Her eyes were brimming with tears. We tried being rational and level-headed: "You're still so young, you've got so much time! Try out ten or twenty men. Then you'll know what's on the market. You'll find out who's really suited to you long-term, and who you're suited to." A weak smile appeared on her gloomy face. I don't think we were able to convince her—not then, anyway.

Unfortunately, we behave far too often like my nanny. Our sample sizes are too small, our decisions rushed—or, in the language of statisticians, not representative. We rely on a false impression of reality, believing that with a few random spot tests we can find the man or woman of our dreams, our ideal job, the best place to live. Sure, it might work out—if so, then I'm thrilled for you—but if it does, it will only be by a stroke of good fortune, and nobody should pin their hopes on that.

The world is much bigger, richer and more diverse than we imagine, so try to take as many samples as you can while you're still young. Your first years of adulthood aren't about earning money or building a career. They're about getting acquainted with the universe of possibility. Be extremely receptive. Taste whatever fate dishes up. Read widely, because novels and short stories are excellent simulations of life. Only as you age should you adapt your modus operandi and become highly selective. By then you'll know what you like and what you don't.

49

MANAGING EXPECTATIONS

The Less You Expect, the Happier You'll Be

New Year's Eve, 1987. My first ever girlfriend had dumped me six months earlier, and I'd been moping around like a lonely ghost ever since. I hung out in my shabby student room (in the attic, with a communal toilet on the floor below) or secreted myself in the library. I couldn't go on like that! I needed a new girlfriend! A sign above the entrance to Rütli, a restaurant in Lucerne, announced a huge New Year's Eve bash. My expectations sky-high, my hair gelled even higher, I bought my ticket. Tonight was the night.

As I rattled through my disco dance moves, trying to be cool but probably pretty clumsy, my eyes swept restlessly from one end of the smoky room to the other. All the good-looking girls were there with their boyfriends, and on the rare occasions they let go of their other half for a few seconds and I threw one of them a smile, they acted like I was invisible. As the minutes ticked down to midnight, I felt more and more like somebody was slowly twisting a corkscrew into my heart. I left the restaurant just before midnight. The evening was a bust. I was twenty francs poorer than before—and I still hadn't landed a girlfriend.

The brain doesn't function without expectations. Essentially it's a veritable expectation machine. When we push down on the handle of a door, we expect the door to open. When we

194

turn on a tap, we expect water to come out. When we board a plane, we expect the laws of aerodynamics to keep us in the air. We expect the sun to rise in the morning and set in the evening. All these expectations are subconscious. The regularities of life are so engraved into our minds that we don't have to think about them actively.

Unfortunately, however, the brain also generates expectations when it comes to out-of-the-ordinary situations, as was painfully brought home to me at the New Year's Eve party. If I'd given myself time to consciously discern my expectations and assess them realistically, I could have spared myself the disappointment.

Research confirms that expectations have a profound impact on happiness, and that unrealistic expectations are among the most effective killjoys. One example: a higher income bolsters wellbeing only up to approximately $75,000 per year, and beyond that point money no longer plays much of a role (Chapter 13). Even below that threshold, wellbeing can be negated in a way that seems paradoxical—if expectations regarding income rise more quickly than income itself, as established by Paul Dolan.

So how best to handle expectations? I recommend organizing your thoughts like an emergency doctor during triage. Constantly distinguish between "I have to have it," "I want to have it" and "I expect it." The first phrase represents a necessity, the second a desire (a preference, a goal) and the third an expectation. Let's address them in turn.

You'll often hear people say things like, "I've absolutely *got* to be CEO" or "I *have* to write this novel" or "I *have* to have children." No, you don't. Besides breathing, eating and drinking, you don't *have* to do anything at all. Few desires are grounded in genuine necessities. So, instead, say, "I want to be

CEO," "I'd like to write a novel" and "My goal is to have children." Seeing desires as musts will only make you a grumpy, unpleasant person to be around. And no matter how intelligent you are, it will make you act like an idiot. The sooner you can erase supposed necessities from your repertoire, the better.

Now, on to desires. A life without goals is a wasted life. Yet we mustn't be shackled to them. Be aware that not all your desires will be satisfied, because so much lies beyond your control. It's not just the board of directors that determines whether you're made CEO; it's the competition, the stock market, the press, your family—none of which you can totally control. The same goes for writing novels and having children. The Greek philosophers had a wonderful expression for the things we want: *preferred indifferents* (indifferent here in the sense of insignificant). So I might have a preference (e.g., I'd *prefer* a Porsche to a VW Golf), but ultimately it's *insignificant* to my happiness.

We now come to the third strand in our triage: expectations. Many of your unhappiest moments are down to sloppily managed expectations—particularly expectations of other people. You can't expect others to conform to them any more than the weather would.

Our expectations possess very limited external force, but hold immense internal sway. Because we're so lax in the way we deal with them, we allow others to gain influence. Advertising, for example, is nothing more than the engineering of expectations; sales is the same. When a banker sells you a financial product, presenting you with complicated projections of future cashflows, that's expectation engineering, plain and simple. So not only are our expectations built on sand, but we also throw open the floodgates and let other people dig around in our sandboxes. Don't.

How do you foster realistic expectations instead? Step one: before every meeting, every date, every project, every party, every holiday, every book and every undertaking, draw a sharp distinction between necessities, desires and expectations. Step two: rate your expectations on a scale from 0 to 10. Are you expecting a disaster (0) or the fulfilment of your life's dream (10)? Step three: deduct two points from your rating, then mentally readjust to that number. The whole exercise takes ten seconds, max. Rating your expectations interrupts the automatic process of plucking them out of thin air, and you're also giving yourself a kind of buffer, because now your expectations are not simply moderate but have actually been lowered fractionally below their proper value. I run through these three steps once a day—with enviable results for my sense of wellbeing.

So what should you take away from all this? That we treat our expectations like helium balloons, letting them climb higher and higher until finally they burst and fall in crumpled shreds from the sky. Stop lumping together necessities, goals and expectations. Keep them meticulously separate. The ability to manage your expectations is part of the *good life*.

50

STURGEON'S LAW

How to Tune Your Bullshit Detector

It's tough being a science-fiction author. Especially if you're writing for the mass market. Literary critics treat you like dirt; and, frankly, much of the vast output of science fiction writing actually *is* third-rate, which makes it all the more difficult for the few works of quality to boost the genre's standing.

Ted Sturgeon was one of the most productive sci-fi authors of the fifties and sixties. With success came malice, and he had to put up with relentless jabs from critics who declared that ninety percent of all sci-fi was crud. Sturgeon's answer: Yeah, that's true—but ninety percent of *everything* that's published is crud, regardless of genre. His answer has gone down in history as *Sturgeon's law.*

At first glance, Sturgeon's assessment seems a trifle harsh—but only at first glance. Think about how few books you enjoy all the way to the end and how many you throw aside in disappointment after a couple of pages. Or think about how few TV movies you watch all the way through, and how many times you channel-hop away. The ratio is probably consistent with *Sturgeon's law.*

According to Daniel Dennett, *Sturgeon's law* holds not just for books and films but more broadly: "90 percent of everything is crap. That is true, whether you are talking about physics, chemistry, evolutionary psychology, sociology, medicine—you name it—rock music, country western." Whether it's exactly ninety percent, a mere eighty-five percent or as much as ninety-five percent is debatable, but it's not worth the argument, and it doesn't matter. For simplicity's sake, let's stick with ninety percent.

Ever since I first heard *Sturgeon's law*, it has been a huge relief. I grew up convinced that most of what people produced was important, well-considered and valuable, so I always assumed I must be in the wrong when something seemed inadequate to me. Today I know it's not because of my lack of sophistication if I think an opera production is a flop. It's not my tenuous grasp of commerce if a business plan makes a shoddy impression. It's not poverty of human kindness if ninety percent of the people at a gala dinner bore me. No, it's not me—it's the world. It bears repeating: ninety percent of all products are junk. Ninety percent of all advertising is tripe. Ninety percent of all e-mails are verbal diarrhea. Ninety percent of all tweets are nonsense. Ninety percent of all meetings are a waste of time. Ninety percent of everything said in those meetings is hot air. Ninety percent of all invitations are traps best circumvented. In short, ninety percent of all the material and intellectual things put into the world are bullshit.

Bearing *Sturgeon's law* in mind will improve your life. It's an excellent mental tool because it "allows" you to pass over most of what you see, hear or read without feeling guilty. The world is full of empty words, but you don't need to listen.

That said, don't try to cleanse the world of nonsense. You won't succeed. The world can stay irrational longer than you can stay sane. So concentrate on being selective, on the few valuable things, and leave everything else aside.

Investors understood this decades before Ted Sturgeon. In his classic 1949 book *The Intelligent Investor*, Benjamin Graham depicts the stock market as an irrational person called Mr. Market. Mr. Market, Graham's imaginary manic-depressive business partner, calls out new stock prices every day, offering to buy or sell shares. Sometimes he's euphorically optimistic, sometimes pessimistic and panicky. His mood goes up and down like a yo-yo. The good news is that as an investor you don't have to accept what Mr. Market is offering. You can simply wait and let the clamor of the market pass you by until Mr. Market makes such a good offer than it would be stupid to refuse. If he offers you a quality stock at an extremely low price—during a market panic, for instance. Ninety percent, even ninety-nine percent, of what Mr. Market yells can be safely ignored. Unfortunately, many investors don't see the stock market as an irrational, manic-depressive hawker but as a reflection of reality; they confuse the price of a stock with its value—and speculate until their money vanishes down the drain.

Of course, you don't just find this sort of thing at the stock exchange. Other markets offer new products, films, games, lifestyles, news items, personal acquaintanceships, leisure activities, holiday destinations, restaurants, sports competitions, TV stars, funny YouTube videos, political opinions, career opportunities and gadgets by the day. You should pass over most of them like rotten apples at a fruit stall. Ninety percent are silly, third-rate and just plain dross. Cover your ears or keep on walking when the din of the market gets too loud. The market isn't an indicator of the relevance, quality or value of its wares.

This is easier said than done. The reason, as it so often does, lies in our past. Imagine yourself among our ancestors, thirty thousand years ago. You were a hunter or gatherer living in a small group of roughly fifty people. Most of what you encountered was highly relevant: plants that were either edible or poisonous; animals you hunted or were hunted by; members of your tribe who saved your life or endangered it. In those days, the reverse of *Sturgeon's law* held true, because ninety percent of everything was relevant. The remaining ten percent of dross consisted primarily of a few stories told around the campfire, bad drawings of animals on the cave wall, or some form of shamanistic practice at which, as an intelligent member of the tribe, you turned up your nose. Ninety percent relevant, ten percent bullshit.

We find it difficult to perceive the world through the radical eyes of a Dan Dennett. Kicking free of all the crap isn't natural behavior. A bullshit detector isn't innate. We've got to deliberately train one.

Let's be unashamedly honest here: *Sturgeon's law* isn't just true of the world outside; it's also true for us. I can only speak for myself, but ninety percent of my ideas are unusable. Ninety percent of my emotions are unfounded. Ninety percent of my desires are twaddle. Because I'm aware of that, I'm much more careful about which of my "inner products" I take seriously and which I pass over with a smile.

So don't just take any old crap that's offered to you. Don't give in to every urge simply because you happen to feel like doing it. Don't try every gadget merely because it exists. Precious few things are valuable, first-rate or essential, and applying *Sturgeon's law* will save you plenty of time and frustration. Recognize the difference between ideas and good ideas, between products and good products, between investments and good investments. Recognize bullshit for what it is. Oh, and one other rule, which in my experience has proved well founded: if you're not sure whether something is bullshit, it's bullshit.

51

IN PRAISE OF MODESTY

The Less Self-Important You Are, the Better Your Life Will Be

Boulevard Haussmann, Avenue Foch, Rue du Dr. Lancereaux, Avenue Paul Doumer, Rue Théodule Ribot, Avenue Kléber, Boulevard Raspail—all the names of large Parisian streets. But who knows these days whom they were named after? Try to guess who those people were.

All major figures of their era, no doubt—city planners, generals, scientists. A dinner invitation from Georges-Eugène Haussmann, for instance, would have thrilled his contemporaries.

And today? Today you step out of the Galeries Lafayette onto the Boulevard Haussmann without a second thought, shopping bags full of things you don't need dangling from the crook of your arm. It's summer, the air shimmers like fluid glass above the boulevard, and your vanilla ice cream drips onto your T-shirt and Bermuda shorts. Your fingers are sticky, and you're annoyed at the throng of tourists, even though you're a tourist yourself. Mostly, however, it's the aggressive, whooshing traffic that gets on your nerves, rushing over the paving stones of the venerable city planner, whose name means nothing to you. Haussmann—who? He's already been consumed by the dust mites of history.

If the expiry date of such important figures as Haussmann, Foch or Raspail extends only four generations or so, then even the colossal names of the present day will have faded in a few more. In a hundred or two hundred years at the most, hardly anybody will know who Bill Gates, Donald Trump or Angela Merkel were. And as for the two of us—you, dear reader, and me—a few decades after we're gone nobody will spare us a second thought.

Imagine two hypothetical types of people: A and B. Type A individuals possess boundless self-esteem. Type B individuals, on the other hand, possess very little. When somebody steals their food, challenges them for their cave or runs off with their mate, the Bs react passively. That's just life, they say. I'll find more food, another cave, a different mate. Type As react in the opposite manner, flying off the handle and vehemently defending their possessions. Which type of person has a better chance of passing on their genes to the next generation? A, of course. It's impossible to live without a certain degree of ego. Try going a single day without using the words "I" or "mine." I tried it, and failed miserably. Simply put, we're Type A.

The problem here is that the sense of self-esteem we've inherited from our Type-A ancestors is so sensitive that it messes things up for us. We explode at the tiniest affronts, even if they're minuscule in comparison to Stone Age threats—we're not praised enough, our attempts to impress aren't met with a suitable response, we're not invited to something. In most cases, other people turn out to be right: we're not as significant as we think.

I recommend viewing your own importance from the perspective of the next century—from a point when your good name will have dwindled to a zero, no matter how fabulous you might be today. A fundamental part of the *good life* is not being too full of yourself. In fact, there's an inverse correlation: the less you stand upon your ego, the better your life will be. Why? Three reasons.

One: self-importance requires energy. If you think overly highly of yourself, you have to operate a transmitter and a radar simultaneously. On the one hand, you're broadcasting your self-image out into the world; on the other, you're permanently registering how your environment responds. Save yourself the effort. Switch off your transmitter and your radar, and focus on your work. In concrete terms, this means don't be vain, don't name-drop, and don't brag about your amazing successes. I don't care if you've just had a private audience with the Pope—be pleased about it, sure, but don't put up the photographs in your apartment. If you're a millionaire, don't donate money so you can have buildings, professorships or football stadiums named after you. It's affected. While you're at it, why not take out TV ads raving about how marvelous you are? At least Haussmann and Co. got their streets for free.

Two: the more self-important you are, the more speedily you'll fall for the *self-serving bias*. You'll start doing things not to achieve a specific goal but to make yourself look good. You often see the *self-serving bias* among investors. They buy stocks in glamorous hotels or sexy tech companies—not because they're solid investments but because they want to enhance their own image. On top of this, people who think highly of themselves tend to systematically overestimate their knowledge and abilities (this is termed *overconfidence*), leading to grave errors in decision-making.

Three: you'll make enemies. If you stress your own importance, you do so at the expense of other people's, because otherwise it would devalue your relative position. Once you're successful, if not before, other people who are equally full of themselves will shit on you. Not a *good life*.

As you can see, your ego is more antagonist than friend. This is hardly news, of course. In fact, it's been the default perspective for 2,500 years. The Stoics, for instance, were always on their guard against overweening self-esteem. A classic example is Marcus Aurelius, who found being a Roman emperor almost unpleasant. By keeping a diary (his *Meditations*), he forced himself to stay modest—no mean feat when you're the most powerful person on Earth. Religion, too, provides intellectual tools to keep the ego in check: in many religions, self-esteem is actually considered a manifestation of the Devil. Yet over the last two hundred years our culture has released the brakes on ego, and today everybody seems to be their own little brand manager.

Think about this: every one of us is merely one person among billions. We're all living inside an infinitesimal sliver of time with a random beginning and a random end. And we have all (the author included) already crammed many stupid things into this brief span. So be glad nobody's named a street after you—it'd only stress you out. Stay modest. You'll improve your life by several orders of magnitude. Self-esteem is so easy that anyone can do it; modesty, on the other hand, may be tough, but at least it's more compatible with reality. And it calms your emotional wave pool.

Self-importance has developed into a malady of civilization. We've got our teeth into our egos like a dog into an old shoe. Let the shoe go. It has no nutritional value, and it'll soon taste rotten.

52

INNER SUCCESS

Why Your Input Is More Important than Your Output

Every country has its own version of the list. In Switzerland it's called the *BILANZ* 300 List, and it identifies the 300 richest people in Switzerland. In Germany, *manager magazin* publishes an annual list of the 500 wealthiest Germans. The *Sunday Times* announces its Rich List in the UK; *Challenges* publishes an equivalent for France. *Forbes* puts together a list each year of all the billionaires in the world. The impression they give is always the same: these, then, are the most successful people in the world, all of them businesspeople (or their heirs).

Similar rankings exist for the most powerful CEOs, the most-cited academics, the most-read authors, the highest-paid artists, the most successful musicians, the most expensive sports stars and the highest-earning actors. Every industry has its own version. Yet how successful are these success stories, really? It depends very much on how you define success.

Society can control the way in which individual people spend their time through the way it measures success and bestows prestige. "It is no accident," writes the American psychology professor Roy Baumeister, "that in small societies struggling for survival, prestige comes with bringing in large amounts of protein (hunting) or defeating the most dangerous enemies (fighting). By the same token, the prestige of mother-hood probably rises and falls with the society's need to increase population, and the prestige of entertainers rises and falls with how much time and money the population can devote to leisure activities." Modern societies brandish the *Forbes* lists (as I'll call these rankings collectively from now on) like bright flags, saying: This is the way!

Why are modern societies trying to steer their sheep toward material success and not, say, toward additional leisure time? Why are there lists of the richest people, but no lists of the most satisfied? Quite simply because economic growth keeps societies together. "The prospect of improvements in living standards, however remote, limits pressure for wealth redistribution," writes former banker Satyajit Das, before quoting Henry Wallick, a former Governor of the U.S. Federal Reserve: "So long as there is growth there is hope, and that makes large income differential tolerable."

If we don't want the *Forbes* lists to drive us crazy, there are two things we've got to understand. First, definitions of success are products of their time. A thousand years ago, a *Forbes* list would have been unimaginable; in another thousand, it will be equally so. Warren Buffett, who along with Bill Gates has topped the *Forbes* list for years, admits he'd never have made it onto the Stone Age equivalent: "If I'd been born thousands of years ago I'd be some animal's lunch because I can't run very fast or climb trees." Depending on the century in which you were born, society would have extolled some other kind of success—but always doing its best to convince you of its particular definition. Don't just blindly follow the flags. Wherever they lead, you certainly won't find the *good life*.

Material success is also 100 percent a matter of chance. We're not fond of chance as an explanation, but it's just a fact. Your genes, your postcode, your intelligence, your willpower—fundamentally there's nothing you can do about any of it, as we saw in Chapter 7. Obviously, successful businesspeople worked hard and made smart decisions. Yet these factors themselves are the results of their genes, their origins and their environmental opportunities. This is why you should regard the *Forbes* lists as basically haphazard. And why you should stop idolizing them.

Recently a friend of mine proudly informed me that he'd been invited to dinner with multimillionaire so-and-so. I shrugged. Why be proud? Why so keen to meet a multimillionaire? The likelihood he'll be given any money is nil. What matters is whether this person is an interesting conversationalist or not—his wealth is utterly irrelevant.

Let me give you a completely different definition of success, one that's at least two thousand years old. Success, according to this definition, neither hinges on how society distributes prestige nor suits vulgar rankings. Here it is: true success is inner success. Voilà.

This has nothing to do with incense sticks, self-contemplation or yoga. Striving for inner success is one of the most sensible approaches there is—and one of the roots of Western thought. As we saw in Chapter 8, Greek and Roman philosophers called this type of success *ataraxia*. Once you've attained *ataraxia*—tranquility of the soul—you'll be able to maintain your equanimity despite the slings and arrows of fate. To put it another way, to be successful is to be imperturbable, regardless of whether you're flying high or crash landing.

How can we achieve inner success? By focusing exclusively on the things we can influence and resolutely blocking out everything else. Input, not output. Our input we can control; our output we can't, because chance keeps sticking its oar in.

Money, power and popularity are things over which we have only limited control. Losing them will send you into a tailspin if they're the focus of your attention. If, however, you've trained yourself to be serene, imperturbable and ataraxic, you'll mostly be happy—no matter what fate throws your way. Simply put, inner success is more stable than the external kind.

John Wooden was far and away the most successful basketball coach in American history. Wooden insisted his players define success in radically different terms: "Success is peace of mind, which is a direct result of self-satisfaction in knowing you made the effort to do your best to become the best that you are capable of becoming." Success in this sense isn't winning titles, collecting medals or being transferred for vast sums of money. It's an attitude. Ironically, President George W. Bush awarded him the Medal of Freedom, the USA's most prestigious accolade—which Bush presumably found more moving than Wooden did.

Let's be honest: nobody's going to strive 100 percent for inner success and pay no heed whatsoever to the external kind. Yet we can edge closer to the ideal of *ataraxia* through daily practice. Every evening, take stock: When did you fail today? When did you let the day be poisoned by toxic emotions? What things beyond your control did you let upset you? And which mental tools are required for self-improvement? You don't have to be the richest person in the cemetery—instead, be the most inwardly successful person in the here and now. "Make each day your masterpiece" was what Wooden hammered into his players' heads. Take his advice. Inner success is never fully attainable, and you'll have to practice it your whole life long. Nobody is going to do that work for you.

Those seeking external success—wealth, a job as CEO, gold medals or honors—are actually striving for inner success too; they just don't realize it. A CEO might use his bonus to buy a 200,000-euro IWC Grande Complication watch—maybe because he likes the way it looks on his wrist, but probably so that he'll be envied. Either way, he wants the IWC because it makes him feel good. Otherwise he wouldn't buy it.

Whichever way you look at it, the truth is that people desire external gain because it nets them internal gain. The question that suggests itself is obvious: why take the long way round? Just take the direct route.

AFTERWORD

The notion that life is easy is a trap into which all of us stray from time to time. When we're young, especially, but not only then. The *good life* is no trivial task. Even intelligent people don't often manage it. Why not?

We've created a world we no longer understand. A world in which our intuition is no longer a reliable compass. A world full of complexity and instability. We attempt to navigate this opaque environment using a brain built for something else entirely—for the world of the Stone Age. Evolution hasn't been able to keep pace with the rapid development of civilization. While our surroundings have altered dramatically over the past ten thousand years, the software and hardware of our inner world, the human brain, has remained unchanged since mammoths grazed the Earth. Viewed from that perspective, it's not surprising we commit systematic errors in both abstract thought and in the concrete way we live our lives.

That's why it's essential to keep a box of mental tools close at hand, something you can turn to again and again. Mental tools make it possible to see the world more objectively and act sensibly in the long-term. As we take possession of these tools through daily practice, we gradually change and improve the structure of our brain. Often termed *heuristics* in the parlance of psychology, these models don't *guarantee* you a *good life*. But, on average, they will *help* you to act better and make better decisions than if you were relying on your intuition alone. I'm convinced that intellectual tools are more important than money, more important than relationships, more important even than intelligence.

Since I started writing about the *good life*, people have been asking me: What exactly is it, then? What's the definition? My answer: I don't know. My approach resembles the negative theology of the Middle Ages. To the question of who or what is God, the theologians answered: it cannot be said precisely what God is, it can only be said what God *isn't*. The same goes for the *good life*. You can't say exactly what the *good life* is, but you can safely say what it's *not*. If you're not leading a *good life*, you'll know it. If one of your friends doesn't have a *good life*, you'll know it. Many readers are bothered by the fact that although I'm writing about the *good life* I don't offer a definition. But frankly, I don't see the point. As Richard Feynman said, "You can know the name of a bird in all the languages of the world, but when you're finished, you'll know absolutely nothing whatever about the bird... So let's look at the bird and see what it's doing—that's what counts. I learned very early the difference between knowing the name of something and knowing something."

Where do the fifty-two mental tools in this book come from? I drew on three main sources. The first is psychological research from the last forty years. This includes mental psychology, social psychology, research into happiness, into heuristics and biases, behavioral economics, and a few approaches from clinical psychology, in particular cognitive behavioral therapy (CBT), which has proved successful.

My second source was Stoicism, a highly practical philosophy that originated in Ancient Greece and blossomed in the Roman Empire in the second century A.D. The biggest names among the Stoics are Zeno (the school's founder), Chrysippus (the most important representative of Stoicism in Ancient Greece), Seneca (who strikes me as the Charlie Munger of ancient Rome), Musonius Rufus (a successful teacher periodically banished by Nero), Epictetus (Rufus's pupil and a former slave), and the Roman emperor Marcus Aurelius. Sadly, the influence of the Stoics vanished with the collapse of the Roman Empire, and Stoicism has never fully recovered. Over the last 1,800 years, it's been insider's knowledge for people seeking a philosophy for practical living.

The Stoics laid great emphasis on practical exercises, such as those I've suggested here, and on maxims. Maxims are valuable because they're accessible, guarding us against carelessness like police tape. At the risk of appearing simplistic, I've allowed myself to add a few maxims of my own to the ones I've quoted here.

My third source was a long tradition of investment literature. Warren Buffett and his business partner, Charlie Munger, are two of the most successful value investors in the world and considered (not just by me) some of the greatest thinkers of our century. For this reason I've taken the liberty of quoting them often. Inventors are especially eager to comprehend the opaque world. Despite everything they don't know, they feel compelled to guess the future as best they can, and the results are reflected in profit or loss. This is why investors since Benjamin Graham have been intent on viewing the world as objectively as possible, and finding intellectual approaches that protect them from impulsive decisions. Over the past hundred years, they have developed a highly workable set of *mental tools* that are relevant far beyond the world of money. It's startling how much life wisdom can be gleaned from the maxims and approaches of value investors.

These three sources—modern psychology, Stoicism and the philosophy of value investing—complement each other perfectly. So perfectly that one might think they came from a single source. Yet they emerged totally independently. There aren't many eureka moments in life, but that was one of my biggest: when I realized how seamlessly and smoothly these three cogs fit together.

Four final observations. First: there are more than fifty-two mental tools. I picked fifty-two because this book has much in common with my previous books *The Art of Thinking Clearly* and *The Art of Acting Wisely*, which (in the original German editions) both contain fifty-two chapters. Those were about cognitive errors; this is about tools. And you'll be well served with these fifty-two. Depending on the situation, you'll need two simultaneously, or three at the most.

Second: many of the foregoing chapters first appeared as newspaper columns in Switzerland and Germany. Columns are obliged to be brief and snappy. That's why the notes and sources aren't in the main text but in the Appendix.

Third: for the sake of simplicity, I've primarily used male pronouns throughout the book, although of course both men and women are intended. Underestimating women is definitely the wrong recipe for a *good life*.

Four: for all the mistakes and omissions in this book, I and I alone am responsible.

—Rolf Dobelli, Bern, Switzerland, 2017

ACKNOWLEDGMENTS

Thanks to my friend Koni Gebistorf, who deftly edited the texts and gave them the necessary polish. Without the weekly pressure of putting my thoughts into a readable format, this book would not exist. I'm grateful to René Scheu, editor of the cultural section at the *Neue Zürcher Zeitung*, which initially published segments of this book as weekly columns. It takes a certain chutzpah to publish a column about practical living in the otherwise highly intellectual environment of the *NZZ*'s cultural pages. I'm grateful also to Gabor Steingart and Thomas Tuma, who gave my writing a lovely home in the *Handelsblatt*. Heartfelt thanks are due to the graphic artist El Bocho for the illustrations that accompanied some of the chapters in the original edition.

I know of no more professional non-fiction editor than Martin Janik at Piper Verlag. As he edited my previous books *The Art of Thinking Clearly* and *The Art of Acting Wisely*, I'm glad he took on this book too. Thanks to Christian Schumacher-Gebler, CEO of Bonnier Deutschland, Felicitas von Lovenberg, my publisher, and all the wonderful people at Piper Verlag. I've never been made more warmly welcome by a publisher.

A huge thanks to my first-class editors, Drummond Moir for the UK edition and the highly professional Michelle Howry for the American edition. Translations are usually a chore for authors. Not so in this case. Working with Drummond and Michelle has been a genuine pleasure.

ACKNOWLEDGMENTS

Thanks to Guy Spier, who gave me the forty-kilogram bronze bust of Charlie Munger that currently adorns our garden. Munger's head is entwined with ivy, making him look a little like a Roman emperor.

Peter Bevelin opened my eyes many years ago to the life wisdom of the classic value investors. I thank him for that. His books are genuine treasure chests, and I've helped myself liberally from them.

This book would not exist without the countless conversations and letters I've had over the years on the topic of the *good life*. I'm grateful to the following people (in no particular order) for their valuable ideas: Thomas Schenk, Kevin Heng, Bruno Frey, Alois Stutzer, Frederike Petzschner, Manfred Lütz, Urs Sonntag, Kipper Blakeley, Rishi Kakar, Schoscho Rufener, Matt Ridley, Michael Hengartner, Tom Ladner, Alex Wassmer, Marc Walder, Ksenija Sidorova, Avi Avital, Uli Sigg, Numa & Corinne Bischof Ullmann, Holger Ried, Ewald Ried, Marcel Rohner, Raffaello D'Andrea, Lou Marinoff, Tom Wujec, Jean-Rémy and Natalie von Matt, Urs Baumann, Erica Rauzin, Simone Schürle, Rainer Mark Frey, Michael Müller, Tommy Matter, Adriano Aguzzi, Viola Vogel, Nils Hagander, Christian Jund, André Frensch, Marc and Monica Bader Zurbuchen, Georges and Monika Kern, Martin Hoffmann, Markus and Irene Ackermann, Robert Cialdini, Dan Gilbert, Carel van Schaik, Markus Imboden, Jonathan Haidt, Joshua Greene, Martin Walser, Angela and Axel Keuneke, Franz Kaufmann and Dan Dennett. I am deeply grateful to all my friends as well as the thinkers, authors, and researchers mentioned above. Everything important in this book came not from me but from them.

My parents Ueli and Ruth are a shining example of how

to live a *good life* over many decades. Thank you so much for everything.

My biggest thanks, however, are due to my wife. Many of the tools discussed here come from Bine's psychological work and life experience. She is my first editor. Her merciless red pencil is a gift to all readers of this book—and her wisdom a gift to our family.

I also thank our three-year-old twins Numa and Avi. They may have robbed me of plenty of sleep during the writing of this book, but, as paradoxical as it sounds, I couldn't have written it without them.

APPENDIX

There are countless scholarly studies from the fields of cognitive psychology and social psychology on almost every mental tool in this book. I've restricted myself here to the most important quotations, technical references, reading recommendations and observations. Most of the quotations I've left in their original language. I see myself primarily as a translator of these scientific studies into everyday language. My goal is to make philosophical ideas and scholarly insights applicable in daily life. I have the greatest respect for the researchers who study these intellectual tools scientifically.

NOTES

Foreword

Charlie Munger is the business partner of legendary investor Warren Buffett, and as far as I'm concerned he's one of the greatest thinkers of our century. Bill Gates said of Charlie Munger: "He is truly the broadest thinker I have ever encountered." (Griffin, Tren: *Charlie Munger— The Complete Investor,* Columbia University Press, 2015, p. 46).

In a lecture given to students in 1994, Charlie Munger revealed the secret behind the way he thinks: "You've got to have models in your head. And you've got to array your experience—both vicarious and direct—on this latticework of models. You may have noticed students who just try to remember and pound back what is remembered. Well, they fail in school and in life. You've got to hang experience on a latticework of models in your head." (Charlie Munger, "A Lesson on Elementary Worldly Wisdom" [1994, lecture]. In: Griffin, Tren: *Charlie Munger,* p. 44).

Munger talks about *mental models*. He doesn't mean models in the sense of architectural models or simulations, however—scaled-down depictions of reality—but rather mental tools, mental tactics, mental strategies and attitudes. For this reason I use the terms "mental tools" and "tools of thought" throughout the book.

I'm convinced that if we don't have a solid mental toolkit to fall back on, the chances are we'll fail at life. I simply cannot imagine how you could be a successful leader without one.

1. Mental Accounting

Richard Thaler is considered the originator of mental accounting theory. (Heath, Chip; and Soll, Jack B.: "Mental Budgeting and Consumer Decisions." In *Journal of Consumer Research,* 1996, Vol. 23, No. 1, pp. 40–52.)

The trick with the parking and speeding tickets was first described in this paper: "A former colleague of mine, a professor of finance, prides himself on being a thoroughly rational man. Long ago he adopted a clever strategy to deal with life's misfortunes. At the beginning of each year he establishes a target donation to the local United Way charity. Then, if anything untoward happens to him during the year, for example an undeserved speeding ticket, he simply deducts this loss from the United Way account. He thinks of it as an insurance policy against small annoyances." (Thaler, Richard H.: "Mental Accounting Matters" in *Journal of Behavioral Decision Making*, 1999, Vol. 12, pp. 183–206).

I touched on the mental accounting fallacy in my book *The Art of Thinking Clearly*, in the essay "The House Money Effect" in Dobelli, Rolf: *The Art of Thinking Clearly*, HarperCollins Publishers, 2013, p. 251.

On the peak–end rule, see: Kahneman Daniel; Fredrickson, Barbara L.; Schreiber, Charles A. and Redelmeier, Donald A.: "When More Pain Is Preferred to Less: Adding a Better End." *Psychological Science*, 1993, Vol. 4, No. 6, pp. 401–405.

On the constructive interpretation of facts: in the past, fluctuations in the price of my stocks and shares would make me nervous. But not anymore. I use mental accounting: if my portfolio doubles or halves in value, it's hardly a tragedy. The portfolio is only one of my many assets. My family, my work as a writer, my WORLD.MINDS foundation and my friends represent at least 90 percent of my true capital. So even if the value of my portfolio halves—through a stock-market crash, for instance—that's actually just 5 percent of my overall assets. Likewise, if stock prices double, I'm not going to be dancing for joy. The value of my assets has increased by only 5 percent.

2. The Fine Art of Correction

Charlie Munger has made a similar observation to Dwight Eisenhower's: "At Berkshire there has never been a master plan. Anyone who wanted to do it, we fired because it takes on a life of its own and doesn't cover new reality. We want people taking into account new information." (Clark, David: *The Tao of Charlie Munger*, Scribner, 2017, p. 141).

Another quotation on the fragility of plans: "life is [...] a game of chess, where the plan we determined to follow is conditioned by the play of our rival—in life, by the caprice of fate. We are compelled to modify our tactics, often to such an extent that, as we carry them out, hardly a single feature of the original plan can be recognized." (Schopenhauer, Arthur, *Counsels and Maxims*, trans. T. Bailey Saunders).

On the connection between diplomas and professional success: "Education is an important determinant of income—one of the most important—but it is less important than most people think. If everyone had the same education, the inequality of income would be reduced by less than 10 percent. When you focus on education you neglect the myriad other factors that determine income. The differences of income among people who have the same education are huge." (Kahneman, Daniel: "Focusing Illusion." In: Brockman, John: Edge Annual Question 2011, *This Will Make You Smarter,* HarperCollins, 2012, p. 49. See also: https://www.edge.org/response-detail/11984 [accessed on 7 July 2017]).

3. The Pledge

In conversation with *The New Yorker*, Clayton Christensen explained why many managers have dysfunctional families. "In three hours at work, you could get something substantial accomplished, and if you failed to accomplish it you felt the pain right away. If you spent three hours at home with your family, it felt like you hadn't done a thing, and if you skipped it nothing happened. So you spent more and more time at the office, on high-margin, quick-yield tasks, and you even believed that you were staying away from home for the sake of your family. He had seen many people tell themselves that they could divide their lives into stages, spending the first part pushing forward their careers, and imagining that at some future point they would spend time with their families—only to find that by then their families were gone. Christensen had made a pledge to God not to work on Sundays, and a pledge to his family not to work on Saturdays and to be home during the week early enough for dinner and to play ball with the kids while it was still light. Sometimes, in order to keep these commitments, he would go to work at three in the morning." (MacFarquhar, Larissa: "When Giants Fail." In: *The New Yorker,* 14 May 2012).

In conversation with Oliver Sacks, the Nobel Prize-winner Robert John remarked on keeping the Sabbath: "It is not even a question of improving society—it is about improving one's own quality of life." ("Oliver Sacks: Sabbath". In: *The New York Times*, 14 August 2015). Oliver Sacks wrote about Robert John: "He was full of entertaining stories about the Nobel Prize and the ceremony in Stockholm, but made a point of saying that, had he been compelled to travel to Stockholm on a Saturday, he would have refused the prize. His commitment to the Sabbath, its utter peacefulness and remoteness from worldly concerns, would have trumped even a Nobel." (Ibid).

On decision fatigue, see: Dobelli, Rolf, *The Art of Thinking Clearly*, HarperCollins, 2013, pp. 1–4 and 158–160.

The example of the truck full of dynamite is taken from Schelling, Thomas C.: "An Essay on Bargaining." In: *The American Economic Review,* 1956, Vol. 46, No. 3, pp. 281–306.

It's easier to stick to pledges 100 percent of the time rather than just 99 percent. Clayton Christensen talks about 98 percent instead of 99 percent: "He told them about how at Oxford he had refused to play basketball on a Sunday, even though it was the national championships, because he had promised God he wouldn't; and how much pressure his coach and teammates had put on him to compromise just that one time. Later, he realized that if he had said yes that time he would have had no standing to say no another time, and what he learned—one of the most important lessons of his life—was that it was easier to do the right thing a hundred percent of the time than ninety-eight percent of the time." (MacFarquhar, Larissa: "When Giants Fail". In: *The New Yorker*, 14 May 2012).

4. Black Box Thinking

On the de Havilland Comet 1 see: https://wikipedia.org/wiki/De _Havilland_Comet (accessed on 7 July 2017).

On accident investigator David Warren, the inventor of the black box, see: https://wikipedia.org/wiki/David_Warren (accessed on 7 July 2017).

The term *black box thinking* was coined by Matthew Syed. He wrote a fabulous book with that title. Syed, Matthew: *Black Box Thinking: The Surprising Truth About Success*, Hodder, 2015. The emphasis of the book is on organizational mistakes, but the mental strategies of *black box thinking* work very well when applied to the personal sphere.

Sullenberger: "Everything we know in aviation, every rule in the rule book, every procedure we have, we know because someone somewhere died…We have purchased at great cost, lessons literally bought with blood that we have to preserve as institutional knowledge and pass on to succeeding generations. We cannot have the moral failure of forgetting these lessons and have to relearn them." (Syed, Matthew: "How Black Box Thinking Can Prevent Avoidable Medical Errors." In: *WIRED*, 12 November 2015. See also: http://www.wired.co.uk/article/preventing-medical-error-deaths [accessed on 7 July 2017]).

Paul Dolan describes how people putting on weight gradually shift their focus: "As people put on weight, they shift the focus of their attention away from parts of their lives that are associated with weight, like health, toward aspects where their weight is less important, like work. This shift in attention explains some of the behaviors we observe; many of us gain weight but do not lose it. The effort needed to lose weight may be greater than the effort required to shift the attention you give to your health and weight." (Dolan, Paul: *Happiness by Design*, Penguin, 2015, E-Book Location 1143.)

"Nobody is immune from self-deception and self-delusion. We all have intricate, subliminal defense mechanisms that allow us to retain beliefs that are dear to us, despite contravening facts." (Koch, Christof: *Consciousness—Confessions of a Romantic Reductionist*, MIT Press, 2012, p. 158.)

On Russell's quotations, see: Russell, Bertrand, *The Conquest of Happiness*.

"If you won't attack a problem while it's solvable and wait until it's unfixable, you can argue that you're so damn foolish that you deserve the problem." (Bevelin, Peter: *Seeking Wisdom*, PCA Publications, 2007, p. 93).

Alex Haley: "If You Don't Deal with Reality, then Reality Will Deal with You." In: *Jet Magazine,* 27 March 1980, p. 30. See also: http://bit.ly/2sXCndR (accessed on 7 July 2017) or in: Bevelin, Peter: *Seeking Wisdom,* PCA Publications, 2007, p. 92.

"We've done a lot of that—scrambled out of wrong decisions. I would argue that that's a big part of having a reasonable record in life. You can't avoid wrong decisions. But if you recognize them promptly and do something about them, you can frequently turn the lemon into lemonade." (Bevelin, Peter: *Seeking Wisdom,* PCA Publications, 2007, p. 101.)

"Because problems aren't like great Bordeaux wines…" See Buffett: "You see, your problem won't improve with age." (Bevelin, Peter: *Seeking Wisdom,* PCA Publications, 2007, p. 93).

5. *Counterproductivity*

On Ivan Illich, see: https://en.wikipedia.org/wiki/Ivan_Illich (accessed on 7 July 2017). Sepandar Kamvar of the MIT Media Lab brought Ivan Illich and the concept of counterproductivity to my attention. See Kamvar's talk: https://www.youtube.com/watch?v=dbB5na0g_6M (accessed on 7 July 2017). Illich even factored in the probability of hospital stays due to road accidents, which also waste time—including additional working hours at the hospital.

On the cost of e-mails, see: "But modern technology has brought a few costs, too, the biggest of which is distraction. A recent study estimated the combined cost of distractions for U.S. businesses to be around $600 billion per year." (Dolan, Paul: *Happiness by Design,* Penguin, 2015, E-Book Location 2644). And: "…e-mail alone costs UK businesses about £10,000 ($16,500) per employee per year." (Ibid., E-Book Location 2633.)

6. *The Negative Art of the Good Life*

Marks, Howard: *The Most Important Thing,* Columbia University Press, 2011, p. 172 f. Howard Marks references an article by Charles D. Ellis titled "The Loser's Game", which appeared in 1975 in *The Financial Analyst's Journal.* See also: http://www.cfapubs.org/doi/pdf/10.2469/faj.v51.n1.1865 (accessed on 7 July 2017).

"In amateur tennis, matches aren't *won*—they're *lost*." The American Admiral Samuel Morison, having analyzed countless wars, has come to a conclusion: war is a bit like amateur tennis. "Other things being equal, the side that makes the fewest strategic errors wins the war." (Morison, Samuel Elison: *Strategy and Compromise,* Little Brown, 1958).

Countless studies have shown that the impact of these misfortunes (paralysis, physical injuries or disabilities, divorce) dissipates more rapidly than we imagine. The most important study is Brickman, Philip; Coates, Dan; Janoff-Bulman, Ronnie: "Lottery Winners and Accident

Victims: Is Happiness Relative?" In: *Journal of Personality and Social Psychologie,* August 1978, Vol. 36, No. 8, pp. 917–927.

"Charlie generally focuses first on what to avoid—that is, on what NOT to do—before he considers the affirmative steps he will take in a given situation." (Peter D. Kaufman in: Munger, Charles T.: *Poor Charlie's Almanack,* The Donning Company Publishers, 2006, p. 63.)

"It is remarkable how much long-term advantage people like us have gotten by trying to be consistently not stupid, instead of trying to be very intelligent." (Munger, Charlie: *Wesco Annual Report 1989.*)

"All I want to know is where I'm going to die, so I'll never go there." (Munger, Charles T.: *Poor Charlie's Almanack,* The Donning Company Publishers, 2006, p. 63.). This line is also the title of one of the best books on Buffett and Munger: Bevelin, Peter: *All I Want to Know Is Where I'm Going to Die so I'll Never Go There: Buffett & Munger— A Study in Simplicity and Uncommon, Common Sense,* PCA Publications, 2016.

7. The Ovarian Lottery

On Buffett's thought experiment: "Imagine there are two identical twins in the womb, both equally bright and energetic. And the genie says to them, 'One of you is going to be born in the United States, and one of you is going to be born in Bangladesh. And if you wind up in Bangladesh, you will pay no taxes. What percentage of your income would you bid to be the one that is born in the United States?' It says something about the fact that society has something to do with your fate and not just your innate qualities. The people who say, 'I did it all myself,' and think of themselves as Horatio Alger—believe me, they'd bid more to be in the United States than in Bangladesh. That's the Ovarian Lottery." (Schroeder, Alice: *The Snowball,* Bantam Books, 2008, E-Book Location 11073.)

Six percent of all the people who have ever lived are alive at this moment. See: https://www.ncbi.nlm.nih.gov/pubmed/12288594 (accessed on 7 July 2017).

Buffett: "If I'd been born thousands of years ago I'd be some animal's lunch because I can't run very fast or climb trees. So there's so much chance in how we enter the world." See: http://www.businessinsider

.com/warren-buffett-nails-it-on-the-importance-of-luck-in-life-2013-10 (accessed on 7 July 2017).

If you make gratitude part of your daily mental practice, you'll mitigate its effect on happiness, because your brain will get used to it. In their paper "It's a Wonderful Life: Mentally Subtracting Positive Events Improves People's Affective States, Contrary to Their Affective Forecasts" (*Journal of Personality and Social Psychology,* November 2008, Vol. 95, No. 5, pp. 1217–1224. doi:10.103), authors Minkyung Koo, Sara B. Algoe, Timothy D. Wilson and Daniel T. Gilbert write: "Having a wonderful spouse, watching one's team win the World Series, or getting an article accepted in a top journal are all positive events, and reflecting on them may well bring a smile; but that smile is likely to be slighter and more fleeting with each passing day, because as wonderful as these events may be, they quickly become familiar—and they become more familiar each time one reflects on them. Indeed, research shows that thinking about an event increases the extent to which it seems familiar and explainable."

8. The Introspection Illusion

English has approximately 300 adjectives for the various emotional states. See: http://www.psychpage.com/learning/library/assess/feelings.html (accessed on 7 July 2017).

Schwitzgebel's quotation: "The introspection of current conscious experience, far from being secure, nearly infallible, is faulty, untrustworthy, and misleading—not just *possibly* mistaken, but massively and pervasively. I don't *think* it's just me in the dark here, but most of us." (Schwitzgebel, Eric: *Perplexities of Consciousness,* MIT Press, 2011, p. 129.)

"Because no one ever scolds us for getting it wrong about our experience and we never see decisive evidence of error, we become cavalier. This lack of corrective feedback encourages a hypertrophy of confidence. Who doesn't enjoy being the sole expert in the room whose word has unchallengeable weight?" (Schwitzgebel, Eric: "The Unreliability of Naive Introspection," 7 September 2007. See: http://www.faculty.ucr.edu/~eschwitz/SchwitzPapers/Naive070907.htm [accessed on 7 July 2017]).

9. The Authenticity Trap

On Charles Darwin's funeral: "He was sitting in the front seat as eldest son and chief mourner, and he felt a draught on his already bald head; so he put his black gloves to balance on the top of his skull, and sat like that throughout the service with the eyes of the nation upon him." (Blackburn, Simon: *Mirror, Mirror,* Princeton University Press, 2016, p. 25.) Blackburn quotes Gwen Raverat, Charles Darwin's granddaughter, writing about his sons. See: Acocella, Joan: "Selfie". In: *The New Yorker,* 12 May 2014. See: http://www.newyorker.com/magazine/2014/05/12/selfie (accessed on 7 July 2017).

"Eisenhower was never a flashy man, but two outstanding traits defined the mature Eisenhower, traits that flowed from his upbringing and that he cultivated over time. The first was his creation of a second self. Today, we tend to live within an ethos of authenticity. We tend to believe that the 'true self' is whatever is most natural and untutored. That is, each of us has a certain sincere way of being in the world, and we should live our life being truthful to that authentic inner self, not succumbing to the pressures outside ourself. To live artificially, with a gap between your inner nature and your outer conduct, is to be deceptive, cunning, and false. Eisenhower hewed to a different philosophy." (Brooks, David: *The Road to Character,* Random House, 2015, p. 67.)

10. The Five-Second No

Munger's quotation: "The other thing is the five-second no. You've got to make up your mind. You don't leave people hanging." (Lowe, Janet: *Damn Right, Behind the Scenes with Berkshire Hathaway Billionaire Charlie Munger,* John Wiley & Sons, 2000, p. 54).

"Charlie realizes that it is difficult to find something that is really good. So, if you say 'No' ninety percent of the time, you're not missing much in the world." (Otis Booth on Charlie Munger, In: Munger, Charlie: *Poor Charlie's Almanack,* Donning, 2008, p. 99).

11. The Focusing Illusion

Kahneman's definition of the *focusing illusion* in Kahneman, Daniel: "Nothing in life is as important as you think it is while you are thinking about it." See: https://www.edge.org/response-detail/11984 (accessed on 7 July 2017). See also: Brockman, John: *This Will Make You Smarter,* Doubleday Books, 2012, p. 49.

I borrowed the windscreen-scraping story from a well-known psychological study entitled "Does Living in California Make People Happy?" Schkade, David A.; Kahneman, Daniel: "Does Living in California Make People Happy? A Focusing Illusion in Judgments of Life Satisfaction." In: *Psychological Science,* 1998, Vol. 9, No. 5, pp. 340–346. In their paper, Professors Kahneman and Schkade described the *focusing illusion* for the first time—there comparing the American Midwest with California. The result? In comparing alternatives A and B, people overestimate the differences and underestimate the commonalities.

12. *The Things You Buy Leave No Real Trace*

How much pleasure do you get from your car? Schwarz, Norbert; Kahneman, Daniel; Xu, Jing: "Global and Episodic Reports of Hedonic Experience." In: Belli, Robert F., Stafford, Frank P. and Alwin, Duane F.: *Calendar and Time Diary,* SAGE Publications Ltd, pp. 156–174.

Buffett: "Working with people who cause your stomach to churn seems much like marrying for money—probably a bad idea under any circumstances, but absolute madness if you are already rich." (Connors, Richard: *Warren Buffett on Business: Principles from the Sage of Omaha,* John Wiley & Sons, 2010, p. 30.)

13. *Fuck-You Money*

"The satiation level beyond which experienced well-being no longer increases was a household income of about $75,000 in high-cost areas (it could be less in areas where the cost of living is lower). The average increase of experienced well-being associated with incomes beyond that level was precisely zero." (Kahneman, Daniel: *Thinking Fast and Slow,* Farrar, Straus and Giroux, 2013, p. 397.)

On the life satisfaction of lottery winners, see: Brickman, Philip; Coates, Dan; Janoff-Bulman Ronnie: "Lottery Winners and Accident Victims: Is Happiness Relative?" In: *Journal of Personality and Social Psychologie,* August 1978, Vol. 36, No. 8, pp. 917–927.

Richard Easterlin: "Income and Happiness: Towards a Unified Theory." In: *The Economic Journal.* Vol. 111, 2001, pp. 465–484.

Other studies have been less absolute than Easterlin, and it seems that increased GDP does improve life satisfaction. The effect is not zero, but it's very low—certainly much lower than most people imagine and than politicians would have us believe. Hagerty, Michael R.; Veenhoven, Ruut: "Wealth and Happiness Revisited—Growing National Income Does Go with Greater Happiness." In: *Social Indicators Research,* 2003, Vol. 64, No. 1, pp. 1–27.

The standard of living nearly doubled between 1946, when GDP was $13,869 per capita, and 1970, when it was $23,024, presented at constant market prices (2009). See: https://www.measuringworth .com/usgdp/ (accessed on 7 July 2017). Johnston, Louis; Williamson, Samuel H.: *What Was the U.S. GDP Then?*, MeasuringWorth, 2017.

On the etymology of *fuck-you money* see: Wolff-Mann, Ethan: "How Much Money Would You Need to Ditch Your Job—Forever?" In: *Money,* 17 October 2016. See: http://time.com/money/4187538/f-u -money-defined-how-much-calculator/ (accessed on 7 July 2017).

Fuck-you money allows you to see and think objectively. Charlie Munger: "Elihu Root, probably the greatest cabinet officer we ever had, said one of my favorite comments: No man is fit to hold public office who isn't perfectly willing to leave it at any time." And: "Is a director really fit to make tough calls who isn't perfectly willing to leave the office at any time? My answer is no." (Bevelin, Peter: *All I Want to Know Is Where I'm Going to Die so I'll Never Go There: Buffett & Munger—A Study in Simplicity and Uncommon, Common Sense,* PCA Publications, 2016, p. 33.)

14. The Circle of Competence

Another quotation from Charlie Munger on the circle of competence: "If you want to be the best tennis player in the world, you may start out trying and soon find out that it's hopeless—that other people blow right by you. However, if you want to become the best plumbing contractor in Bemidji, that is probably doable by two-thirds of you. It takes a will. It takes the intelligence. But after a while, you'd gradually know all about the plumbing business in Bemidji and master the art. That is an attainable objective, given enough discipline. And people who could never win a chess tournament or stand in center court in a respectable tennis tournament can rise quite high in life by slowly developing a circle of competence—which results partly from what they were born with and partly from what they slowly develop through work." In: Farnham Street Blog: *The "Circle Of Competence" Theory Will Help You Make Vastly Smarter Decisions,* quoted in: *Business Insider,* 5 December 2013. See: http://www.businessinsider.com/the-circle-of-competence-theory-2013-12 (accessed on 7 July 2017).

Tom Watson's quotation: "I'm no genius. I'm smart in spots—but I stay around those spots."

Evans, Dylan: *Risk Intelligence,* Atlantic Books, 2013, p. 198.

Debbie Millman: "Expect anything worthwhile to take a long time." See Brain Pickings: http://explore.brainpickings.org/post/53767000482/the-ever-wise-debbie-millman-shares-10-things-she (accessed on 8 July 2017).

Anders Ericsson has researched the famous 10,000 hours rule. Ericsson, Anders; Pool, Robert: *Peak: Secrets of the New Science of Expertise,* Eamon Dolan/Houghton Mifflin Harcourt, 2016.

Kevin Kelly has written extensively on obsession: "Obsession is a tremendous force; real creativity comes when you're wasting time and when you're fooling around without a goal. That's often where real exploration and learning and new things come from." (Edge.org: "The Technium: A Conversation with Kevin Kelly," with a foreword by John Brockman, 2 March 2014. See: https://www.edge.org/conversation/kevin_kelly-the-technium (accessed on 8 July 2017).

15. *The Secret of Persistence*

"Charlie and I just sit around and wait for the phone to ring." (Hagstrom, Robert: *The Essential Buffett,* Wiley, 2001, p. 34).

"As a result, we systematically overemphasize doing above not-doing, zeal above deliberation, and action above waiting." This is rooted in our evolutionary past: our ancestors survived not by persistence and cooling their heels but by decisive action. Better to run away once too often than to pause and reflect. Better to strike once too often than to stop and think. Hence *action bias,* our automatic inclination towards action in uncertain situations, which I described in a previous book: Dobelli, Rolf: *The Art of Thinking Clearly,* HarperCollins, 2013, pp. 128–130.

On the bestselling books of all time, see https://www.die-besten-aller-zeiten.de/buecher/meistverkauften/ (accessed on 8 July 2017). The

bestselling products: http://www.businessinsider.com/10-of-the-worlds
-best-selling-items-2014-7 (accessed on 8 July 2017). For drinks, Coca-
Cola is at the top. Since its launch in 1886, Coke has sold an estimated
30,000 billion bottles and cans. For food, Lay's crisps are at the top (an
estimated 4,000 billion packets since 1932). For games, it's the Rubik's
Cube (350 million units sold since 1980).

"Long-term successes are like making cakes with baking powder." In
financial jargon this is known as compound interest; Einstein called
it "the eighth wonder of the world." See: http://www.goodreads
.com/quotes/76863-compound-interest-is-the-eighth-wonder-of-the
-world-he (accessed on 8 July 2017).

Russell, Bertrand, *The Conquest of Happiness*.

"A positive correlation between raucous behavior and good ideas,
between restlessness and insight, between activity and results, cannot be found." See Warren Buffett's quotation: "We don't get paid
for activity, just for being right. As to how long we'll wait, we'll wait
indefinitely." (Buffett, Warren: *Berkshire Hathaway Annual Meeting
1998*).

The final quotation in this chapter, from Charlie Munger: "You
don't have to be brilliant, only a little bit wiser than the other guys, on
average, *for a long, long time*." (Bevelin, Peter: *All I Want to Know Is
Where I'm Going to Die so I'll Never Go There: Buffett & Munger—
A Study in Simplicity and Uncommon, Common Sense*, PCA Publications, 2016, p. 7).

16. *The Tyranny of a Calling*

On Anthony see: https://en.wikipedia.org/wiki/Anthony_the_Great
(accessed on 8 July 2017).

I first read about John Kennedy Toole's tragic end in Ryan Holiday's
book *Ego Is the Enemy*. (Holiday, Ryan: *Ego Is the Enemy*, Portfolio,
2016, p. 180.) Holiday's wonderful book is a perfect introduction to
modesty and therefore relevant to Chapters 7, 16, and 51.

"One of the symptoms of approaching nervous breakdown is the
belief that one's work is terribly important." In: Russell, Bertrand: *The
Conquest of Happiness, 1930.* See: https://en.wikiquote.org/wiki/
The_Conquest_of_Happiness (accessed on 8 July 2017).

I have written extensively about survivorship bias and self-selection bias in another book. See: Dobelli, Rolf: *The Art of Thinking Clearly*, HarperCollins, 2013, pp. 1–4 and 139–141.

"You'll do better if you have passion for something in which you have aptitude. If Warren had gone into ballet, no one would have heard of him." (Bevelin, Peter: *All I Want to Know Is Where I'm Going to Die so I'll Never Go There: Buffett & Munger—A Study in Simplicity and Uncommon, Common Sense*, PCA Publications, 2016, p. 75).

17. The Prison of a Good Reputation

Bob Dylan quotation in: *Dylan bricht sein Schweigen, Die Zeit*, 29 October 2016. See: http://www.zeit.de/kultur/literatur/2016-10/nobelpreis-bob-dylan-interview-stockholm (accessed on 8 July 2017).

Buffett: "Would you rather be the world's greatest lover, but have everyone think you're the world's worst lover? Or would you rather be the world's worst lover but have everyone think you're the world's greatest lover? Now, that's an interesting question. Here's another one. If the world couldn't see your results, would you rather be thought of as the world's greatest investor but in reality have the world's worst record? Or be thought of as the world's worst investor when you were actually the best? In teaching your kids, I think the lesson they're learning at a very, very early age is what their parents put the emphasis on. If all the emphasis is on what the world's going to think about you, forgetting about how you really behave, you'll wind up with an Outer Scorecard. Now, my dad: He was a hundred percent Inner Scorecard guy. He was really a maverick. But he wasn't a maverick for the sake of being a maverick. He just didn't care what other people thought. My dad taught me how life should be lived. I've never seen anybody quite like him." (Schroeder, Alice: *The Snowball*, Bantam Books, 2008, pp. 30–31.)

"Next time you're meeting a friend, keep track: you'll spend 90 percent of the time talking about other people." What do mathematicians chat about at lunchtime in the university cafeteria? "Millennium problems?" Hardly. They gossip about their colleagues: who's having an affair with whom, who's pinched whose ideas, and who—yet again—has missed out on an honorary doctorate.

Brooks, David: *The Road to Character*, Penguin, 2016, E-Book Location 4418.

18. The "End of History" Illusion

On the *end of history illusion*, see: Quoidbach, Jordi; Gilbert, Daniel T.; Wilson, Timothy D.: "The End of History Illusion." In: *Science,* 4 January 2013, Vol. 339 (6115), pp. 96–98.

For many years psychologists assumed that a personality (after the age of about thirty) was set in stone. They talked about the so-called five stable personality traits, the Big Five: openness to experience, conscientiousness, extraversion, agreeableness and neuroticism. Today, however, we know that all our personality traits are subject to development across the course of our lives. We just don't notice it, because we're in our own skin every day and don't perceive the marginal changes. Over decades, however, as with an airport, dramatic alterations become visible. No, if anything is set in stone, it's our political beliefs (see Haidt, Jonathan: *The Righteous Mind: Why Good People Are Divided by Politics and Religion,* Pantheon, 2012). We learn that the earth revolves around the sun, we accept new opinions, but not political ones. My tip to all politicians: save your money and stop trying to win over voters by arguing rationally. You'll never manage it.

You can exercise some influence over changes in your personality. "My old boss, Ben Graham, when he was 12 years old, wrote down all of the qualities that he admired in other people and all the qualities he found objectionable. And he looked at that list and there wasn't anything about being able to run the 100-yard dash in 9.6 or jumping 7 feet. They were all things that were simply a matter of deciding whether you were going to be that kind of person or not... Always hang around people better than you and you'll float up a little bit. Hang around with the other kind and you start sliding down the pole." (Warren Buffett quoted in: Lowe, Janet: *Warren Buffett Speaks: Wit and Wisdom from the World's Greatest Investor,* John Wiley & Sons, 2007, p. 36).

Another thought experiment from Warren Buffett. Think back to your schooldays. Imagine your old class. Let's say the teacher has set the following assignment: you can receive 10 percent of the earned income from any student you choose across the rest of their lifetime; similarly you will give them 10 percent of your earned income. What criteria would you use to pick a student? Try to ignore the knowledge you have today—like knowing that one of your former classmates has become a billionaire, or something. You didn't know that back then. This is about the criteria you would use to do the assignment. Would you have chosen the best footballer in your class, a once highly prestigious position? Would you have chosen the boy with the biggest muscles? Would you have chosen the heartthrob? The girl with the wealthiest parents? The most intelligent one? The one you liked the best? The teacher's pet? The most hard-working kid? The most trustworthy? One thing you immediately notice with this experiment is that the criteria that were so vital back then—football skills, strength, beauty, rich parents—play no part in the assignment. What matters are criteria like trustworthiness, diligence, intelligence and, most of all, whether you really like the person. With the exception of intelligence, none of these qualities is innate; they are available to all human beings. To quote Buffett: "You are all second-year MBA students, so you have gotten to know your classmates. Think for a moment that I granted you the right—you can buy 10 percent of one of your classmate's earnings for the rest of their lifetime. You can't pick someone with a rich father; you have to pick someone who is going to do it on his or her own merit. And I gave you an hour to think about it. Will you give them an IQ test and pick the one with the highest IQ? I doubt it. Will you pick the one with the best grades? The most energetic? You will start looking for qualitative factors, in addition to (the quantitative) because everyone has enough brains and energy. You would probably pick the one you responded the best to, the one who has the leadership qualities, the one who is able to get other people to carry out their interests. That would be the person who is generous, honest and who gave credit to other people for their own ideas. All types of qualities. Whomever you admire the most in the class. Then I would throw in a hooker. In addition to this person you had to go short one of your classmates. That is more fun. Who do I want to go short? You wouldn't pick the person with the lowest IQ, you would think about the person who turned you off, the person who is egotistical, who is greedy, who cuts corners, who is slightly dishonest. As you look at those qualities on the left and right hand side, there is one interesting thing about them; it is not the ability to throw a football 60 yards, it is not the ability the run the 100 yard dash in 9.3 seconds, it is not being the best looking person in the class—they are all qualities that if you really want to have the ones on the left hand side, you can have them. They are qualities of behavior, temperament, character that are achievable; they are not forbidden to anybody in this group. And if you look at the qualities on the right hand side, the ones that turn you off in other people, there is not a quality there that you have to have. You can get rid of it. You can get rid of it a lot easier at your age than at my age, because most behaviors are habitual. The chains of habit are too light to be felt until they are too heavy to be broken. There is no question about it. I see people with these self-destructive behavior patterns at my age or even twenty years younger and they really are entrapped by them." (Connors, Richard: *Warren Buffett on Business: Principles from the Sage of Omaha,* John Wiley & Sons, 2010, pp. 171–172.)

Hire for attitude, train for skill. In: Taylor, Bill: "Hire for Attitude, Train for Skill." In: *Harvard Business Review,* 1 February 2011.

Buffett: "We don't try to change people. It doesn't work well...We accept people the way they are." (Bevelin, Peter: *All I Want to Know Is Where I'm Going to Die so I'll Never Go There: Buffett & Munger— A Study in Simplicity and Uncommon, Common Sense,* PCA Publications, 2016, p. 107).

On the vignette about the social butterfly who married an introverted woman. He should have listened to Charlie Munger, who said: "If you want to guarantee yourself a life of misery, marry somebody with the idea of changing them." (Bevelin, Peter: *All I Want to Know Is Where I'm Going to Die so I'll Never Go There: Buffett & Munger—A Study in Simplicity and Uncommon, Common Sense,* PCA Publications, 2016, p. 108.)

"Oh, it's just so useful dealing with people you can trust and getting all the others the hell out of your life. It ought to be taught as a catechism...But wise people want to avoid other people who are just total rat poison, and there are a lot of them." (Clark, David: *The Tao of Charlie Munger,* Scribner, 2017, p. 177).

19. The Smaller Meaning of Life

"When I called Gary's house to thank him, I connected with an old-style answering machine with a new-style message: 'Hi, this is Gary, and this is not an answering machine, it is a questioning machine! The two questions are, "Who are you?" and "What do you want?" Then there was a pause, and the message added, 'and if you think those are trivial questions, consider that 95 percent of the population goes through life and never answers either one!'" (Pearce, Terry: *Leading Out Loud,* Jossey-Bass; 3rd edition, 2013, p. 10).

NOTES

"Let all your efforts be directed to something, let it keep that end in mind." Seneca, On the Tranquility of Mind, 12.5 (Holiday, Ryan: *The Daily Stoic,* Portfolio, 2016, E-Book-Location 215).

Life goals are massively important. Nickerson, Carol; Schwarz, Norbert; Diener, Ed et al.: "Happiness: Financial Aspirations, Financial Success, and Overall Life Satisfaction: Who? and How?" In: *Journal of Happiness Studies,* December 2007, Vol. 8, pp. 467–515.

"The same principle applies to other goals—one recipe for a dissatisfied adulthood is setting goals that are especially difficult to attain." (Kahneman, Daniel: *Thinking Fast and Slow,* Farrar, Straus and Giroux, 2013, p. 402).

20. *Your Two Selves*

Daniel Kahneman coined the terms "experiencing self" and "remembering self." (Kahneman, Daniel: *Thinking Fast and Slow,* Farrar, Straus and Giroux, 2013, p. 380ff.)

Researchers studied happiness among students during the holidays. See: Wirtz, Derrick; Kruger, Justin; Napa Scollon, Christie; Diener, Ed: "What to Do on Spring Break? The Role of Predicted, On-line, and Remembered Experience in Future Choice." In: *Psychological Science,* September 2003, Vol. 14, No. 5, pp. 520–524.

On the *peak–end rule*: Kahneman, Daniel; Fredrickson, Barbara L.; Schreiber, Charles A.; Redelmeier, Donald A.: "When More Pain Is Preferred to Less: Adding a Better End." In: *Psychological Science,* November 1993, Vol. 4, No. 6, p. 401–405.

21. *The Memory Bank*

Zhang, Jia Wei and Howel, Ryan T.: "Do Time Perspectives Predict Unique Variance in Life Satisfaction Beyond Personality Traits?." In: *Personality and Individual Differences,* June 2011, Vol. 50, No. 8, pp. 1261–1266.

22. *Life Stories Are Lies*

The American psychologist Thomas Landauer was the first scientist to formulate a thesis regarding the amount of information an average person can store. "Every technique he tried led to roughly the same answer: 1 gigabyte. He didn't claim that this answer is precisely correct. But even if it's off by a factor of 10, even if people store 10 times more or 10 less than 1 gigabyte, it remains a puny amount. It's just a tiny fraction of what a modern laptop can retain. Human beings are not warehouses of knowledge." (Sloman, Steven; Fernbach, Philip: *The Knowledge Illusion,* Riverhead Books, 2017, p. 26.)

23. The "Good Death" Fallacy

Researchers in the USA confronted students with similar life stories. See: Diener, Ed; Wirtz, Derrick; Oishi, Shigehiro: "End Effects of Rated Life Quality: The James Dean Effect." In: *Psychological Science,* March 2001, Vol. 12, No. 2, pp. 124–128.

24. The Spiral of Self-Pity

If you find yourself in a hole, stop digging. See: https://en.wikipedia .org/wiki/Law_of_holes (accessed on 8 July 2017).

"Self-pity gets pretty close to paranoia, and paranoia is one of the very hardest things to reverse. You do not want to drift into self-pity. I have a friend who carried a big stack of linen cards—about this thick—and when somebody would make a comment that reflected self-pity, he would take out one of the cards, take the top one off the stack and hand it to the person, and the card said, 'Your story has touched my heart. Never have I heard of anyone with as many misfortunes as you.' Well you can say that's waggery, but I suggest that every time you find you're drifting into self-pity, and I don't care the cause—your child could be dying of cancer, self-pity is not going to improve the situation—just give yourself one of those cards. [Self-pity is] a ridiculous way to behave, and when you avoid it you get a great advantage over everybody else, almost everybody else, because self-pity is a standard condition and yet you can train yourself out of it." (Munger, Charlie: Commencement Address at USC Law School, 2007, in Farnam Street Blog: "The Munger Operating System: How to Live a Life That Really Works," 13 April 2016. See: https://www.valuewalk .com/2017/02/10-ways-can-think-succeed-like-charlie-munger/4/ (accessed on 30 August 2017).

Five hundred years ago, a million of your direct, blood-related ancestors were alive on Earth. Five centuries of four generations each = twenty generations.

Even undeniably awful childhood events are minimally correlated with success or satisfaction in adult life. See: Clarke, Ann M.: *Early Experience: Myth and Evidence*. Free Press; Rutter, Michael: "The long-term effects of early experience." In: *Developmental Medicine and Child Neurology,* 1980, Vol. 22, pp. 800–815.

"I think that the events of childhood are overrated; in fact, I think past history in general is overrated. It has turned out to be difficult to find even small effects of childhood events on adult personality, and there is no evidence at all of large—to say nothing of determining—effects." (Seligman, Martin: *Authentic Happiness,* Free Press, 2002, E-Book-Location 1209ff.)

"Things will get thrown at you and things will hit you. Life's no soft affair." (Seneca, Moral Letters to Lucilius, Letter 107.)

"What point is there in 'being unhappy, just because once you were unhappy?'" Seneca, quoted in: Irvine, William B.: *A Guide to the Good Life,* Oxford University Press, 2008, p. 220.

Charlie Munger's iron prescription: "Whenever you think that some situation or some person is ruining your life, it is actually you who are ruining your life...Feeling like a victim is a perfectly disastrous way to go through life. If you just take the attitude that however bad it is in any way, it's always your fault and you just fix it as best you can—the so-called iron prescription." See: http://latticeworkinvesting.com/quotes/ (accessed on 9 July 2017).

25. Hedonism and Eudemonia

Plato and Aristotle both believed that people should be as temperate, courageous, just and prudent as possible. See: https://en.wikipedia.org/wiki/Eudaimonia (accessed on 9 July 2017).

What became known as the cardinal virtues. See: St. Ambrose: *De officiis ministrorum*. See: https://en.wikipedia.org/wiki/Cardinal_virtues (accessed on 9 July 2017).

"By muddling causes and consequences, philosophers have been forced to construct tortured defenses of some truly astonishing claims—for example, that a Nazi war criminal who is basking on an

Argentinean beach is not really happy, whereas the pious missionary who is being eaten alive by cannibals is." (Gilbert, Dan: *Stumbling on Happiness*, Vintage, 2007, p. 34.)

Paul Dolan: "So experiences of pleasure and purpose are all that matter in the end. Hedonism is the school of thought that holds that pleasure is the only thing that matters in the end. By adding sentiments of purpose to pleasure, I define my position as sentimental hedonism. I am a sentimental hedonist and I think that, deep down, we all are." (Dolan, Paul: *Happiness by Design*, Penguin, 2015, E-Book-Location 1442.)

"I know it when I see it" is the most famous sentence in the whole history of the American Supreme Court. It was used not in the sense of "meaning" but of porn. See: https://en.wikipedia.org/wiki/I_know_it _when_I_see_it (accessed on 9 July, 2017).

Kahneman: "The novel idea is to consider 'meaningful' and 'meaningless' as experiences, not judgments. Activities, in his view, differ in a subjective experience of purposefulness—volunteer work is associated with a sense of purpose that channel-surfing lacks. For Dolan, purpose and pleasure are both basic constituents of happiness. This is a bold and original move." (Paul Dolan, *Happiness by Design*, Penguin, 2015, foreword by Daniel Kahneman, E-Book-Location 75.)

On recent film scholarship: Oliver, Mary Beth; Hartmann, Tilo: "Exploring the Role of Meaningful Experiences in Users' Appreciation of 'Good Movies.'" In: *Projections*, Winter 2010, Vol. 4, No. 2, p. 128–150.

26. The Circle of Dignity—Part I

The Miracle of Dunkirk. See: https://en.wikipedia.org/wiki/Dunkirk _evacuation (accessed on 9 July 2017).

For the story of the telegram, see: Stockdale, Jim: *Thoughts of a Philosophical Fighter Pilot*, Hoover Institution Press, 1995, E-Book-Location 653.

One of Warren Buffett's principles, according to his biographer Alice Schroeder: "Commitments are so sacred that by nature they should be rare." (Schroeder, Alice: *The Snowball*, Bantam Books, 2008, p. 158.)

If social change is your mission, you'll end up tangling with thousands of people and institutions who are doing everything they can to uphold the status quo. Ideally, you want to keep your mission narrowly focused. You can't rebel against all aspects of the dominant order. Society is stronger than you are. You can only achieve personal victories in clearly defined moral niches.

"If an individual has not discovered something that he will die for, he isn't fit to live." (Martin Luther King, speech at the Great March on Detroit, 23 June 1963.)

27. The Circle of Dignity—Part II

Jim Stockdale describes his jet being shot down and his capture, see: https://www.youtube.com/watch?v=Pc_6GDWl0s4 (accessed on 9 July 2017).

Stockdale: "I laid down and I cried that night, right on that floor. I was so happy that I had had the guts to get it all together and make it impossible for them to do what they were going to try to do." See: https://www.youtube.com/watch?v=Pc_6GDWl0s4 (timestamps 9:50 and 13:30).

Vučić: "Erbost über abschätzige Kommentare auf einer Website, forderte er während eines Interviews den Chefredakteur des Staatsfernsehens auf, die Unverschämtheiten gleich selbst einmal vorzulesen. Der begann, merkte dann, dass er sich unmöglich machte, und weigerte sich fortzufahren." / "Furious at the contemptuous comments on a website, during an interview he demanded the editor-in-chief of state television read the outrageous comments out loud. The man began, but realized he was in an impossible situation and refused to continue." See: https://www.nzz.ch/international/wahl-in-serbien-durchmarsch-von-vucic-ins-praesidentenamt-ld.155050 (accessed on 10 July 2017).

In his book The Road to Character, David Brooks describes the life of politician Frances Perkins. In 1933, Franklin D. Roosevelt made her the first female Cabinet secretary in the USA. Perkins used a similar strategy. "When opponents made vicious charges against her, she asked them to repeat their question, believing that no person can be scurrilous twice." (Brooks, David: The Road to Character, Penguin, 2016, p. 44.)

28. The Circle of Dignity—Part III

One woman in America, for instance, accepted 10,000 dollars to get the name of an online casino tattooed on her forehead. See: Sandel, Michael J.: What Money Can't Buy, Farrar, Straus and Giroux, 2012, p. 184.

29. The Book of Worries

On the experiment with the sparrows, see: Zanette, Liana Y.; White, Aija F.; Allen, Marek C.; Clinchy, Michael: "Perceived Predation Risk Reduces the Number of Offspring Songbirds Produce per Year," *Science*, 9 December 2011, Vol. 334, No. 6061, p. 1398–1401. See also: Young, Ed: "Scared to Death: How Intimidation Changes Ecosystems," In: *New Scientist*, 29 May 2013.

"'Don't worry, be happy' bromides are of no use; notice that people who are told to 'relax' rarely do." (Gold, Joel: *Morbid Anxiety*. In: Brockman, *What Should We Be Worried About?*, Harper Perennial, 2014, p. 373.)

Russell, Bertrand: *The Conquest of Happiness*, Suhrkamp, 1977, p. 56.

Mark Twain: "I am an old man and have known a great many troubles, but most of them have never happened." See: http://quoteinvestigator.com/2013/10/04/never-happened/ (accessed on 9 July, 2017).

30. The Opinion Volcano

"When people are given difficult questions to think about—for example, whether the minimum wage should be raised—they generally lean one way or the other right away, and then put a call in to reasoning to see whether support for that position is forthcoming." (Haidt, Jonathan: *The Happiness Hypothesis*, Basic Books, 2006, E-Book Location 1303.)

I described the affect heuristic in an earlier books: Dobelli, Rolf: *The Art of Thinking Clearly*, HarperCollins, 2013.

31. Your Mental Fortress

Boethius: *The Consolation of Philosophy*.

The term "mental fortress" derives from "inner fortress," which comes from Marcus Aurelius's *Meditations*. It has also been translated as "inner citadel."

32. Envy

Gore Vidal: "Whenever a friend succeeds a little something in me dies." Quoted in: *The Sunday Times Magazine*, 16 September 1973.

In case you've forgotten, here's a brief recap of the *Snow White* tale: Snow White's stepmother (and current queen of the land) is jealous of her stepdaughter's beauty. She hires a contract killer (a hunter) to bump her off, but he reneges on their agreement and lets Snow White go. Running into the forest, Snow White finds the Seven Dwarves. After her disagreeable experience with outsourcing (the hunter), the stepmother decides to take matters into her own hands. She poisons the beautiful Snow White.

Bertrand Russell considered jealousy one of the most important sources of unhappiness. "Envy is, I should say, one of the most universal and deep-seated of human passions." Russell, Bertrand: *The Conquest of Happiness.*

Also Russell: "In an age when the social hierarchy is fixed, the lowest classes do not envy the upper classes so long as the division between rich and poor is thought to be ordained by God. Beggars do not envy millionaires, though of course they will envy other beggars who are more successful. The instability of social status in the modern world, and the equalitarian doctrines of democracy and socialism, have greatly extended the range of envy... Our age is therefore one in which envy plays a peculiarly large part."

"Researchers recently made employees at the University of California feel worse off by providing them with a Web link to the salaries of their colleagues (made possible by the state's 'right-to-know law'). Those who were earning less than the median wage were less satisfied with their jobs after they viewed that link." (Dolan, Paul: *Happiness by Design,* Penguin, 2015, E-Book Location 2352.)

"We find that 'envy' emerges as the category of the highest importance with 29.6 percent of respondents mentioning it as a major reason behind frustration and exhaustion of 'others'. Feelings of envy by far surpass such causes, as *'lack of attention'* (19.5 percent), *'loneliness'* (10.4 percent), and *'time loss'* (13.7 percent)." (Krasnova, Hanna, et al.: "Envy on Facebook: A Hidden Threat to Users' Life Satisfaction?", publication by TU Darmstadt, 2013, pp. 1477–1491.)

Munger: "The idea of caring that someone is making money faster than you are is one of the deadly sins. Envy is a really stupid sin because it's the one you could never possibly have any fun at. There's a lot of pain and no fun. Why would you want to get on that trolley?"

(Munger, Charles T.: *Poor Charlie's Almanack,* Donning 2008, S. 431.)

I've already written about envy in a previous book. See: Dobelli, Rolf: *The Art of Thinking Clearly,* HarperCollins, 2013, pp. 257–259.

33. Prevention

Albert Einstein: "A clever person solves a problem. A wise person avoids it." See: http://www.azquotes.com/quote/345864 (accessed on 11 July 2017). It's not certain that Einstein said this.

A similar quotation from the polymath (and Founding Father) Benjamin Franklin can be found in an anonymous letter to the readers of the *Philadelphia Gazette* that recommends setting up fire services on a voluntary basis: "An ounce of prevention is worth a pound of cure." See: https://www.goodreads.com/quotes/247269-an-ounce-of-prevention-is-worth-a-pound-of-cure (accessed on 11 July 2017).

Munger: "I have a rule in life, if there is a big whirlpool you don't want to miss it with 20 feet—you round it with 500 feet." (Bevelin, Peter: *All I Want to Know Is Where I'm Going to Die so I'll Never Go There: Buffett & Munger—A Study in Simplicity and Uncommon, Common Sense*, PCA Publications, 2016, p. 58.)

Howard Marks: "I tell my father's story of the gambler who lost regularly. One day he heard about a race with only one horse in it, so he bet the rent money. Halfway around the track, the horse jumped over the fence and ran away. Invariably things can get worse than people expect. Maybe 'worst-case' means 'the worst we've seen in the past.' But that doesn't mean things can't be worse in the future." (Marks, Howard: *The Most Important Thing, Uncommon Sense for the Thoughtful Investor*, Columbia Business School Publishing, 2011, p. 55, quoted in: Bevelin, Peter: *All I Want to Know Is Where I'm Going to Die so I'll Never Go There: Buffett & Munger—A Study in Simplicity and Uncommon, Common Sense*, PCA Publications, 2016, p. 62.)

Munger: "You may well say, 'Who wants to go through life anticipating trouble?' Well, I did, trained as I was. All my life I've gone through life anticipating trouble...It didn't make me unhappy to anticipate trouble all the time and be ready to perform adequately if trouble came. It didn't hurt me at all. In fact it helped me." (Bevelin, Peter: *All I Want to Know Is Where I'm Going to Die so I'll Never Go There: Buffett & Munger—A Study in Simplicity and Uncommon, Common Sense*, PCA Publications, 2016, p. 62.)

On pre-mortems see: https://en.wikipedia.org/wiki/Pre-mortem (accessed on 11 July 2017). The idea of the pre-mortem has a long history. The Stoics called it *premeditato malorum* (negative visualization).

34. Mental Relief Work

On the volunteer's fallacy or volunteer's folly, see: Dobelli, Rolf: *The Art of Thinking Clearly*, HarperCollins, 2013, pp. 193–195.

Richard Feynman: "[John] von Neumann gave me an interesting idea: that you don't have to be responsible for the world that you're in. So I have developed a very powerful sense of social irresponsibility as a result of von Neumann's advice. It's made me a very happy man ever since. But it was von Neumann who put the seed in that grew into my *active* irresponsibility!" (Feynman, Richard: *Surely, You're Joking, Mr. Feynman!*, W. W. Norton & Company, 1997, p. 132.)

35. The Focus Trap

"Then at dinner, Bill Gates Sr. posed the question to the table: What factor did people feel was the most important in getting to where they'd gotten in life? And I said, 'Focus.' And Bill said the same thing. It is unclear how many people at the table understood 'focus' as Buffett lived that word. This kind of innate focus couldn't be emulated. It meant the intensity that is the price of excellence. It meant the discipline and passionate perfectionism that made Thomas Edison the quintessential American inventor, Walt Disney the king of family entertainment, and James Brown the Godfather of Soul. It meant single-minded obsession with an ideal." (Schroeder, Alice: *The Snowball,* Bantam Books, 2008, E-Book-Location 19788.)

"If a person gave your body to any stranger he met on his way, you would certainly be angry. And do you feel no shame in handing over your own mind to be confused and mystified by anyone who happens to verbally attack you?" (Epictetus, tr. Elizabeth Carter, https://en.wikiquote.org/wiki/Epictetus, accessed on 13 August 2017.)

Kevin Kelly: "Here's something else that's interesting. Everybody who's watching me right now, you and I, we all spend four, maybe more, five years with deliberate study and training to learn how to read and write, and that process of learning how to read and write actually has rewired our brains. We know that from plenty of studies of literate and illiterate people from the same culture—that reading and writing changes how your brain works. That only came about because of four or five years of deliberate practice and study, and we shouldn't expect necessarily that the real mastery of this new media is something we can deduce by hanging around. You can't learn calculus just hanging around people who know calculus, you actually have to study it. It may be that for us to really master the issues of attention management, critical thinking, learning how technological devices work and how they bite back, all this techno-literacy may be something that we have to spend several years being trained to do. Maybe you can't just learn it by hanging around people who do it or else just hanging around trying to learn it by osmosis. It may require training and teaching, a techno-literacy, and learning how to manage your attention and distractions is something that is probably going to require training." In: Edge.org: *The Technium,* A Conversation with Kevin Kelly, 2 March 2014, Foreword by John Brockman. See: https://www.edge.org/conversation/kevin _kelly-the-technium (accessed on 8 July 2017).

"Your happiness is determined by how you allocate your attention. What you attend to drives your behavior and it determines your happiness. Attention is the glue that holds your life together." (Dolan, Paul: *Happiness by Design,* Penguin, 2015, E-Book Location 224.)

"The production process for happiness is therefore how you allocate your attention...The same life events and circumstances can affect your happiness a lot or a little depending on how much attention you pay to them." (Dolan, Paul: *Happiness by Design,* Penguin, 2015, E-Book Location 891.)

Munger: "I did not succeed in life by intelligence. I succeeded because I have a long attention span...the idea of multitasking my way to glory has never occurred to me." (Bevelin, Peter: *All I Want to Know Is Where I'm Going to Die so I'll Never Go There: Buffett & Munger— A Study in Simplicity and Uncommon, Common Sense,* PCA Publications, 2016, p. 6.)

36. Read Less, But Twice—on Principle

On Dostoyevsky's reception of Holbein's painting, see: *Literarischer Spaziergang in Basel* SRF, Schweizer Radio & Fernsehen. See: https://www.srf.ch/radio-srf-2-kultur/srf-kulturclub/streifzug-literarischer -spaziergang-in-basel (accessed on 13 July 2017).

37. The Dogma Trap

Rozenblit, Leonid; Keil, Frank: "The Misunderstood Limits of Folk Science: An Illusion of Explanatory Depth." In: *Cognitive Science,* 1 September 2002, Vol. 26, No. 5, pp. 521–562.

Here's another example of irrefutability: "The world was created by the undisprovable Flying Spaghetti Monster. The Spaghetti Monster is merciful and all-powerful. When good things happen, it's thanks to the Spaghetti Monster. Bad things only appear bad from the small, limited perspective of human beings, not from the omnipotent perspective of the Spaghetti Monster. Believe resolutely in the Spaghetti Monster and you'll have a good life—if not on Earth, then in the Beyond." (Tenets summarized by Rolf Dobelli.) The Flying Spaghetti Monster cannot be refuted, just as God, Zeus and Allah cannot be refuted. At first glance, this appears to be a strength. In fact it's a weakness. The Church of the Flying Spaghetti Monster is a parody religion founded by the American physicist Bobby Henderson. See: https://en.wikipedia.org/wiki/Flying_Spaghetti_Monster (accessed on 13 August 2017).

For the quotation from Hans Küng, see: *Does God Exist? An Answer for Today,* trans. Edward Quinn (Garden City, NY: Doubleday, 1980), p. 185.

Munger: "When you announce that you're a loyal member of some cult-like group and you start shouting out the orthodox ideology, what you're doing is pounding it in, pounding it in, pounding it in." (Bevelin, Peter: *All I Want to Know Is Where I'm Going to Die so I'll Never Go There: Buffett & Munger—A Study in Simplicity and Uncommon, Common Sense,* PCA Publications, 2016, p. 113.)

For a similar heuristic to my imaginary TV talk show, see Munger: "I have what I call an 'iron prescription' that helps me keep sane when I drift toward preferring one intense ideology over another. I feel that I'm not entitled to have an opinion unless I can state the arguments against my position better than the people who are in opposition. I think that I am qualified to speak only when I've reached that state." (Bevelin, Peter: *All I Want to Know Is Where I'm Going to Die so I'll Never Go There: Buffett & Munger—A Study in Simplicity and Uncommon, Common Sense,* PCA Publications, 2016, p. 114.) This approach is generally acknowledged as an antidote to confirmation bias, which I discussed in a previous book. See: Dobelli, Rolf: *The Art of Thinking Clearly,* HarperCollins, 2013, pp. 19–23.

38. Mental Subtraction

The practical exercise for *mental subtraction*: I got the idea for this specific exercise from my wife several years ago, when she was working with senior executives as a psychotherapist.

On the *psychological immune system*: "Human beings have the ability to make the best of a bad situation. After anticipating a devastating divorce, say, people find that their spouses were never really right for them. I like to say that people have a psychological immune system. We suffer the slings and arrows of outrageous fortune more capably than we might predict." (Fiske, Susan: *Forecasting the Future,* interview with Daniel Gilbert, in: *Psychology Today,* 1 November 2002. See: https://www.psychologytoday.com/articles/200211/forecasting-the -future (accessed on 11 July 2017).

On getting used to gratitude: in their paper "It's a Wonderful Life: Mentally Subtracting Positive Events Improves People's Affective States, Contrary to Their Affective Forecasts" (*Journal of Personality and Social Psychology,* November 2008, Vol. 95, No. 5, pp. 1217–1224. doi:10.103), authors Minkyung Koo, Sara B. Algoe, Timothy D. Wilson and Daniel T. Gilbert write: "Having a wonderful spouse, watching one's team win the World Series, or getting an article accepted in a top journal are all positive events, and reflecting on them may well bring a smile; but that smile is likely to be slighter and more fleeting with each passing day, because as wonderful as these events may be, they quickly become familiar—and they become more familiar each time one reflects on them. Indeed, research shows that thinking about an event increases the extent to which it seems familiar and explainable."

On medalists at the Barcelona Olympics, see Ibid.

On life expectancy (at birth) across history, see: https://en.wikipedia .org/wiki/Life_expectancy (accessed on 11 July 2017).

"Our happiness is sometimes not very salient, and we need to do what we can to make it more so. Imagine playing a piano and not being able to hear what it sounds like. Many activities in life are like playing a piano that you do not hear…" (Dolan, Paul: *Happiness by Design,* Penguin, 2015, E-Book Location 1781.)

39. *The Point of Maximum Deliberation*

"Experience is what you get when you didn't get what you wanted." This aphorism has been attributed to various sources: https://www .aphorismen.de/zitat/73840 and https://en.wikiquote.org/wiki/Randy _Pausch (accessed on 11 July 2017).

40. *Other People's Shoes*

To understand the other person's position, you have to step into it. See Ben Horowitz on how to do so: "The very next day I informed the head of Sales Engineering and the head of Customer Support that they would be switching jobs. I explained that, like Jodie Foster and Barbara Harris, they would keep their minds, but get new bodies. Permanently. Their initial reactions were not unlike the remake where Lindsay Lohan and Jamie Lee Curtis both scream in horror." (Horowitz, Ben: *The Hard Thing About Hard Things,* HarperCollins, 2014, E-Book Location 3711.)

Schwitzgebel, Eric; Rust, Joshua: "The Behavior of Ethicists," In: *The Blackwell Companion to Experimental Philosophy,* Wiley-Blackwell, 2014.

41. *The Illusion of Changing the World—Part I*

Nelson Mandela: "We can change the world and make it a better place. It is in your hands to make a difference." (http://www.un.org/en/events/ mandeladay/2011/sg_message2011.shtml.)

Steve Jobs: "The people who are crazy enough to think that they can change the world, are the ones who do."

On the *focusing illusion*, see: Kahneman, Daniel: *Focusing Illusion.* In: Brockman, John: Edge Annual Question 2011, *This Will Make You Smarter,* HarperCollins, 2012, p. 49. See: https://www.edge.org/ response-detail/11984 (accessed on 12 July 2017).

On the *intentional stance:* It's worth noting that this is also one of the reasons why we're so susceptible to religion. Gods jump in to fill the void where there's no visible human or animal agency. Why does a volcano explode? Today we know it's caused not by gods but by plate tectonics.

"...we tend to give too much credit to whichever clever person is standing nearby at the right moment." (Ridley, Matt: *The Evolution of Everything,* HarperCollins, 2015, E-Book Location 61.) See also the WORLD.MINDS video: https://www.youtube.com/watch?v=rkqq8x X98lQ (accessed on 12 July 2017).

"'Martin Luther is credited with the Reformation,' he wrote. 'But it had to happen. If it had not been Luther it would have been someone else.' The chance result of a battle could bring forward or delay the ruin of a nation, but if the nation was due to be ruined it would happen anyway. Montesquieu thus made the distinction between ultimate and proximate causes that became such a useful concept in social science." (Ridley, Matt: *The Evolution of Everything,* HarperCollins, 2015, E-Book-Location 3162.)

On Cortez: A similar use of biological weapons—again completely unintended and accidental—is the reason why the USA is currently an independent state. Victory over the British in 1776 cannot be credited to the "great man" George Washington. No, independence was won thanks to mosquitos. The British attacked the American army via the southern states. In coastal areas in particular, the swampy ground is ripe with malaria-carrying mosquitoes—which promptly bit the British soldiers. The Americans, meanwhile, were garrisoned largely in the North, where there was less danger of malaria. Local soldiers stationed in the South were primarily black slaves, who had developed a certain level of immunity to malaria after thousands of years in Africa. The Americans thus have mosquitos, not "great men," to thank for their independence. (Paraphrased and summarized, ibid., E-Book-Location 3242.) "'Mosquitoes,' says McNeill, 'helped the Americans snatch victory from the jaws of stalemate and win the Revolutionary War, without which there would be no United States of America. Remember that when they bite you next Fourth of July.'" (Ridley, Matt: *The Evolution of Everything,* HarperCollins, 2015, E-Book-Location 3242.)

In Switzerland after WW II there was hardly an inn that didn't hang a framed portrait of General Guisan on the wall, mostly above the dining table. As a child, the old man with the stiff embroidered collar—popping up more commonly than Jesus, up and down the land—seemed to me like a hero. The portraits of Guisan only began to disappear in the 1970s, leaving an unbleached rectangle on the wallpaper for years in many buildings. Squinting your eyes and using your imagination, you could still project the image of the "great man" onto it. Was Guisan a decisive figure in Swiss history? No. The popular general had nothing to do with keeping Switzerland out of the Second World War. It was chance, fate, luck. Germany had more important places to conquer than Switzerland. Any other general staff officer would have been equally deserving of a portrait hanging on the wall of a smoky pub.

42. The Illusion of Changing the World—Part II

"A less pragmatically Marxist version of Deng might have delayed the reform, but surely one day it would have come." (Ridley, Matt: *The Evolution of Everything,* HarperCollins, 2015, E-Book Location 3188.)

On the invention of the lightbulb: "... it was utterly inevitable once electricity became commonplace that lightbulbs would be invented when they were. For all his brilliance, Edison was wholly dispensable and unnecessary. Consider the fact that Elisha Gray and Alexander Graham Bell filed for a patent on the telephone on the very same day. If one of them had been trampled by a horse en route to the patent office, history would have been much the same." (Ridley, Matt: *The Evolution of Everything,* HarperCollins, 2015, E-Book-Location 1739.)

Warren Buffett: "My conclusion from my own experiences and from much observation of other businesses is that a good managerial record (measured by economic returns) is far more a function of what business boat you get into than it is of how effectively you row (though intelligence and effort help considerably, of course, in any business, good or bad). Some years ago I wrote: 'When a management with a reputation for brilliance tackles a business with a reputation for poor fundamental economics, it is the reputation of the business that remains intact.' Nothing has since changed my point of view on that matter. Should you find yourself in a chronically-leaking boat, energy devoted to changing vessels is likely to be more productive than energy devoted to patching leaks." (Greenwald, Bruce C. N.; Kahn, Judd; Sonkin, Paul D.; van Biema, Michael: *Value Investing: From Graham to Buffett and Beyond,* John Wiley & Sons, 2001, p. 196.)

Matt Ridley's observation about CEOs: "Most CEOs are along for the ride, paid well to surf on the waves their employees create, taking occasional key decisions, but no more in charge than the designers, middle managers and above all customers who chose the strategy. Their careers increasingly reflect this: brought in from the outside, handsomely rewarded for working long hours, then ejected with little ceremony but much cash when things turn sour. The illusion that they are feudal kings is maintained by the media as much as anything. But it is an illusion." (Ridley, Matt: *The Evolution of Everything,* HarperCollins, 2015, E-Book Location 3279.)

43. The "Just World" Fallacy

In Germany, for example, half of all reported crimes are cleared up (not including unreported cases). See: http://www.tagesspiegel.de/politik/neue-polizeistatistik-wie-gefaehrlich-ist-deutschland/8212176.html (accessed on 11 July 2017).

Gray, John: *Straw Dogs: Thoughts on Humans and Other Animals,* Granta Books, 2002, p. 106f.

44. Cargo Cults

On the Moleskine notebooks, see: https://www.welt.de/wirtschaft/article146759010/Der-kleine-Schwindel-mit-Hemingways-Notizbuechern.html (accessed on 11 July 2017).

For Robert Greenberg's comment about Jean-Baptiste Lully, see: https://robertgreenbergmusic.com/scandalous-overtures-jean-baptiste-lully/ (accessed on 11 July 2017).

45. If You Run Your Own Race, You Can't Lose

On the specialization of scribes: the oldest cuneiform writing preserves not poetry but financial accounts.

Kevin Kelly: https://www.edge.org/conversation/kevin_kelly-the-technium (accessed on 11 July 2017).

46. The Arms Race

When Warren Buffett bought the unprofitable textile company Berkshire-Hathaway at a bargain-basement price in 1962, he immediately invested in new, more efficient textile machines. His intention was to drastically lower production costs and bring the company back into the black. Production costs did fall, but they still didn't make a profit. Where had the added value of this million-dollar investment gone? To the manufacturers of the new textile machines and to the consumers. Warren Buffett's metaphor for this arms race: "We always had new machinery that held the promise of increasing our profit, but never did because everyone else bought the same machinery. It was sort of like being in a crowd, and everyone stands on tip-toes—your view doesn't improve, but your legs hurt." (Berkshire Hathaway Annual Meeting, 2004, notes by Whitney Tilson at www.tilsonfunds.com.)

Lewis Carroll's *Through the Looking Glass*: "Now, here, you see, it takes all the running you can do, to stay in the same place." See: *Through the Looking-Glass, and What Alice Found There*. London, 1871.

John Cassidy: "If almost everybody has a college degree, getting one doesn't differentiate you from the pack. To get the job you want, you might have to go to a fancy (and expensive) college, or get a higher degree. Education turns into an arms race, which primarily benefits the arms manufacturers—in this case, colleges and universities." (Cassidy, John: "College Calculus: What's the Real Value of Higher Education?" In: *The New Yorker,* 7 September 2015.)

On the original affluent society see: https://en.wikipedia.org/wiki/Original_affluent_society (accessed on 11 July 2017).

In many places in Switzerland, Germany and many other countries, people put two-year-old children into private kindergartens, hoping to get them into the best private primary schools, then through the selection process for the best secondary schools, and finally a place at an elite university—all because their neighbors are doing it too. This means even tiny children are being recruited into the *arms race*, but it's the private schools that profit, not them.

47. Making Friends with Weirdos

On Spinoza's excommunication, see: https://en.wikipedia.org/wiki/Baruch_Spinoza (accessed on 17 August 2017).

48. The Secretary Problem

If no candidate is better than the top applicant from the previous 37 percent, you'll obviously have to hire the final one. But statistically speaking, if you run through the procedure enough times, on average you'll achieve the best results with this technique.

I'm grateful to Professor Rudolf Taschner for his observation about how candidates can turn the secretary algorithm to their advantage. "An applicant who doesn't stand out professionally but who has read Dobelli's article could make sure she's invited to interview straight after the first thirty-seven percent. Then she'll have given herself an advantage that the mathematical model, with its very precise-sounding solution, hasn't envisaged" (private correspondence on 7 July 2017).

Experiments with the *secretary problem* have shown that most people plump for a candidate too soon—especially in online dating. See: https://en.wikipedia.org/wiki/Secretary_problem#cite_note-0 (accessed on 11 July 2017).

As you age, change your modus operandi: become highly selective. There's a lovely anecdote from Marshall Weinberg about going to lunch with Warren Buffett that's worth repeating here. "He had an exceptional ham-and-cheese sandwich. A few days later, we were going out again. He said, 'Let's go back to that restaurant.' I said, 'But we were just there.' He said, 'Precisely. Why take a risk with another place? We know exactly what we're going to get.' That is what Warren looks for in stocks, too. He only invests in companies where the odds are great that they will not disappoint." (Lowe, Janet: *Warren Buffett Speaks: Wit and Wisdom from the World's Greatest Investor,* John Wiley & Sons, 2007, p. 142.)

49. Managing Expectations

On the New Year's Eve party: a study by Jonathan Schooler, Dan Ariely and George Loewenstein came to a similar conclusion. In their paper, they describe a New Year's Eve party in 1999/2000. In retrospect, the people at the party who had the highest expectations and put in the most effort had the least fun. "The results of this field study suggest that high expectations can lead to disappointment and that spending time and effort (and perhaps money) on an event can increase dissatisfaction." (Schooler, Jonathan; Ariely, Dan; Loewenstein, George: "The pursuit and assessment of happiness can be self-defeating." In: *The Psychology of Economic Decisions,* OUP, 2003, Vol. 1, p. 60.)

Research confirms that expectations have a profound impact on well-being: "People evaluate their situation with regard to an aspiration level that is formed by their hopes and expectations. If people attain their aspiration levels they are satisfied with their lives."

(Frey, Bruno S.; Stutzer, Alois: *Happiness and Economics,* Princeton University Press, 2001, p. 12.)

"There is also evidence, again using reports of life satisfaction and mental health, that the gains from increases in income can be completely offset if your expectations about gains in income rise faster than does income itself." (Dolan, Paul: *Happiness by Design,* Penguin, 2015, E-Book Location 1690.)

Even the notorious U curve of life satisfaction is connected to false expectations. Young people are happy because they believe things can only ever improve—higher income, more power, greater opportunity. In middle age, between forty and fifty-five, they reach a low point. They're forced to accept that the high-flying aspirations of their youth cannot be realized. On top of that they have children, a career, income pressures—all unexpected dampers on happiness. In old age, people are reasonably happy once more, because they've exceeded those unrealistically low expectations. (Schwandt, Hannes: "Unmet Aspirations as an Explanation for the Age U-shape in Wellbeing." In: *Journal of Economic Behavior & Organization,* 2016, Vol. 122, edition C, pp. 75–87.)

On "preferred indifferents": "The Stoics mark the distinction between the way we ought to opt for health as opposed to virtue by saying that I select *(eklegomai)* the preferred indifferent but I choose *(hairoûmai)* the virtuous action." In: *Stanford Encyclopedia of Philosophy.* See: https://plato.stanford.edu/entries/stoicism/ (accessed on 11 July 2017).

When it comes to New Year's resolutions, deduct three points rather than two from your expectation rating. New Year's resolutions (e.g. getting fit, drinking less, quitting smoking) rarely work. See: Polivy, Janet; Herman, C. Peter: "If at First You Don't Succeed—False Hopes of Self-Change." In: *American Psychologist,* September 2002, Vol. 57, No. 9, p. 677–689. See also: Polivy, Janet: "The False Hope Syndrome: Unrealistic Expectations of Self-Change." In: *International Journal of Obesity and Related Metabolic Disorders,* May 2001, 25 suppl. 1, p. 80–84.

According to Warren Buffett, even marriage is a question of expectation management. "What's the secret of a great marriage? It's not looks, nor intelligence, nor money—it's low expectations." (Sellers,

Patricia: "Warren Buffett's Wisdom for Powerful Women." In: *Fortune*, 6 October 2010. See: http://fortune.com/2010/10/06/warren-buffetts -wisdom-for-powerful-women/ (accessed on 11 July 2017).

50. *Sturgeon's Law*

The original quotation from Ted Sturgeon: "When people talk about the mystery novel, they mention *The Maltese Falcon* and *The Big Sleep*. When they talk about the western, they say there's *The Way West* and *Shane*. But when they talk about science fiction, they call it 'that Buck Rogers stuff,' and they say 'ninety percent of science fiction is crud.' Well, they're right. Ninety percent of science fiction is crud. But then ninety percent of everything is crud, and it's the ten percent that isn't crud that is important, and the ten percent of science fiction that isn't crud is as good as or better than anything being written anywhere." (Dennett, Daniel: *Intuition Pumps and Other Tools for Thinking*, W. W. Norton, 2013, E-Book Location 639).

Daniel Dennett: "90 percent of everything is crap. That is true, whether you are talking about physics, chemistry, evolutionary psychology, sociology, medicine—you name it—rock music, country western. 90 percent of everything is crap." See: https://en.wikipedia.org/wiki/ Sturgeon percent27s_law#cite_ref-5 (accessed on 11 July 2017).

Harry Frankfurt, professor of philosophy at Princeton University, published a bestseller a few years back that was snappily titled *On Bullshit*. (Frankfurt, Harry G.: *On Bullshit*, Princeton University Press, 2005, p. 61.) In the book he demonstrates that lies aren't the main enemy of truth; *bullshit* is. Frankfurt defines bullshit as speech devoid of content that nonetheless pretends to be relevant, but I think the definition can usefully be broadened. *Bullshit* is the ninety percent that *Sturgeon's law* dictates is irrelevant—no matter whether you're talking about books, fashion trends or lifestyles.

The world can stay irrational longer than you can stay sane. I came up with this phrase as a counterpart to *Sturgeon's law*. It's an adaptation of a quotation from John Maynard Keynes: "The market can stay irrational longer than you can stay solvent." See: https://www.maynard keynes.org/keynes-the-speculator.html (accessed on 11 July 2017).

On Benjamin Graham's idea about *Mr. Market* see: https://en.wikipedia .org/wiki/Mr._Market (accessed on 11 July 2017).

51. In Praise of Modesty

Think about how important you would have had to be in order to be invited to the official opening ceremonies of the Eiffel Tower (complete with a gourmet banquet) in 1889, the Taj Mahal in 1648 or the Great Pyramid of Giza in 2581 B.C. Khufu himself invited you! You sit there on the stage, gazing at the newly constructed pyramid as slaves waft a warm desert breeze into your face, hoping that the ceremony—the dances, the speeches, the dull parade of soldiers—will soon be over and you can move on to the "relaxing part." How important you must have felt! How baselessly important.

Here's a nice example of modesty and rationality: the American general George Marshall (after whom the Marshall Plan to help rebuild Europe was named) had to sit for an official portrait, as was customary in those days. "After appearing many times and patiently honoring the requests, Marshall was finally informed by the painter that he was finished and free to go. Marshall stood up and began to leave. 'Don't you want to see the painting?' the artist asked. 'No, thank you,' Marshall said respectfully and left." (Holiday, Ryan: *Ego Is the Enemy,* Portfolio, 2016, E-Book Location 1628.) "Who has time to look at a picture of himself? What's the point?" (ibid., E-Book Location 1634.)

I described the *self-serving bias* and *overconfidence* in another book. Dobelli, Rolf: *The Art of Thinking Clearly,* HarperCollins Publishers, 2012, pp. 134–136 and pp. 43–45.)

52. Inner Success

"By linking prestige and esteem to particular activities or accomplishments, a culture can direct many people to devote their energies in those directions. It is no accident that in small societies struggling for survival, prestige comes with bringing in large amounts of protein (hunting) or defeating the most dangerous enemies (fighting). By the same token, the prestige of motherhood probably rises and falls with the society's need to increase population, and the prestige of entertainers rises and falls with how much time and money the population can devote to leisure activities." (Baumeister, Roy: *The Cultural Animal,* Oxford University Press, 2005, p. 146.)

Why are there lists of the richest people but not lists of the most satisfied people? Well, there are life satisfaction rankings, but only on a national rather than individual level. The OECD regularly publishes a superbly compiled ranking—Norway and Switzerland have been vying for the top spot for years. See: http://www.oecdbetterlifeindex.org (accessed on 12 July 2017).

"Growth is needed to maintain social cohesion. The prospect of improvements in living standards, however remote, limits pressure for wealth redistribution. As Henry Wallick, a former Governor of the U.S. Federal Reserve, accurately diagnosed: 'So long as there is growth there is hope, and that makes large income differential tolerable.' " (Das, Satyajit: "A World Without Growth?" In: Brockman, *What Should We Be Worried About?*, Harper Perennial, 2014, p. 110.)

Warren Buffett: "If I'd been born thousands of years ago I'd be some animal's lunch because I can't run very fast or climb trees. So there's so much chance in how we enter the world." See: http://www.businessinsider.com/warren-buffett-nails-it-on-the-importance-of-luck-in-life-2013-10 (accessed on 11 July 2017).

John Wooden: "Success is peace of mind, which is a direct result of self-satisfaction in knowing you made the effort to do your best to become the best that you are capable of becoming." (Wooden, John: *The Difference Between Winning and Succeeding*, TED-Talk, 2009. See: https://www.youtube.com/watch?v=0MM-psvqiG8 (time: 3:00).

You don't have to be the richest person in the cemetery; be the most inwardly successful person in the here and now. Adapted from a quotation from John Spears: "You don't have to be the richest guy in the cemetery." (Green, William; O'Brian, Michael: *The Great Minds of Investing*, Finanzbuch Verlag, 2015, p. 72.)

John Wooden: "Make each day your masterpiece." See: https://en.wikipedia.org/wiki/John_Wooden#cite_note-94 (accessed on 11 July 2017).

Afterword

Richard Feynman: "You can know the name of a bird in all the languages of the world, but when you're finished, you'll know absolutely nothing whatever about the bird...So let's look at the bird and see what it's doing—that's what counts. I learned very early the difference between knowing the name of something and knowing something." See: https://www.youtube.com/watch?v=ga_7j72Cvlc and http://www.quotationspage.com/quote/26933.html (accessed on 11 July 2017).

One of the best definitions I know of the *good life* comes from Epictetus, the Stoic: "A life that flows gently and easily." (Epictetus, *Discourses*, 1.4). Another definition came to me over lunch with a friend, an entrepreneur who had built up a fortune of several hundred million. It was summer. We were sitting outside. The pub had metal tables that had been repainted several times, our shoes crunched on the gravel, and we had to be careful that no wasps had crawled over the rims of our glasses when we lifted our ice tea to our lips. We talked mostly about my work—plans for this book—and his: investment strategies, financial interests, asset management, issues with donations, problems with employees, drivers, servants, maintenance on his private jet and, on top of this, his time-consuming positions on various boards of directors, whose prestigious membership he had earned not merely because of his wealth. Suddenly the words tumbled from my lips: "Why, my dear friend, do you do it all? If I had all your millions, I'd spend my time doing nothing but reading, thinking and writing." It wasn't until I was on the way home that I realized, oddly startled, that that's exactly what I do. So that would be a definition of the *good life*: somebody hands you a few million, and you don't change anything at all.